IMAGES
of America

FAIRVIEW PARK

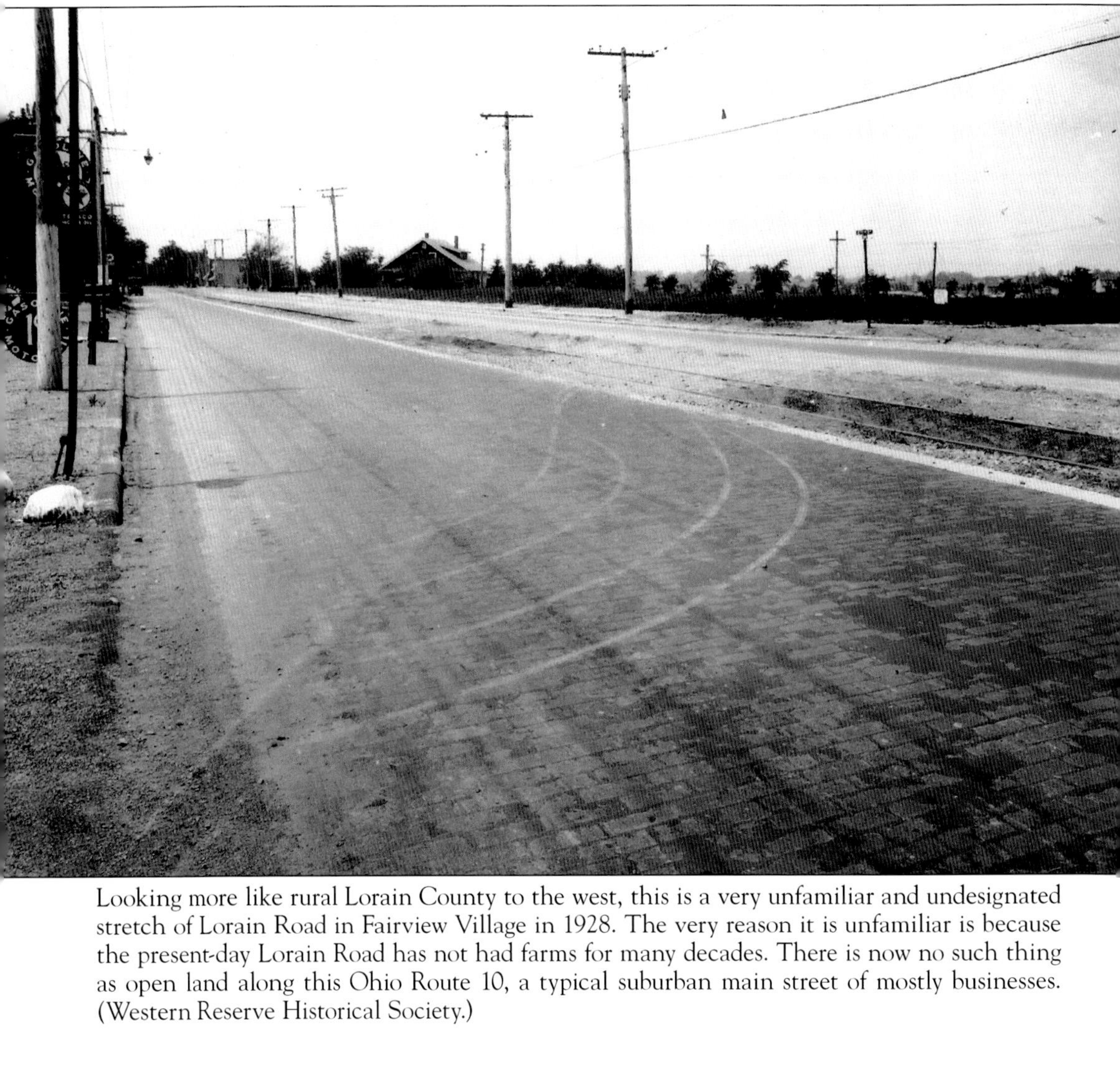

Looking more like rural Lorain County to the west, this is a very unfamiliar and undesignated stretch of Lorain Road in Fairview Village in 1928. The very reason it is unfamiliar is because the present-day Lorain Road has not had farms for many decades. There is now no such thing as open land along this Ohio Route 10, a typical suburban main street of mostly businesses. (Western Reserve Historical Society.)

On the cover: The Fairview Village Fire Department got its first mechanized pumper in 1924. This is one of three group pictures at the time, so they obviously wanted to proudly pose with their new purchase. It also necessitated building the first fire station. The village's first fire chief, Jack Schneider, in the white hat and uniform, included his little son George up next to the driver. (Fairview Park Historical Society.)

IMAGES
of America

FAIRVIEW PARK

Frank Barnett

ARCADIA
PUBLISHING

ISBN 978-0-7385-5204-0

Published by Arcadia Publishing
Charleston, South Carolina

Printed in the United States of America

Library of Congress Catalog Card Number: 2008927340

For all general information contact Arcadia Publishing at:
Telephone 843-853-2070
Fax 843-853-0044
E-mail sales@arcadiapublishing.com
For customer service and orders:
Toll-Free 1-888-313-2665

Visit us on the Internet at www.arcadiapublishing.com

To Herman and Margaret Barnett,
who first moved us to Fairview Park in 1963.

Contents

ACKNOWLEDGMENTS

I simply could not have done this without the Fairview Park Historical Society. Thanks to Leah Trainer, Debbie Hammerle, and Deb Shell for allowing me to dig through their files for a few months. And, like most of the Cleveland area Arcadia books, I have to thank Lynn Duchez Bycko at the Cleveland Press Archives at Cleveland State University. In addition to the names credited with each picture, thanks to Dennis Hrubiak, James Widmer, Marilyn Yesberger, Diane Peplin, Darlene Waugh, Kevin Kelley, Gary Swilik, and Al Dahlhausen.

A little competition helps. I must thank friends who did other Arcadia books. Tom Matowitz, Matt Grabski, Wayne Kehoe, Reginnia Williams, and Bill Becker, all historians to varying degrees, inspired and made suggestions. And my Arcadia editor, Melissa Basilone, patiently guided me through the occasionally overwhelming process. It is harder than it looks.

I am not sure exactly how this works, but there must be some karmic connection to my memory of the author of the "other" Fairview Park book of 30 years ago. The late Margaret Schaefer Goebelt wrote *Fairview Park in Historic Review* in 1978. I notice we both left the school system the same year; in 1974, she retired, and I graduated. She worked for the whole school system. In third grade, our teacher once let four of us into the teachers' lounge across the hall to discuss a small group project. Just as Mrs. Goebelt walked in, I was in a playful shoving match with the other boy in the group, and she immediately scolded us for "wrassling on the davenport." I assured her we were working on a project, but she insisted, "No you're not, you were wrassling on the davenport." Not only did I feel falsely accused, but, though I knew what a davenport was, I used the word "couch." And I never thought of anything I did as "wrassling." But she promptly disappeared into a back room. Did she plant a seed some 40 years before my book came out? It seems like there must be some deep magical connection. Thanks Mrs. Goebelt, wherever you are.

Introduction

A book about Fairview Park cannot just start in 1948 when it got that name. The area had been evolving for a number of years, from township government through the establishment of Fairview Village in 1910, the name change in 1948 (because there was another Fairview in Ohio), and becoming a city in 1951. Although this book focuses mostly on what is called Fairview Park, a little sense of what was already established when it got a new label is needed. In fact, labels like city and village can get kind of fuzzy. When does a village become a city? And when is the oldest designation, the township, no longer a township?

Fairview Park was originally part of the much-larger Rockport Township. Although townships still exist in Ohio, in the early days when it was all wilderness, the land was first divided into counties then further divided into equal-sized townships. Early Ohio was so thick and indistinguishable with endless wilderness that the earliest settlers most likely came by boat from the north off Lake Erie and from the south off the Ohio River. The land that the first white settlers saw in the mid-18th century was so thickly forested that, according to Ralph Pfingsten's *From Rockport to West Park*, "Realistic estimates indicate that as much as 95% of the land area was covered with trees." It took the almost incomprehensible task of digging the two Ohio canal systems by hand across the entire state to start opening up the wilderness in between, an easier-said-than-done connecting of these two very different bodies of water. The Ohio River in turn connected to the Mississippi River, while Lake Erie connected to the St. Lawrence River and eventually the Atlantic Ocean. So the state became a major link. With the canals and later the railroads, the state started to evolve like some biological form, with borders expanding and contracting as people settled in and interacted with the land, some becoming urban, and some becoming rural.

Borders evolved with technology. Trains and later trucks and cars on paved roads may have replaced the canals, but even they had to evolve. Before railroad tracks spread throughout the vanishing wilderness of Ohio, wagons and stagecoaches rumbled across plank roads, parallel strips of lumber just wide enough apart to support wagon wheels. These were toll roads, with the tolls paying for the upkeep. What is now Lorain Road had a tollbooth at Wooster Road where people had to pay. Obviously it was a lot of work to lay the roads and keep replacing rotted and broken lumber. This also created a big market for lumber from all the trees that were cleared as cities grew. But railroad tracks were eventually an improvement over plank roads, and electric trains called the interurban were an improvement over steam trains. People too young to remember the streetcars throughout Cleveland have an even harder time imagining the interurban, which were essentially long-distance streetcars. People started traveling, commuting for fun or business between Cleveland and Rockport to Oberlin or Sandusky or further out. People simply take for granted today that roads are paved.

And then there is the technology of bridges. One thing about Rockport was its beautiful river, the Rocky, running right through the middle of the township. Any area with a major river valley has an obstacle to contend with until bridges can be built. In Rockport's case, west of the river was that much more isolated, so east of the river saw the earliest development. The northeast part of Rockport Township evolved into the city of Lakewood. South of Lakewood became the city of West Park, which annexed to Cleveland in 1923. The entire township west of the Rocky River was originally the hamlet and later the village of Rocky River. Eventually, the land south of Center Ridge Road took on the name Goldwood Township, which became Fairview. The first bridges were always at the valley level. As engineering improved and the population grew, high-level bridges were stretched across the valley at several points, including the three interstates that came through in the 1960s and 1970s.

And yet, other than needing high-level bridges to overcome crossing the river valley, people are not complaining of the obstacle. Everyone refers to the section of Cleveland Metroparks that rub up against Fairview Park as, simply, the valley. It has always been good for the soul to go down in the valley to enjoy nature. The valley cuts a long diagonal edge across Fairview Park, and realtors have developed some very dynamic properties along the valley rim. Starting in the northeast corner of town, several networks of cul-de-sacs along the outside edge of Story Road start reaching like twisting fingers as far to the valley rim as they can get, allowing for big, beautiful houses with backyards that tumble into the hills overlooking the valley (although that tumbling does include contending with erosion). The southern end of that diagonal swath of the valley is off of West 210th Street near Mastick Road, with more cul-de-sacs reaching toward the valley. In between these two ends of the diagonal, the valley brushes up alongside a stretch of Lorain Road, creating dynamic locations for apartments, office buildings, and the cemetery.

Oddly, the borders of Fairview Village in 1910 left fragments of Goldwood Township to both the north and south, as if Fairview seceded from the middle. The north part was eventually annexed by Rocky River, and the southern part became Parkview Village in 1925 until it was annexed to Fairview Park in 1966. Goldwood Township had only been established since April 6, 1910, when Fairview Village broke off five months later on September 10. The village population in 1910 was 300, the city population was 9,311 in 1950, and by 2000, it was 17,572.

Lastly, the area suggests a few assumptions that surprisingly are not true. It is odd enough that the name West Park, a Cleveland neighborhood that borders Fairview Park, was named for John West, and had nothing to do with it being on the west side. And Mastick Woods Golf Course may be among the woods of the Metroparks, but Woods as well as Mastick were old family names in Rockport. Directly on that West Park border across the valley from Fairview Park is the former Fairview Park Hospital, now simply Fairview Hospital. The names, believe it or not, are not related. It sounds absolutely impossible, but the hospital started in Ohio City near downtown Cleveland alongside a park called Fairview Park. Fairview Village had already become the city of Fairview Park long before the hospital was built in its present location. So the examination of Fairview Park starts off with a coincidence to end all coincidences.

Welcome to zip code 44126.

One

BUSINESSES

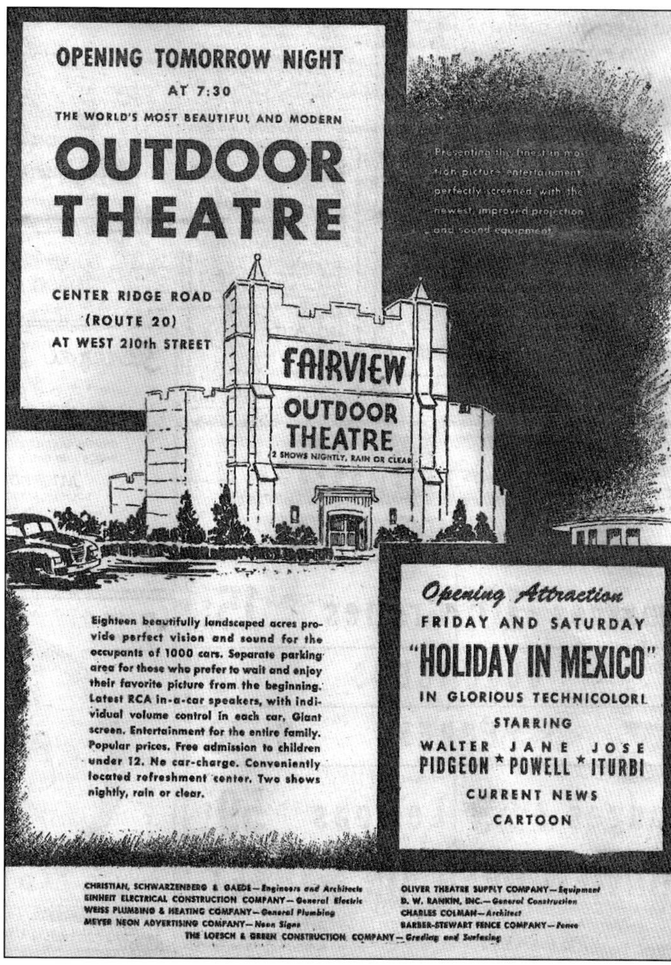

This movie advertisement is from the old *Fairview Herald* in 1947. Just six years later, Westgate Shopping Center opened here and was redeveloped a couple more times over the next 50 years. (Fairview Park Historical Society.)

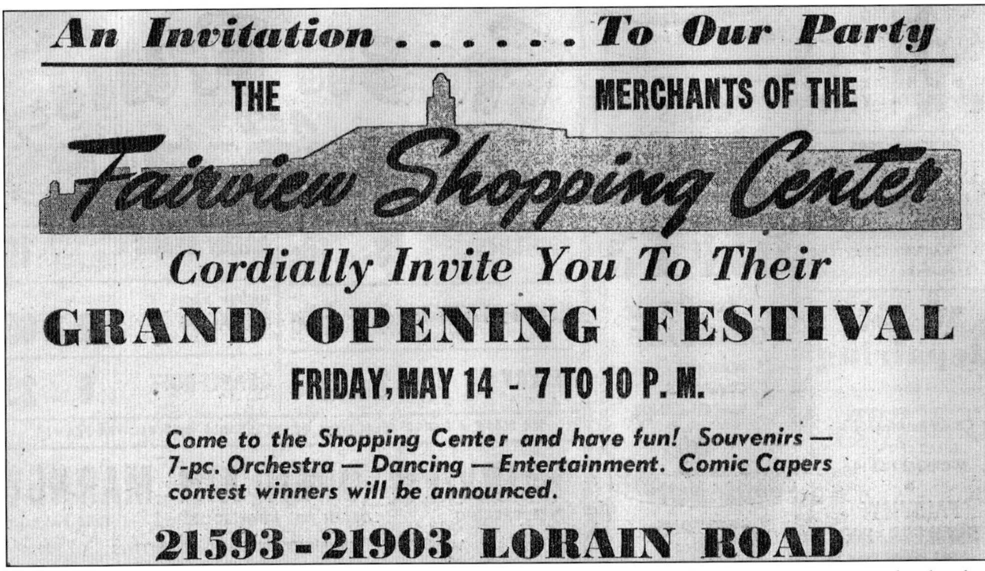

One could say this evolving suburb helped establish the fact that shopping centers and suburbia tend to go together. In the fall of 1947, the Fairview Shopping Center became the first of its kind in Cuyahoga County. It was built on the former property of Willis Potter, the last of the many farms on Lorain Road. With such a major development, the village became the city of Fairview Park in 1950. Many years later, when half the shopping area was rebuilt in the 1990s, it evolved yet again to become Fairview Centre, complete with French spelling. This image is from the *Fairview Herald*. (Fairview Park Historical Society.)

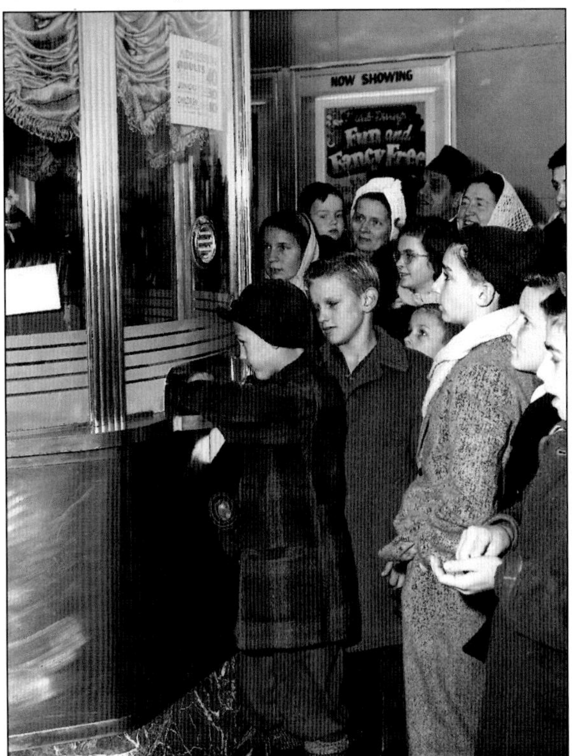

Gradually the shopping center started opening one store at a time before the movie theater was complete. This theater opened at Thanksgiving in 1947, becoming the first area theater to open since West Park's Riverside Theater in 1938. It was over 20 years before Westgate opened a movie theater. It was built about where the Potter farmhouse used to stand before the house was moved to the rear of the property where Hillsdale Avenue now runs. When the theater was torn down in the 1990s, the letter *F*, which had been atop the theater marquee, was reinstalled above the middle of the shopping center. (Fairview Park Historical Society.)

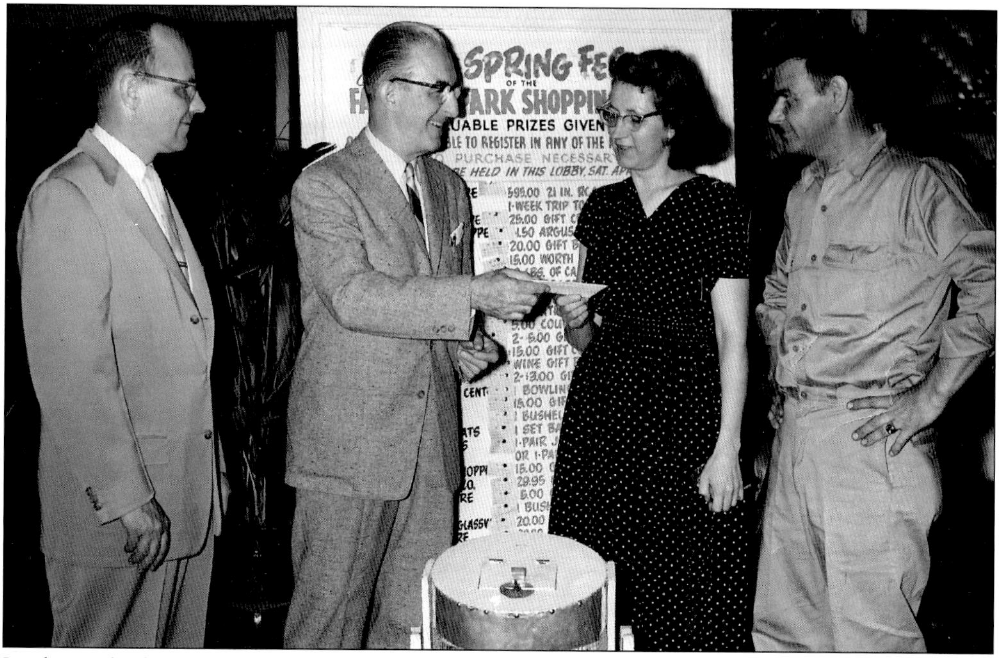

In the early days of the Fairview Theater, Wednesday nights were usually called Bank Night, where adults could put their name in a large drum to be drawn for cash prizes. The names stayed in the drum forever, so a name could be drawn any week, but one had to be present to win. (Fairview Park Historical Society.)

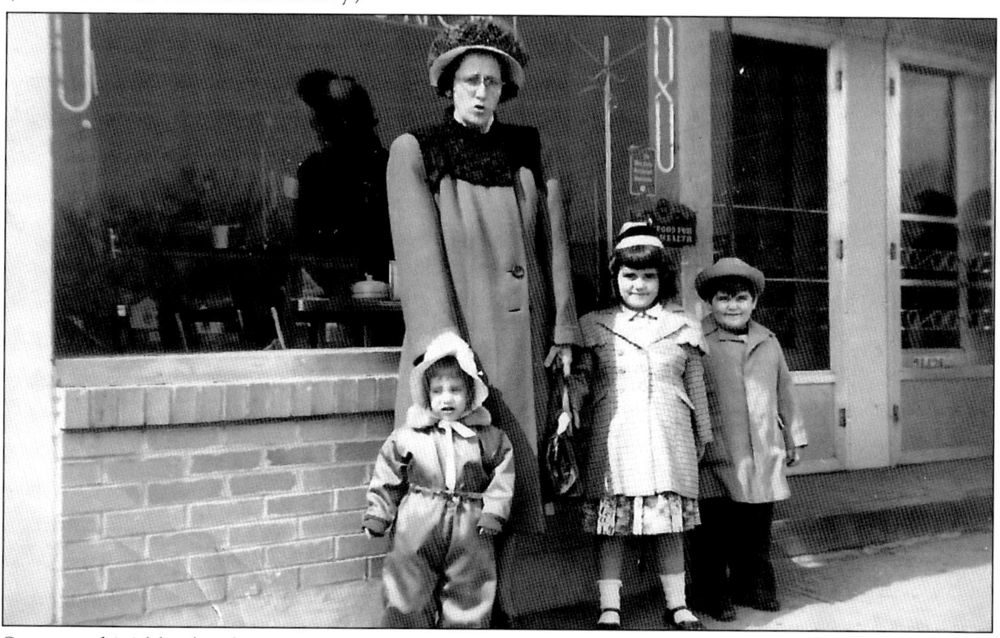

Steve and Mildred Lakios, pictured here with their children in the mid-1950s, opened Stevens Lunch at 21438 Lorain Road in May 1946. In addition to good food, it prospered because of its location. Being on Route 10 near a new shopping center, it brought more business than expected. Although they sold the restaurant in 1957, the truck traffic increased in 1955 with the Ohio Turnpike opening several miles down Lorain Road. (Joy Gdovin.)

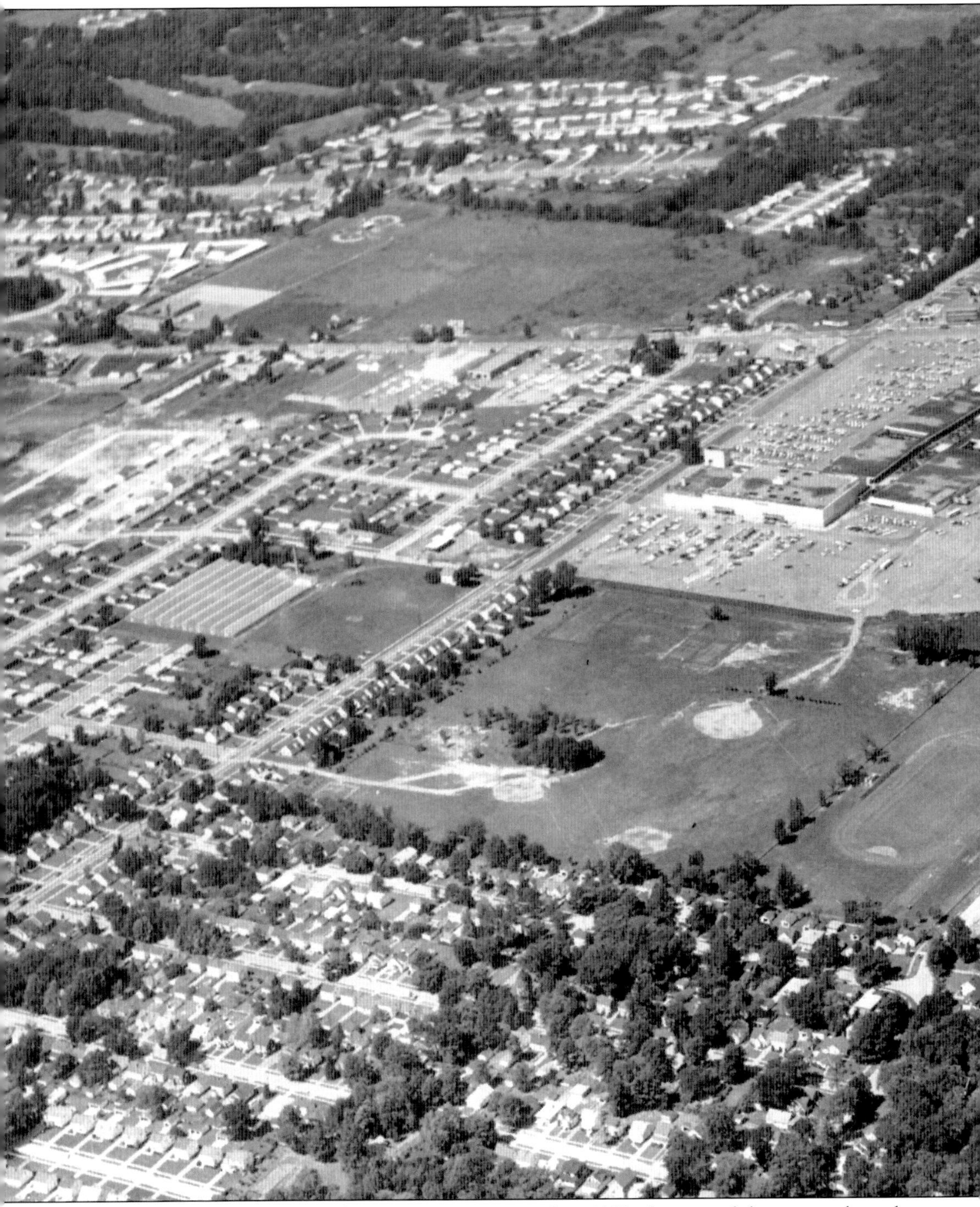

Taken soon after Westgate Shopping Center opened in 1953, the rest of the city and southern Rocky River seems to radiate from its core in this photograph. Running horizontally across the top third of the picture is the Fairview/Rocky River border and the easternmost stretch of Center Ridge Road, ending at Wooster Road just beyond the right edge of this picture. A newly developing Bohlken Park is taking shape just below Westgate. In fact, a lot of the dirt

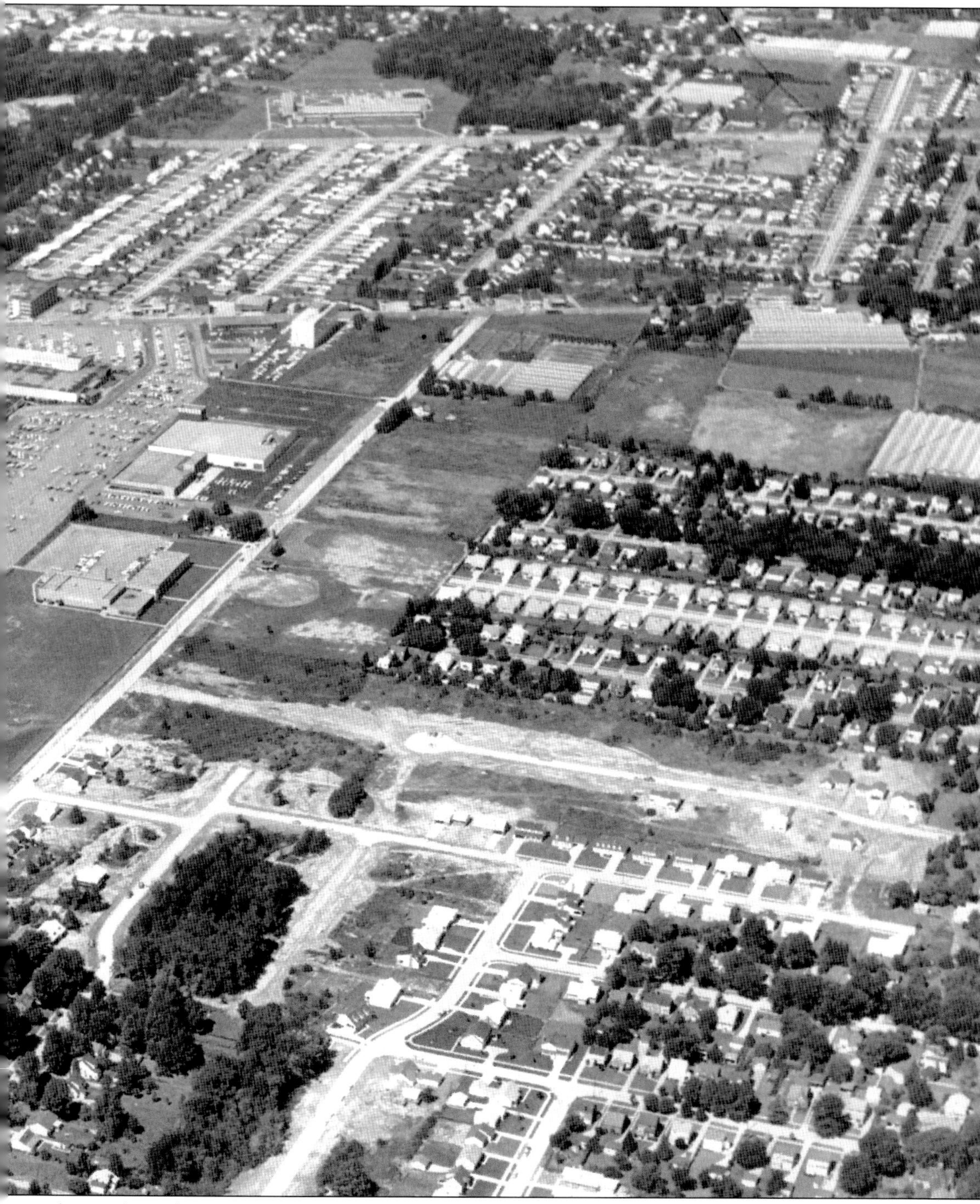

dug up from the Westgate construction was used as fill to make the park usable for its playing fields and playground. As usual, comparing scenes from then and today, all that open land is unfamiliar because it is now the typical suburban stretch of stores and restaurants. (Cleveland Press Archives, Cleveland State University.)

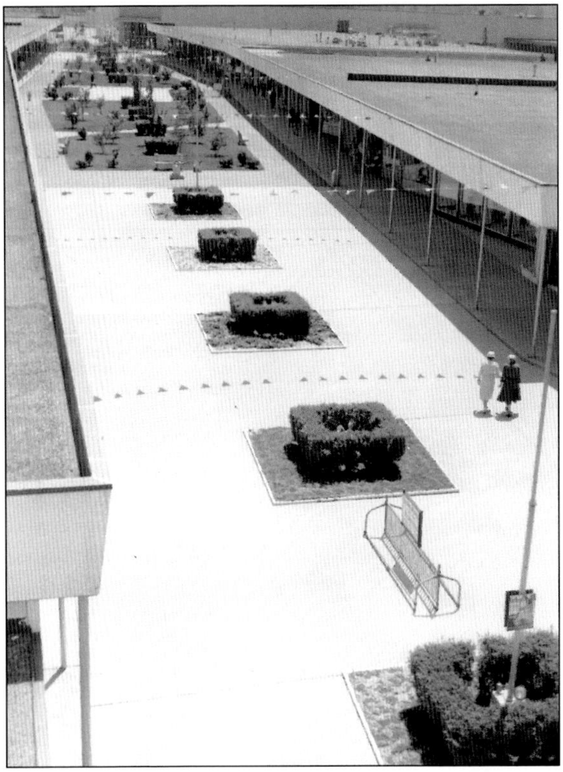

The Fairview Shopping Center had been the first in Cuyahoga County in 1947. Then in 1953, developers built the state's first open-air landscaped shopping plaza, Westgate. It was essentially a mall without a roof, with strips of stores facing into a landscaped plaza. Westgate Shopping Center has since gone through two other phases, reflecting suburban shopping trends. It was eventually roofed in 1969, making it one of the area's first enclosed malls. As the 21st century began, the outdoor plaza once again became popular. Westgate was torn down and redeveloped back into an outdoor plaza in 2007. (Cleveland Press Archives, Cleveland State University.)

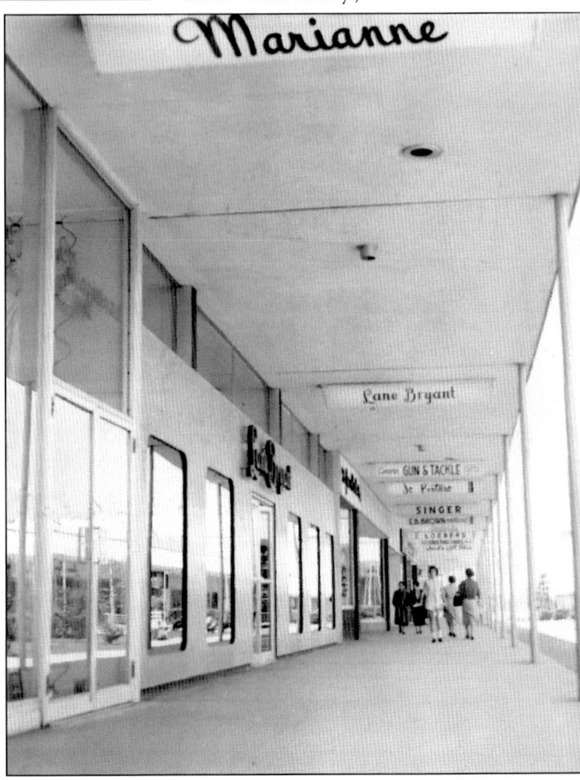

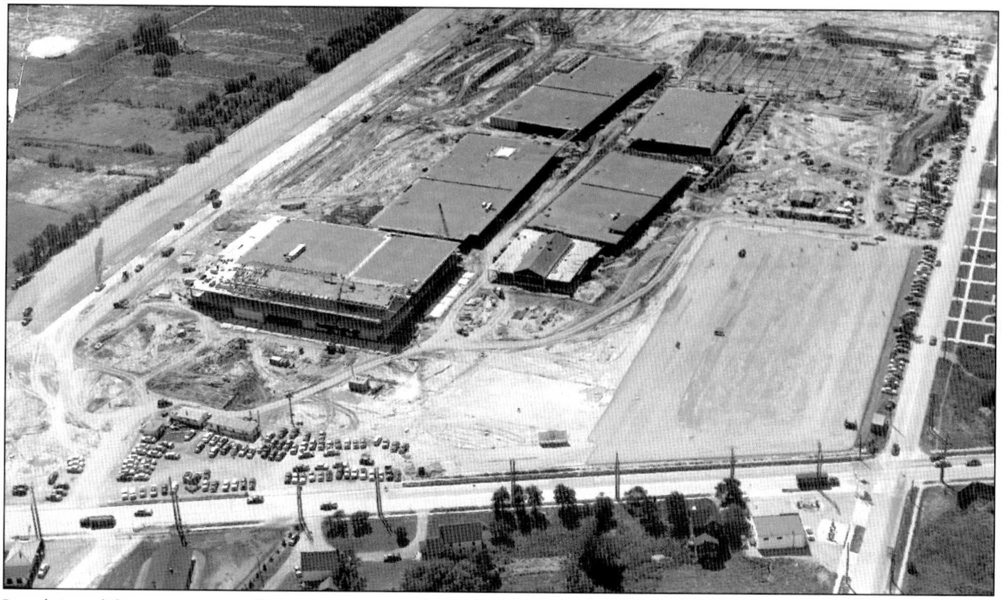

Looking like some nondescript rectangles, the original Westgate Shopping Center begins to take shape. (Cleveland Press Archives, Cleveland State University.)

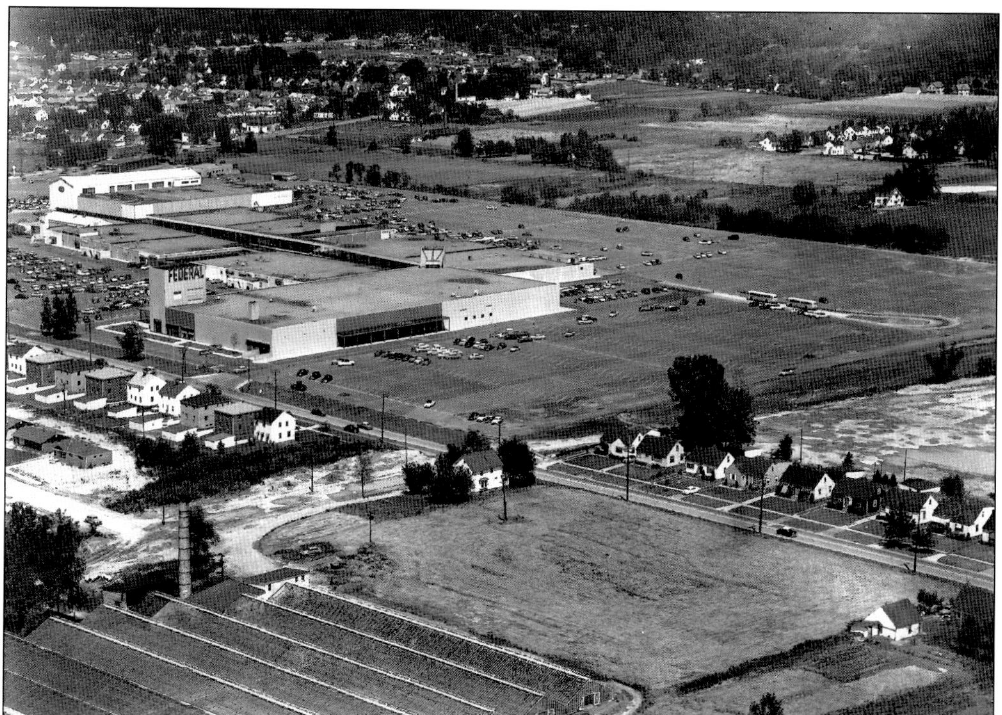

This mid-1950s view not only shows all the land yet to be developed east of Westgate Shopping Center in the upper half of the picture but also the greenhouses, lower left corner, that were there before the Addington Place condominiums were built on the site. Greenhouses were very common throughout the area long after the farms were gone. (Fairview Park Historical Society.)

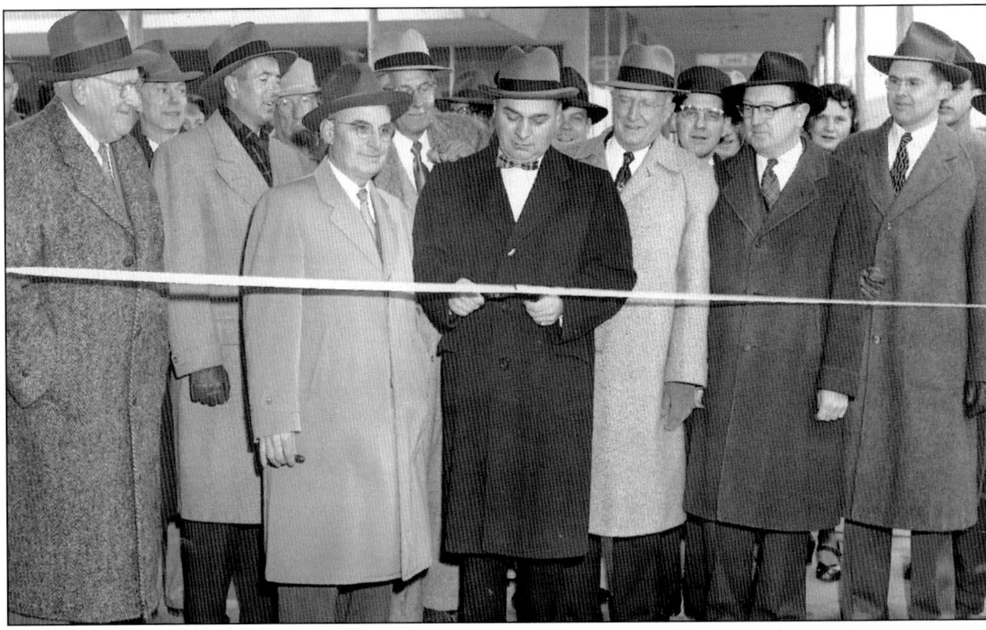

County commissioner Henry W. Speeth cuts the ribbon to open up the $10 million Westgate Shopping Center in 1954. Flanking him from left to right are Mayor Karl A. Bohlken, the three developers of the project, the president of the project's builders, the head of the new Westgate Merchants Association, and the representative of the insurance company. (Cleveland Press Archives, Cleveland State University.)

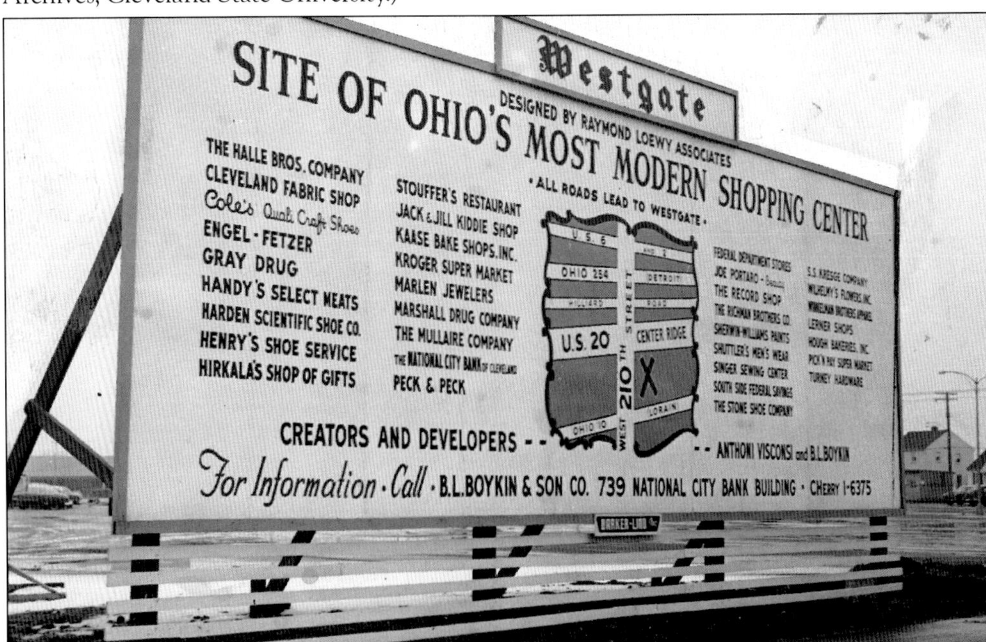

A sign for Fairview Park's newest accomplishment in January 1954 also shows how much has changed since then. So many of those stores listed are no longer in business. By 2007, Westgate Shopping Center came full circle, being completely torn down and redeveloped as a modern open-air complex of stores. (Cleveland Press Archives, Cleveland State University.)

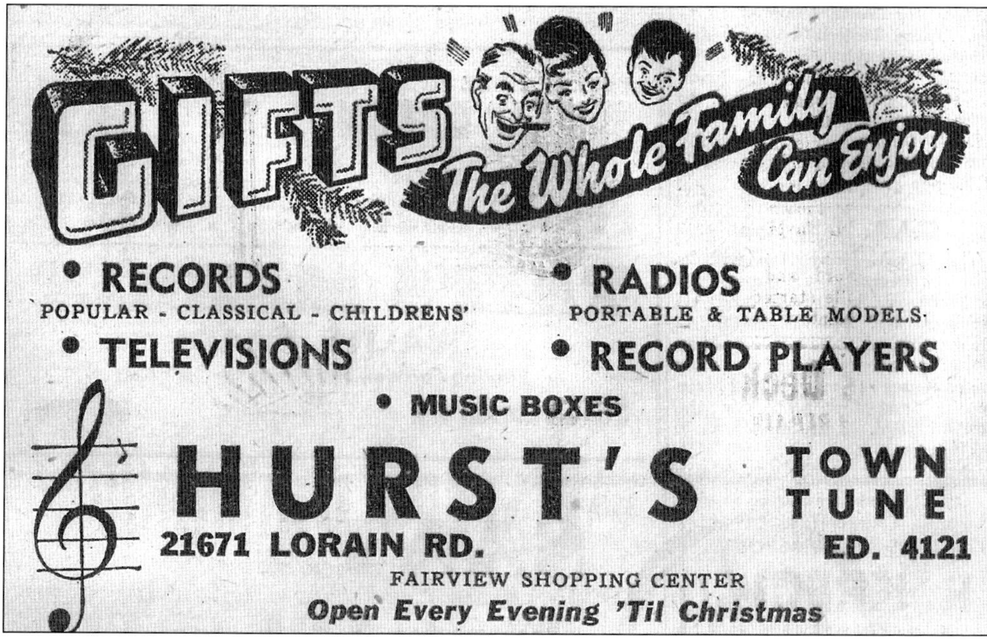

Hurst's Tune Town closed in the early 1970s. Musician Mike Hay remembers, "I bought all my records from Hurst. I was in a local band in the early 60s called the TreeStumps. A new Bob Dylan record would be on the radio and the TreeStumps would be playing it the next week. Hurst Tune Town was my virtual link to the music world." This image is from the *Fairview Herald*. (Fairview Park Historical Society.)

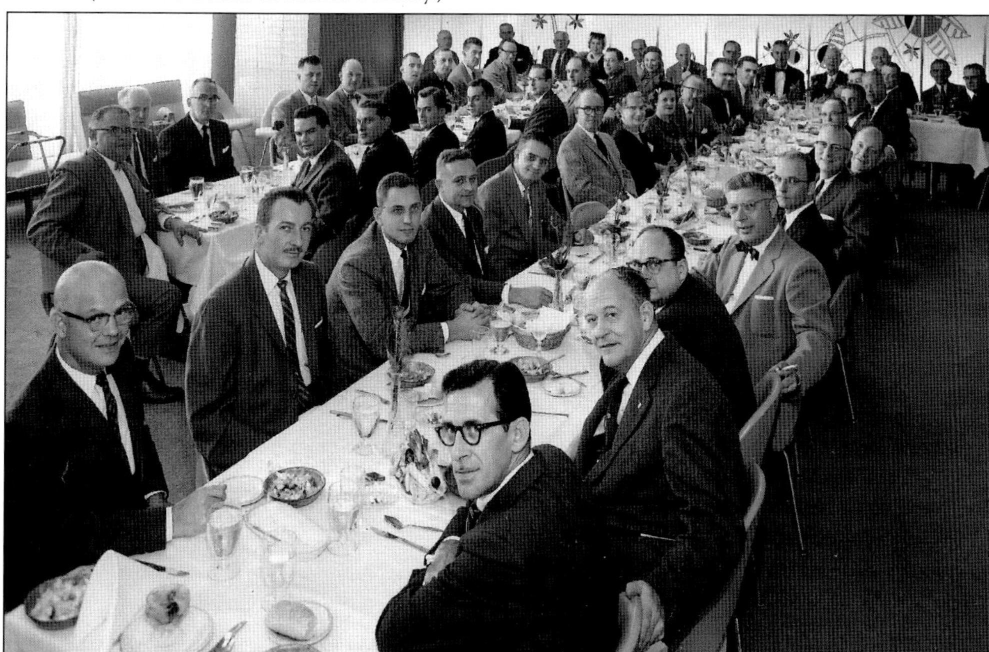

Pictured is a luncheon at the long-gone Chung's Restaurant after the new Society Bank branch was opened on October 6, 1958. School superintendent Lewis F. Mayer sits at the lower left. (Fairview Park Historical Society.)

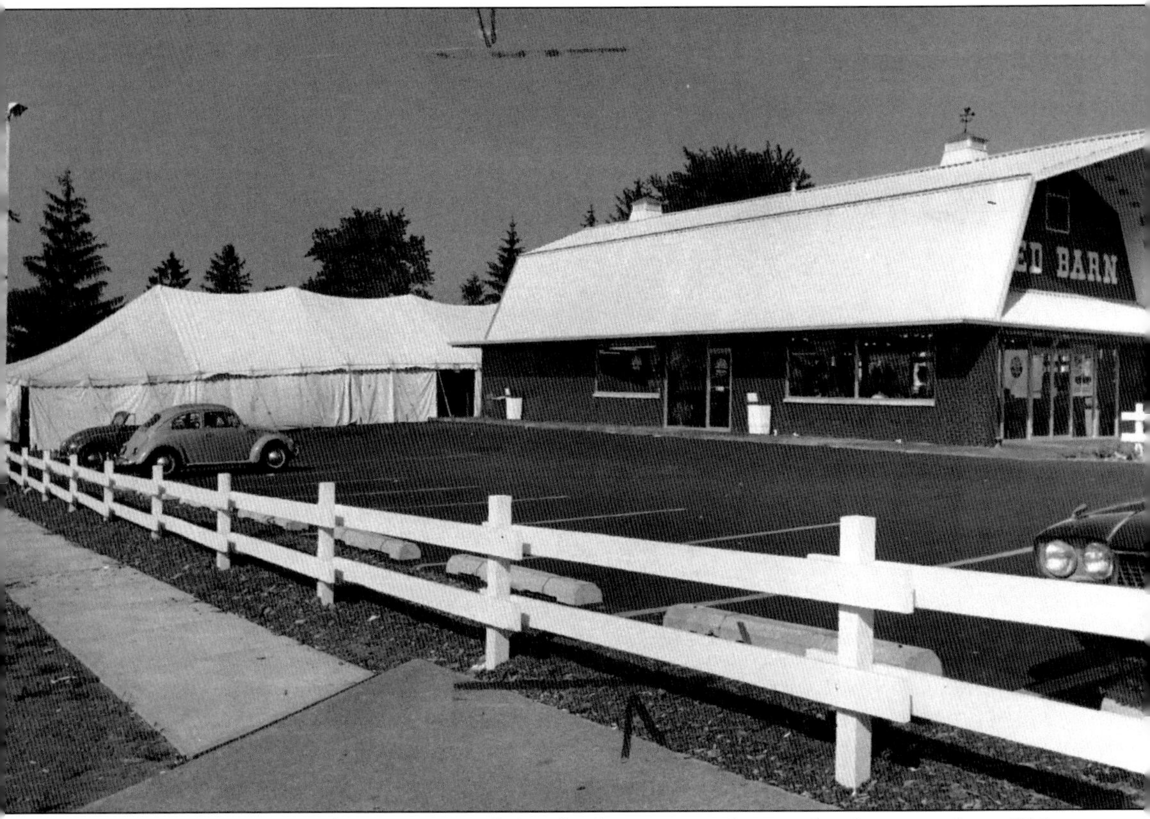

This is not just a popular Fairview Park fast-food restaurant that used to be across from Ohliger Drug Store at West 217th Street and Lorain Road. Although the whole chain of Red Barns went out of business, their barn-shaped buildings continued to be recognizable throughout Greater Cleveland as various other restaurants utilized the buildings. When this picture was taken, the tent in the back was controversial. Since the nearby high school cafeteria was being enlarged, the Red Barn anticipated increased business, and the 40-foot-by-100-foot tent could hold 600 people. But the city took the restaurant to court, saying it was against zoning and fire-prevention codes. (Cleveland Public Library.)

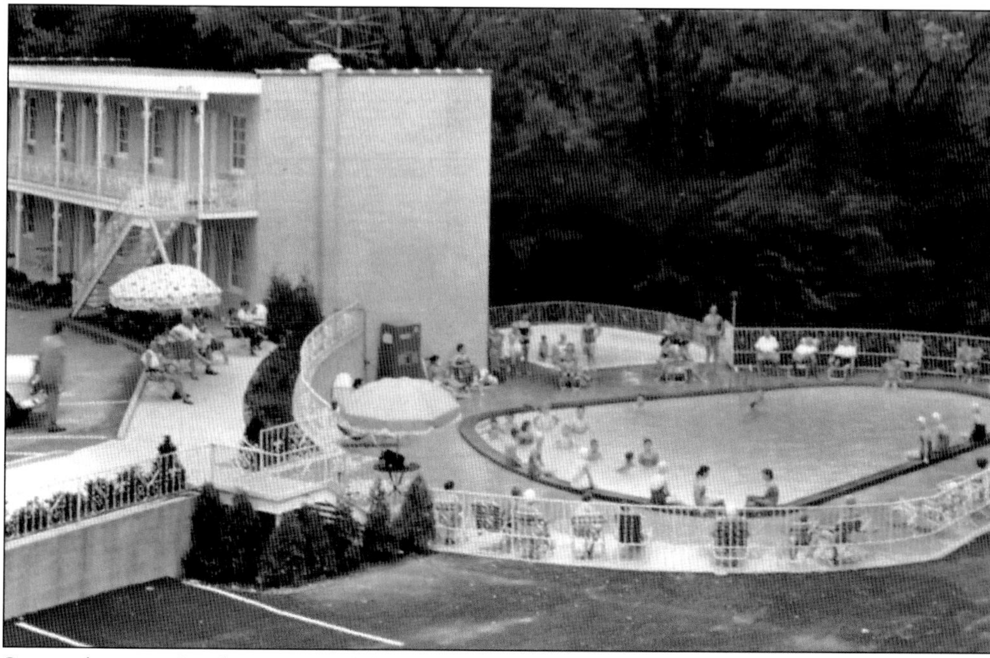

Some photographs document subtle changes, such as a building that has been replaced by another. Then there are the more extreme changes like the long-gone Valley View Motel along Lorain Road, complete with a swimming pool alongside the Rocky River Reservation of the Cleveland Metroparks. (Gordon Kramp postcard collection.)

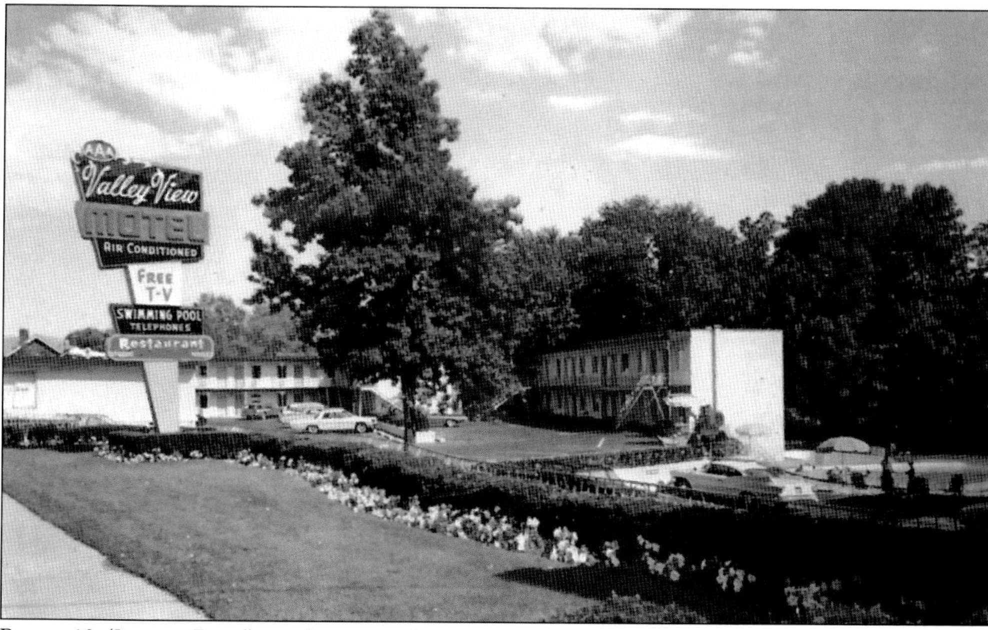

Route 10 (Lorain Road) used to get a lot of the cross-country traffic before the interstates of the 1960s and 1970s arrived. Travelers could stop and stay the night at motels like the Valley View. The main building prospered for a few short years in the 1990s as one of the finest Indian restaurants in Greater Cleveland, the Clay Oven, before it was torn down. (Gordon Kramp postcard collection.)

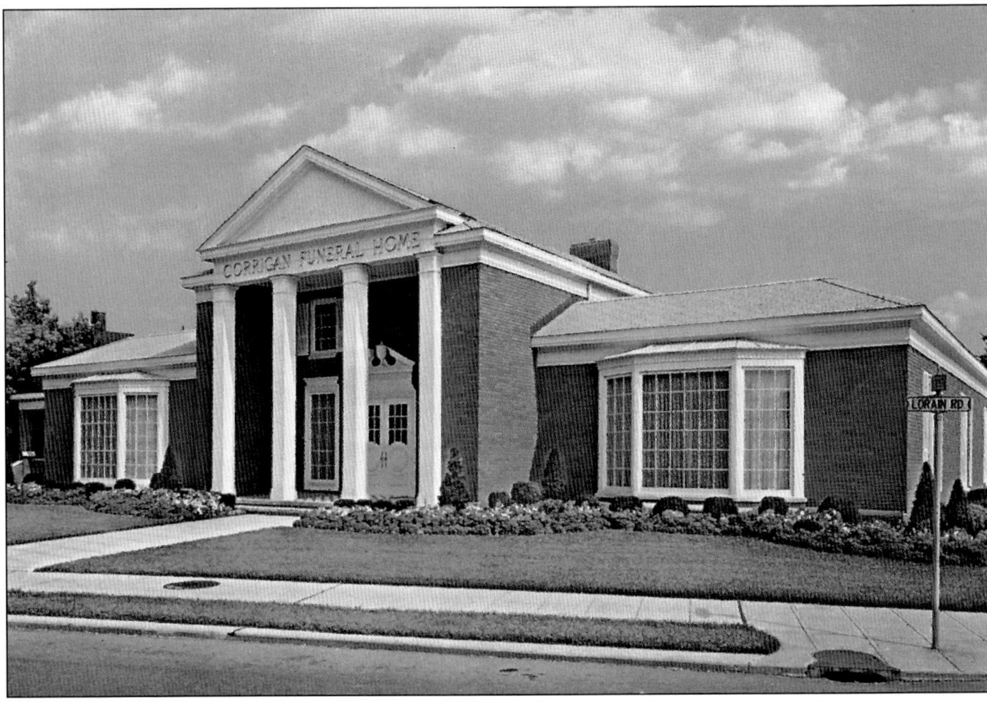

The classical exterior of Corrigan Funeral Home's new building was a striking addition to Lorain Road, another bold step away from the farmland of recent decades. (Gordon Kramp postcard collection.)

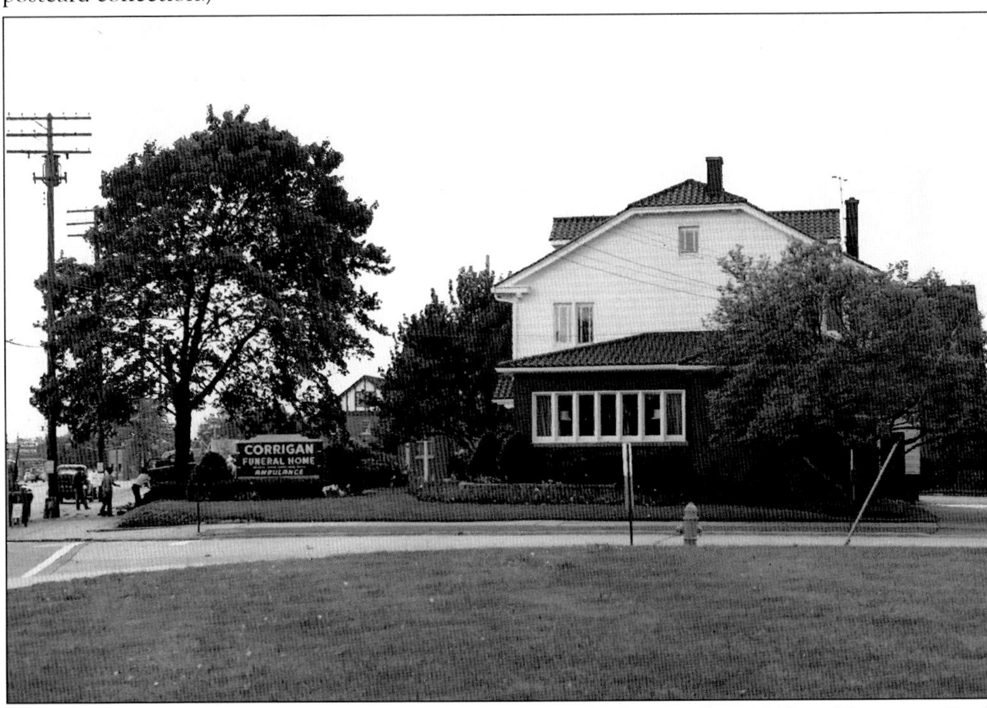

This is Corrigan Funeral Home before it was rebuilt in the 1960s. (Fairview Park Historical Society.)

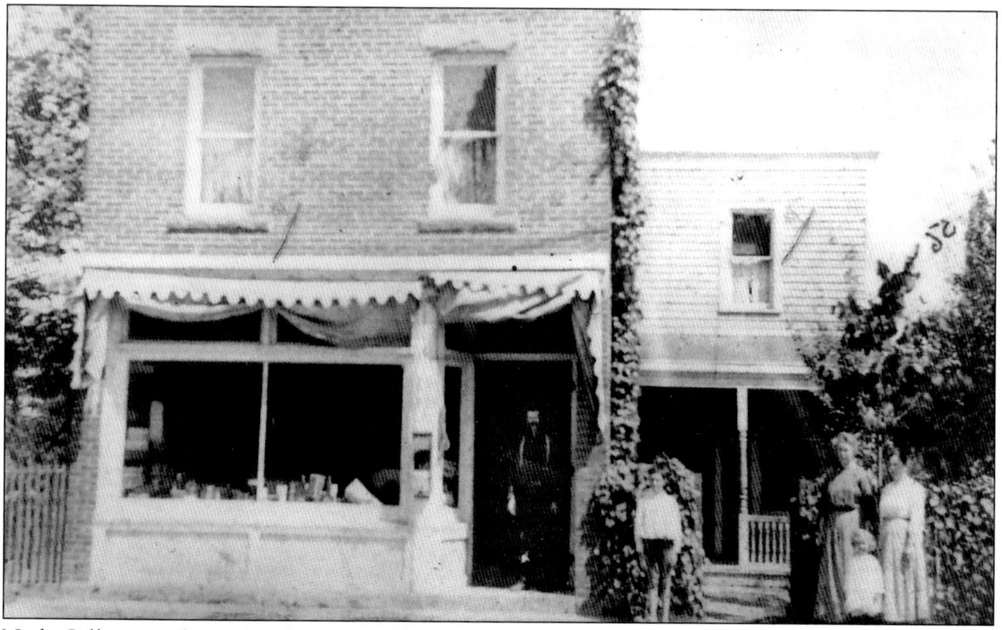

Nick Gilles stands in the doorway of his grocery store, the first in Fairview, at the northwest corner of the Lorain Road bridge. More people remember the second-oldest grocery, the Pantry, because it operated into the 1960s. Gilles was the village treasurer for the first 21 years. His son Fred, center, died in World War I. The Gilles-Sweet School was named after him. This building is now a bed-and-breakfast. (Fairview Park Historical Society.)

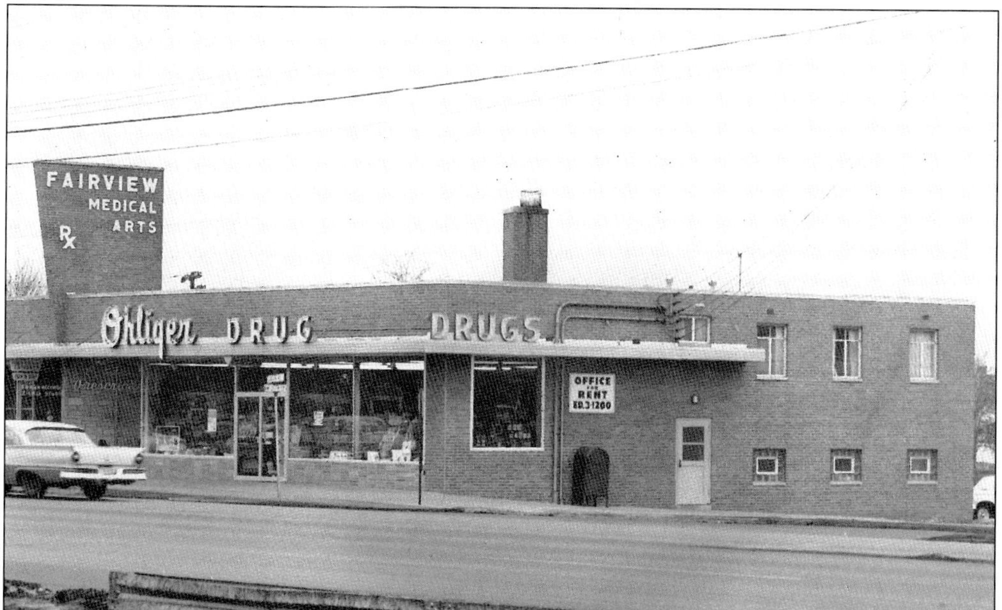

This photograph is from early 1961. It has not changed too much from this original look, although in later years, that slab on the front edge of the roof was removed, and more decorative material was added above the awning. Not only was Ohliger Drug Store on friendly terms with its competitor, Pierstorf's, just a few blocks away, but it also was among the few successful independent drugstores up against the huge chain stores. (Tom Ohliger.)

GRAND OPENING

Saturday, March 26

PIERSTORF PHARMACY

BRANCH No. 2

22432 LORAIN AVENUE

A modern up-to-date drug store for your convenience. Drugs, Perfumes, Sundries, Cigars, Cigarettes and Ice Cream at reasonable prices. A registered pharmacist to serve you, Mr. Herman Pierstorf—Miss C. E. McDowell.

SOUVENIRS

A box of candy free with every purchase of 50c or over. A big Lolly Pop for the children with every purchase of 25c or over.

OPENING DAY SPECIAL

A 35c tooth brush free with every 39c tube of Chlora-Dixo tooth paste. A 25c Aladdin Knife Sharpener with every 25c box of Nature's Remedy. A 75c box of Brazil Nuts or Bon Bons, 39c. Woodbury's Soap, per bar, 19c.

The best Ice Cream Soda in Fairview Village for 10c. A modern up-to-date refrigerated fountain serving Peerless Best Ice Cream.

A longtime familiar sight near West 220th Street and Lorain Road, Pierstorf's original location in 1927 was a few blocks to the west. It was started by Herman Pierstorf. (Fairview Park Historical Society.)

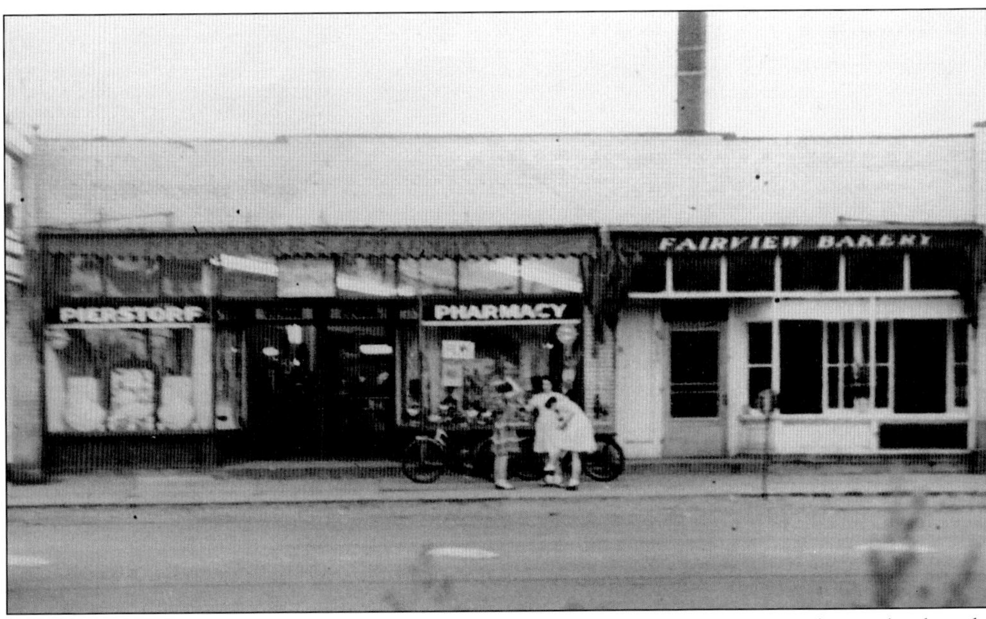

Pierstorf brothers Clarence and Ervin started Fairview Photo Service in the early days by developing film themselves in the pharmacy basement after hours. In those days, Kodak focused all its retailing in pharmacies, but the driver who picked up film from the Pierstorfs for developing thought it was too long a drive out of Cleveland, so the Pierstorfs bought their own equipment and started a very successful business. (Fairview Park Historical Society.)

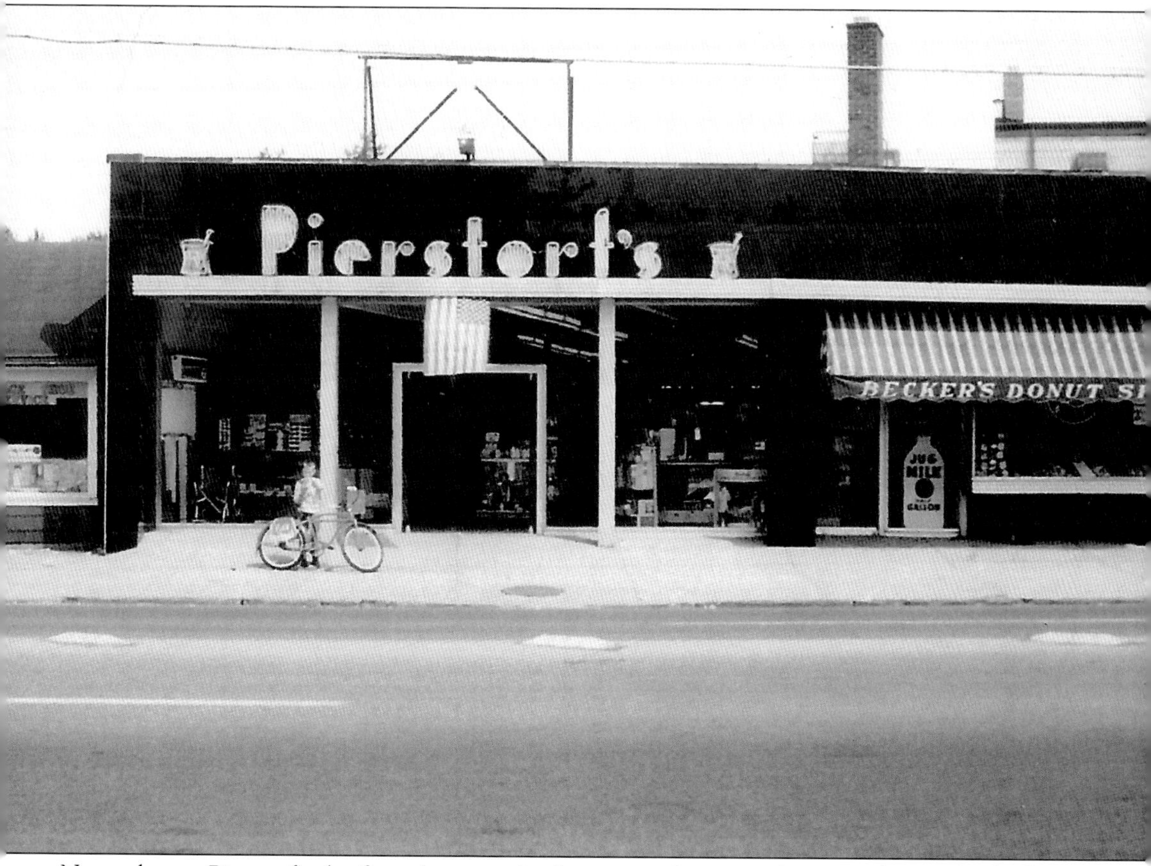

Not only was Pierstorf's the first pharmacy in the area with air conditioning, but it also had a distinctive storefront of black carrera glass, and it was the first pharmacy with full-drop windows. And the sign, consisting of the name Pierstorf's and a pharmacist's mortar and pestle formed in stainless steel, was the only one of its kind. The manufacturer had to tell the Pierstorf brothers to quit referring customers to them who wanted a similar sign because it was too hard to try making again. Pierstorf's closed in 1993 after 66 years in business. It was the longest continually open business in Fairview Park. Ervin and Clarence Pierstorf ran it from 1927 to 1975, at which point Bill Hall ran it 18 more years. (Ervin Pierstorf.)

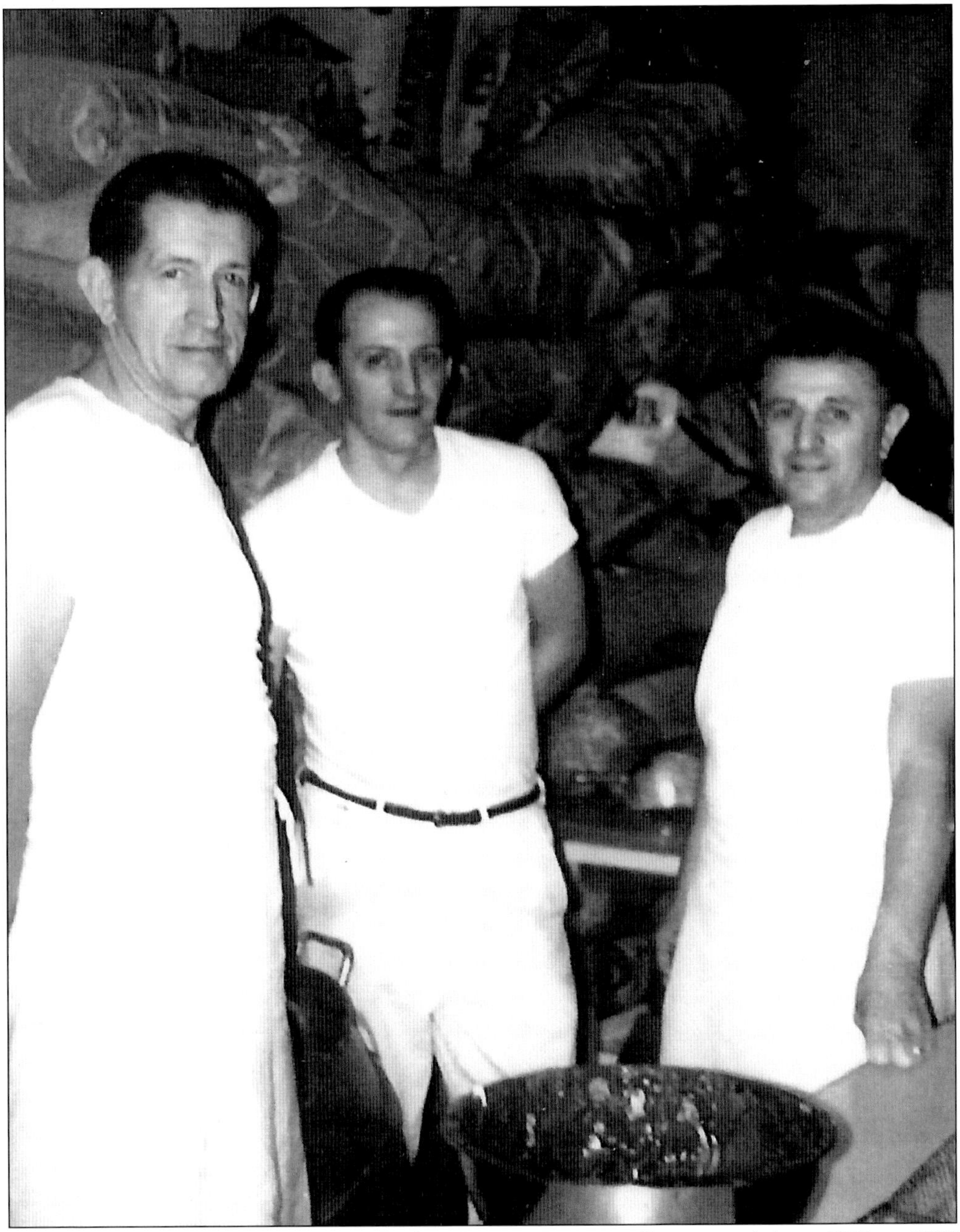

Beckers Donut Shop has a long but broken history. It originally operated from 1957 to 1988 next to Pierstorf's pharmacy. Then it merged with a bakery on the east side of Cleveland. But after about 10 years, it was able to move back into the old space as if it never left. Here Becker brothers, from left to right, Louie, Bob (owner), and Bill pose before bags of all-important flour and sugar. Fairview Photo used the storefront for a few years, and in 2006, Beckers returned with the same phone number it used to have. (Tom Becker.)

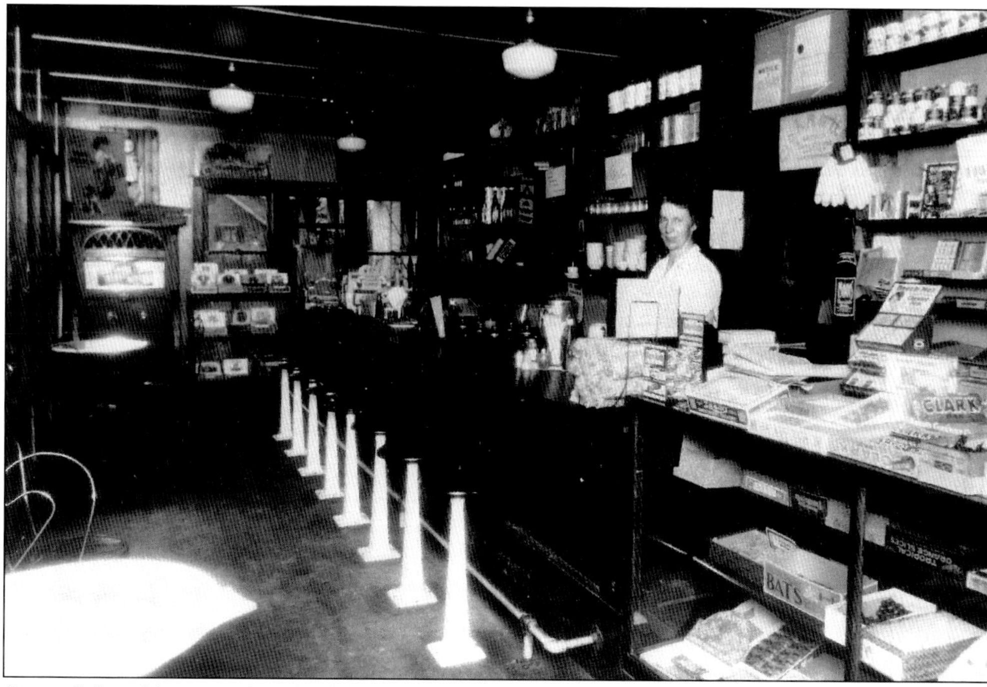

One of the oldest-standing buildings in Fairview, Midnite Barbecue later became Alma's and then Gina's Place. Esther Hogstram stands behind the counter. It is said that the day it opened in 1927, Charles Lindbergh landed his airplane in Paris. (Fairview Park Historical Society.)

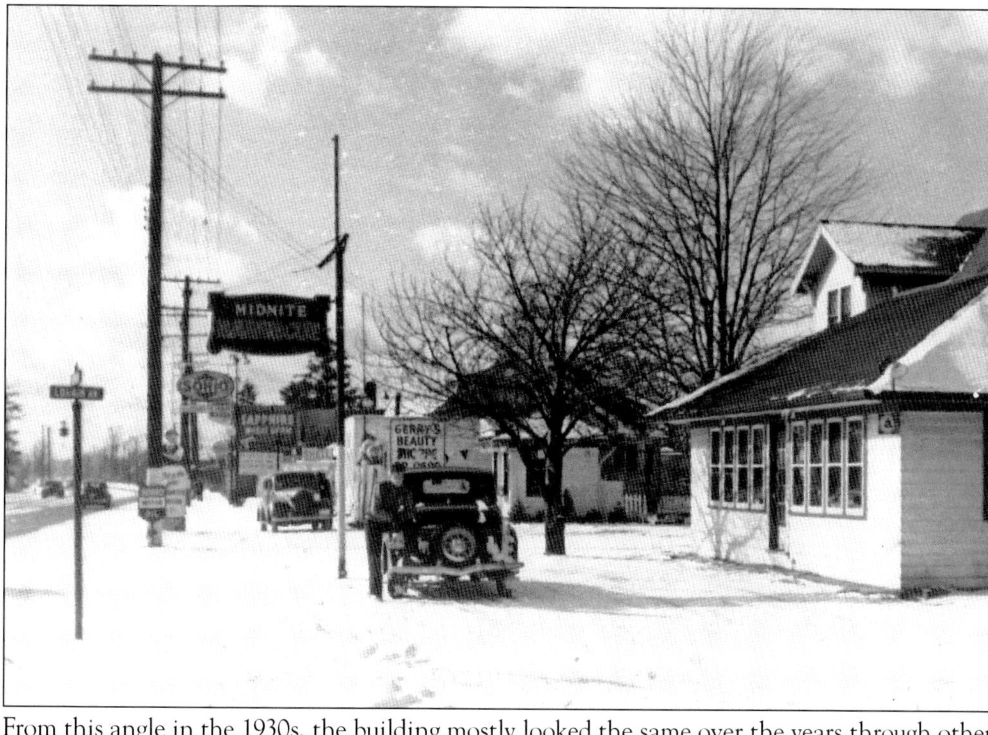

From this angle in the 1930s, the building mostly looked the same over the years through other owners. (Fairview Park Historical Society.)

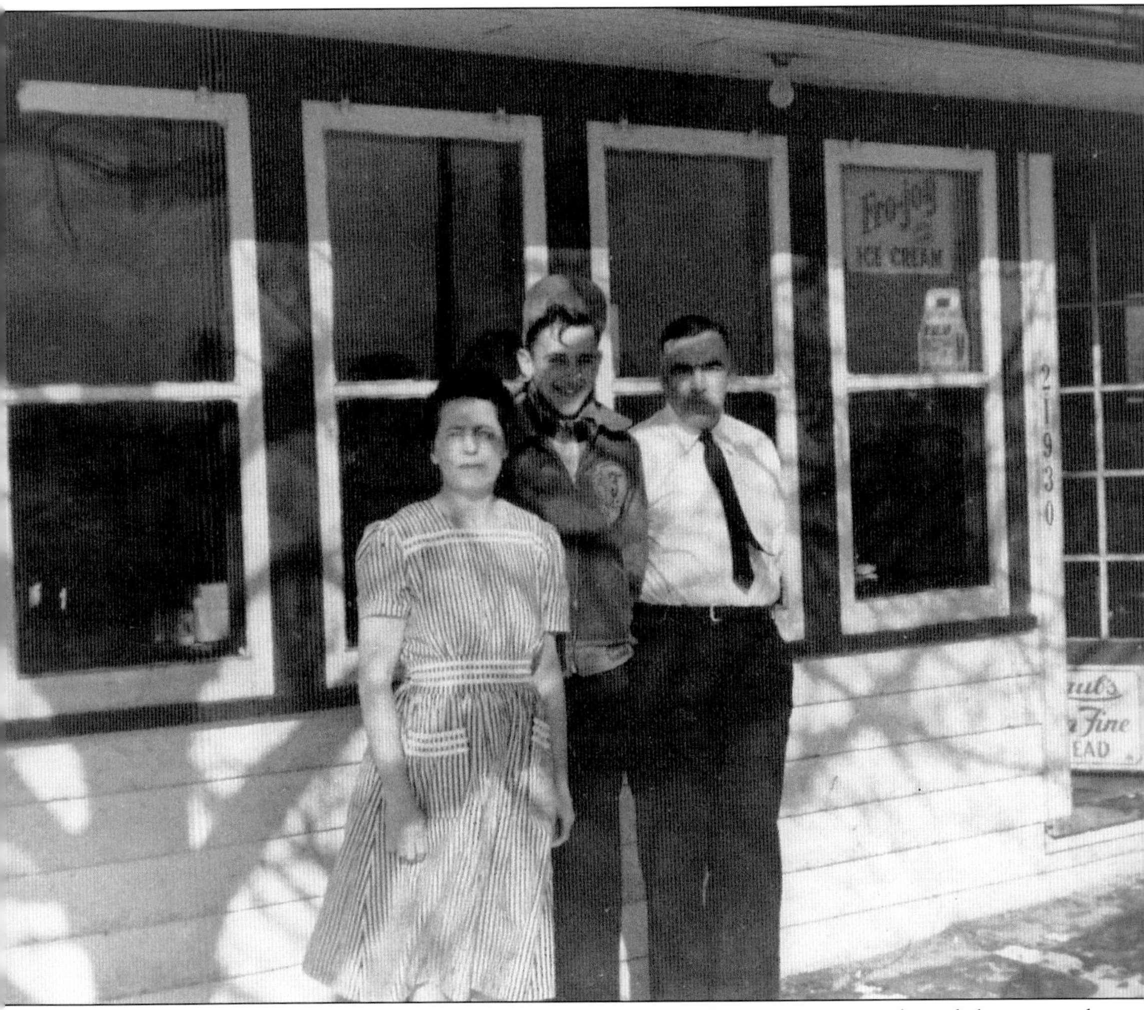

Amelia and Walter Thomson ran Midnite Barbecue at the easternmost edge of the original Spencer land. Amelia was a Spencer, and this land was her wedding gift. The young man standing in between Amelia and Walter around 1941 is Joe Mayer, who later became a radio personality in Cleveland. (Fairview Park Historical Society.)

Two

BAIN PARK CABIN

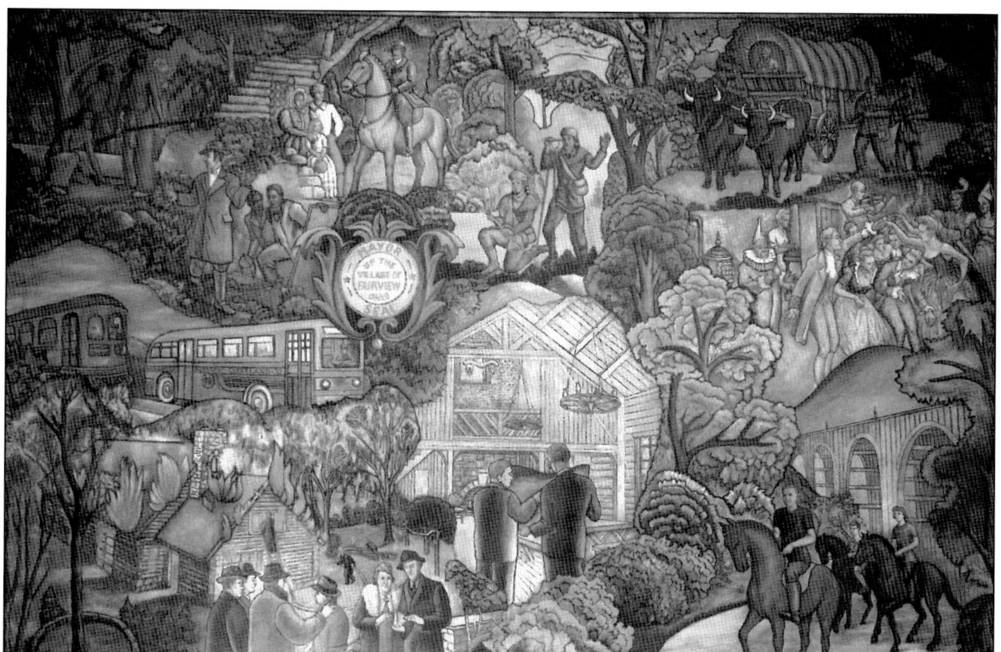

It is safe to say that the most unique work of art in Fairview Park is the mural in Bain Park Cabin. Designed by Earl Neff and painted by Works Progress Administration artist Michael Rozdilsky, it depicts the history of Fairview Village up until 1940 when the mural was painted for the opening of the cabin. It features Native Americans, a preacher on horseback, Conestoga wagons, the Underground Railroad, the mayor's seal, costume parties and dances, the interurban, the North Olmsted Municipal Bus Line, the first cabin burning, Mayor David Bain reviewing blueprints, and Neff riding horses under the Lorain Road bridge with his wife and son. (David Barnett.)

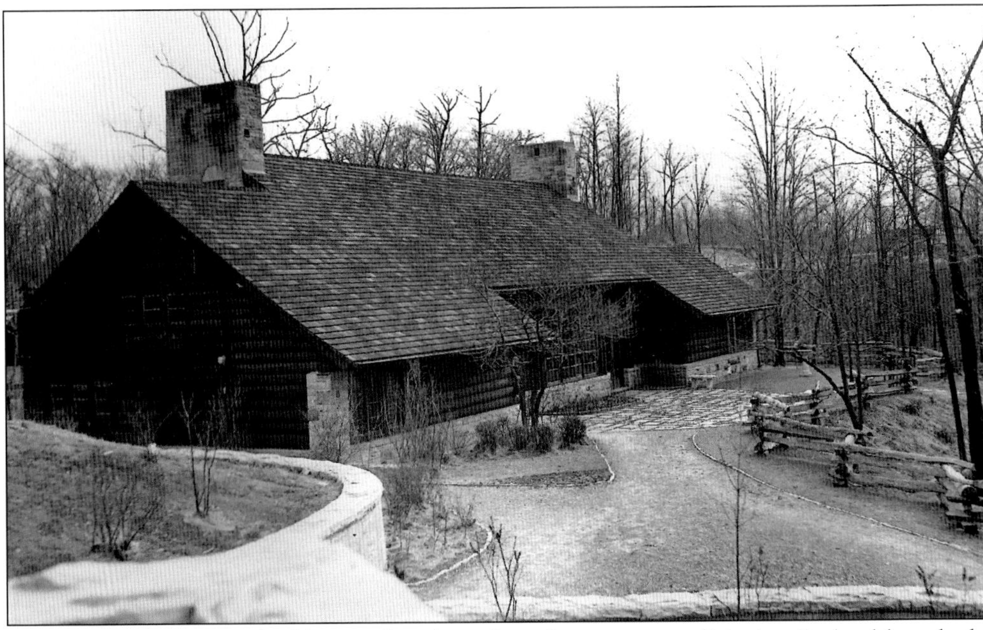

The city's most historic building and park predate the city name, Fairview Park, although the village's park was called Fairview Park from its dedication in 1928 until the park and cabin were renamed in 1953. The Community Cabin was ready to open in 1937, but the brand-new building was mysteriously destroyed by fire just a day before its dedication. (Fairview Park Historical Society.)

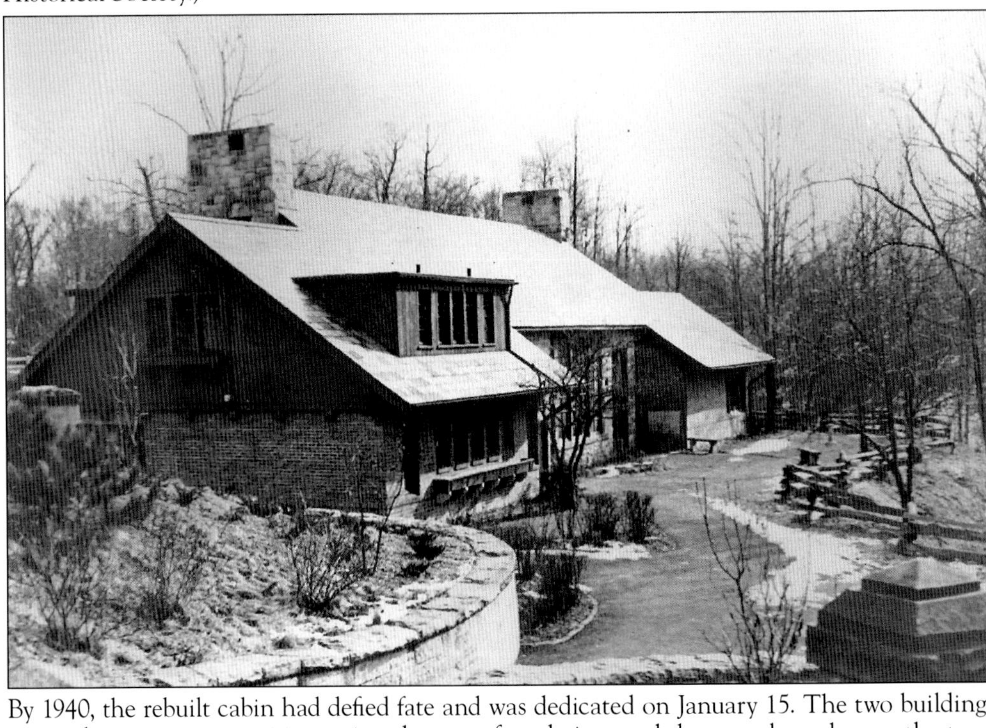

By 1940, the rebuilt cabin had defied fate and was dedicated on January 15. The two buildings are in the exact same position, using the same foundation, and the same branches on the trees are seen in these two shots. (Fairview Park Historical Society.)

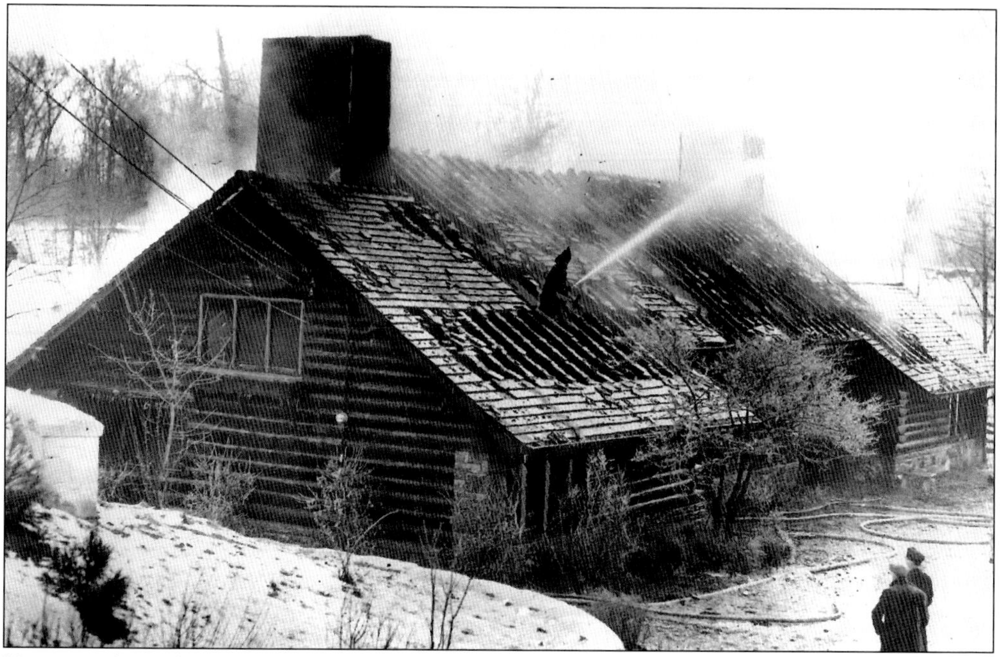

Here is a shot of the first Community Cabin on fire on December 14, 1937. It was not insured yet because it was a Works Progress Administration project that had not yet been taken over by the village. But the community refused to be defeated, quickly mobilizing to rebuild. (Fairview Park Historical Society.)

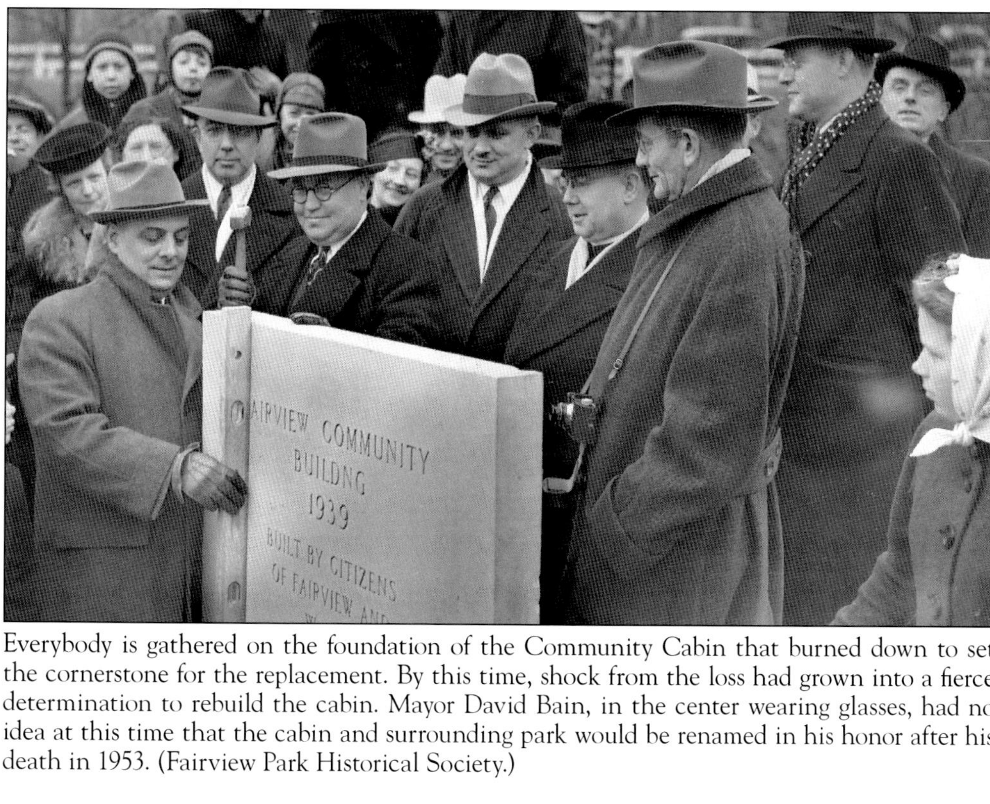

Everybody is gathered on the foundation of the Community Cabin that burned down to set the cornerstone for the replacement. By this time, shock from the loss had grown into a fierce determination to rebuild the cabin. Mayor David Bain, in the center wearing glasses, had no idea at this time that the cabin and surrounding park would be renamed in his honor after his death in 1953. (Fairview Park Historical Society.)

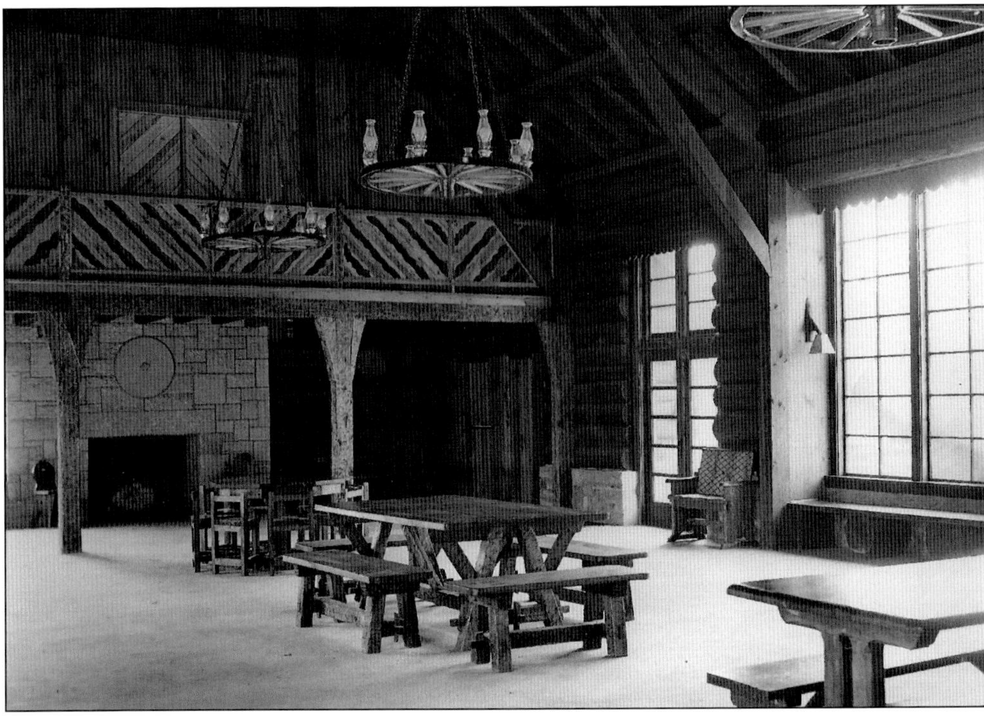

Little did the photographer realize that this picture preserved a rare image of the Community Cabin interior seen by few people before it disappeared in a fire. (Fairview Park Historical Society.)

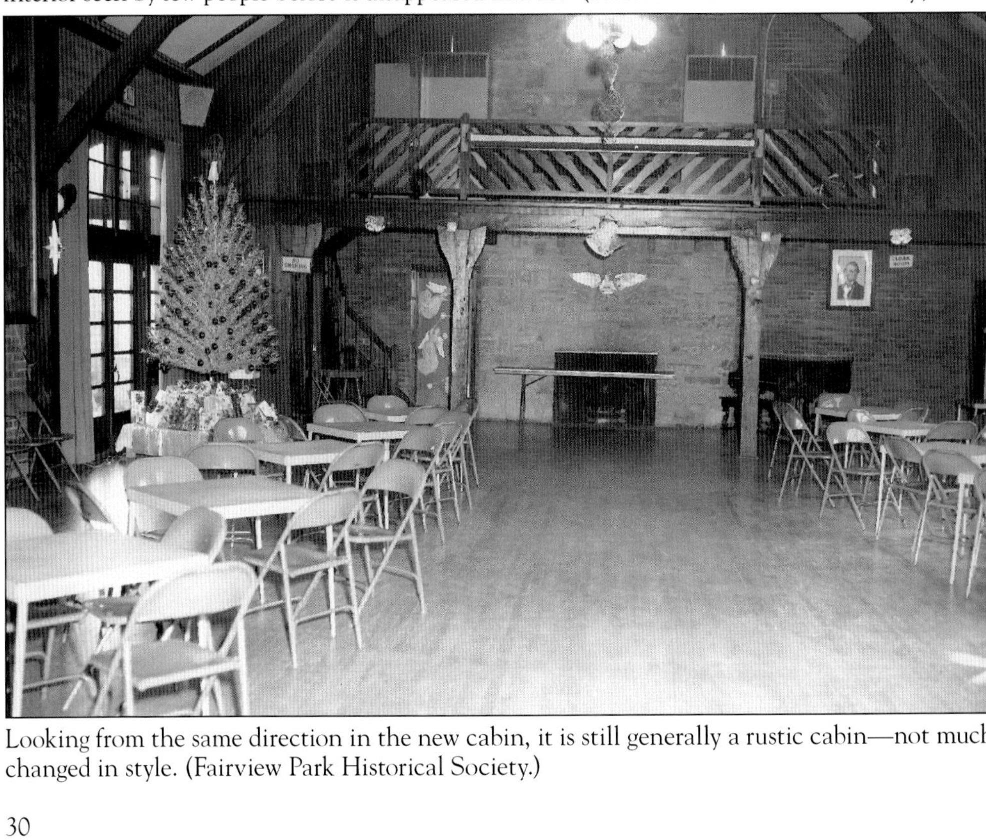

Looking from the same direction in the new cabin, it is still generally a rustic cabin—not much changed in style. (Fairview Park Historical Society.)

Three

Century Homes

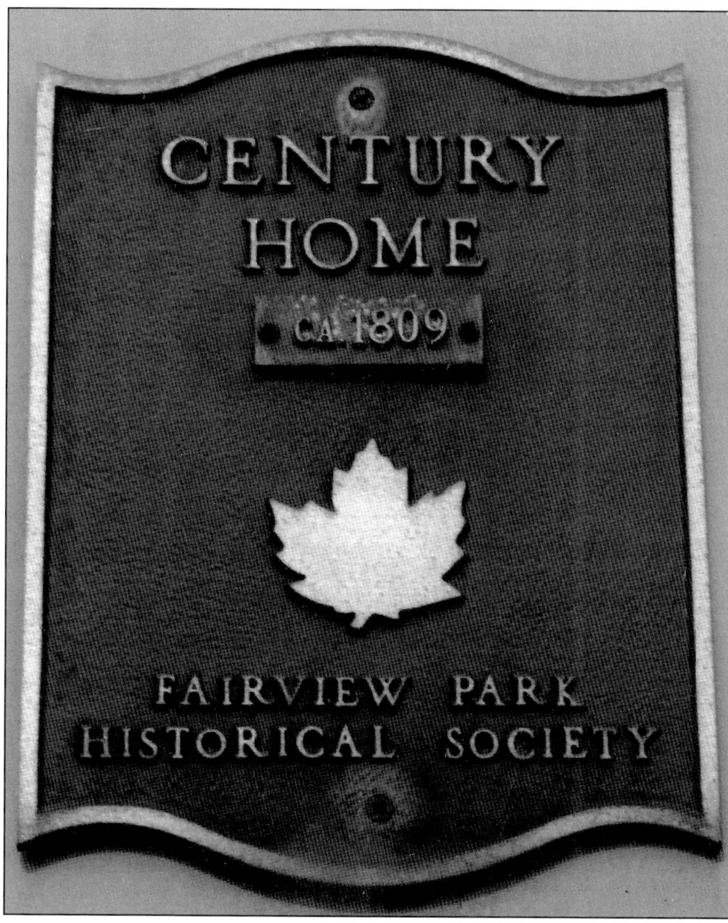

In 1976, the Fairview Park Historical Society started to recognize significant century homes with a plaque. To qualify, the house cannot have had extensive alterations so that it retains its historical status. The following are the first 10 houses to get this designation. (Fairview Park Historical Society.)

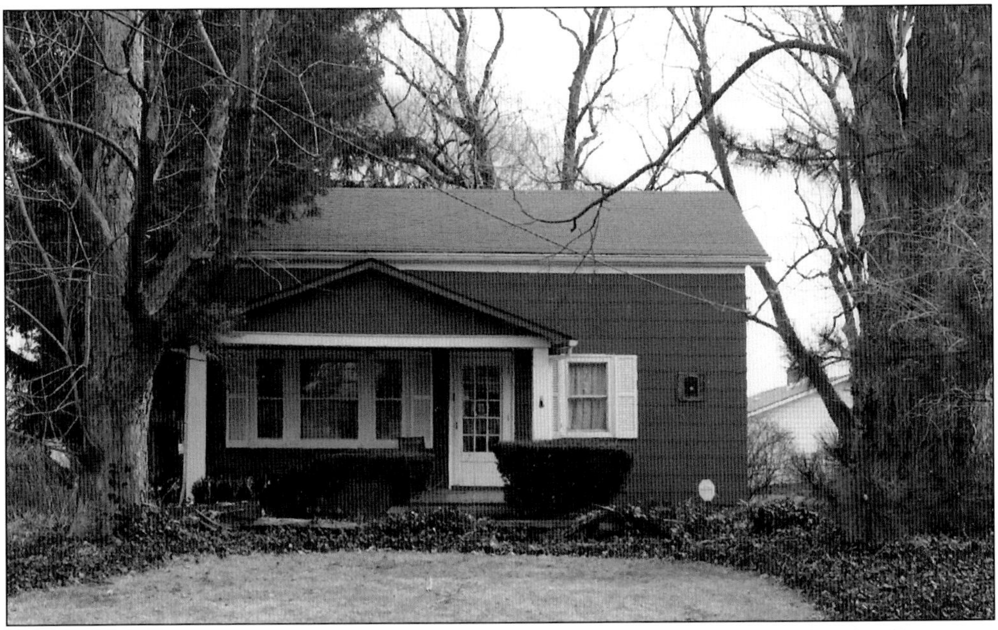

John Place Spencer was the first in his family to settle in the area. His older brother Benjamin Spencer followed, building this farmhouse on Spencer Road (now 5167 West 220th Street) in 1831. When his wife, Sally, died in 1840, he sold the house and built another down the road. Moses C. Baker eventually acquired this house, and it was part of the Underground Railroad, helping slaves escape to Canada. (Fairview Park Historical Society.)

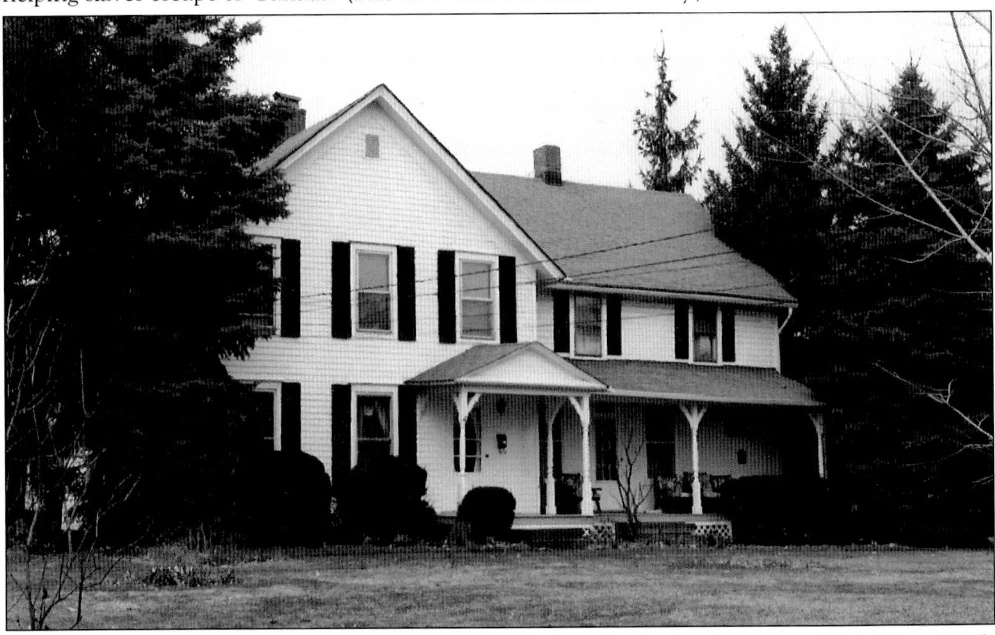

Having remarried in 1850 to Diana, Benjamin Spencer built this house at 4924 West 220th Street in 1866. Their daughter Minnie married the son of James and Almira Eaton. They lived here with their sons and her parents. Minnie's reputation as a great cook brought people here from afar for chicken dinners every Sunday in the early 1900s at what was called Lilac Acres. (Fairview Park Historical Society.)

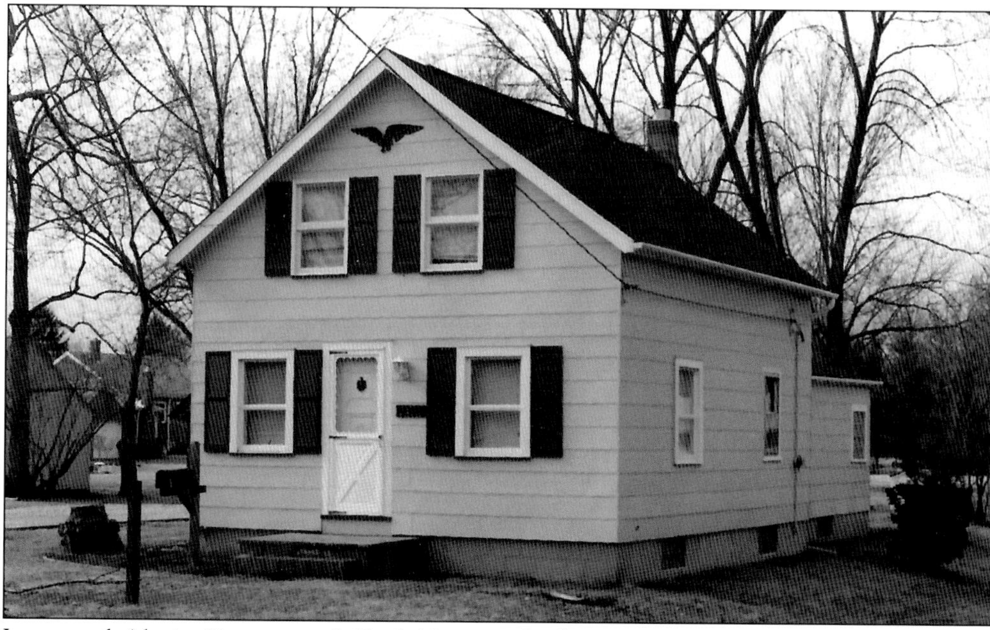

James and Almira Eaton raised 12 children in the house at 5532 West 220th Street, which was built around 1865. At one time, they lived in the valley beneath where the Lorain Road high-level bridge was later built. As people could only ford the river at that point, Eaton was always helping people. This distracted enough time and money that the family almost starved one winter. So they relocated first to Bay Village then here. (Fairview Park Historical Society.)

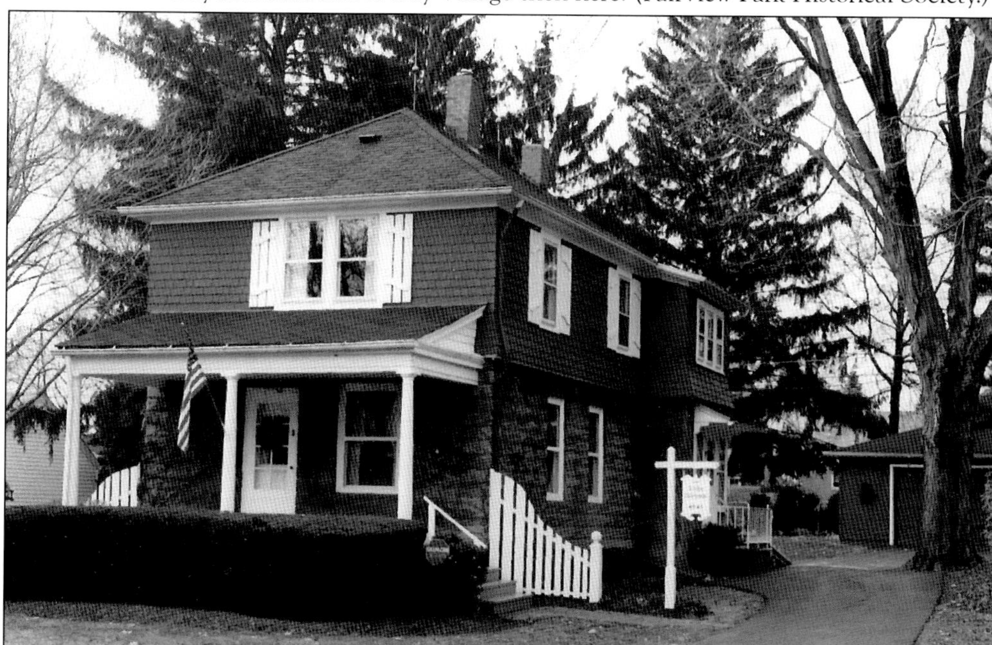

In 1953, James and Gloria Grant bought this house at 4648 West 220th Street, naming it Little Fairlawn after a golf course it reminded James of. Built in 1895, Vernon Spencer, grandson of John Place Spencer, made the bricks himself. He farmed here for a few years with his wife and five sons before relocating to Westlake. (Fairview Park Historical Society.)

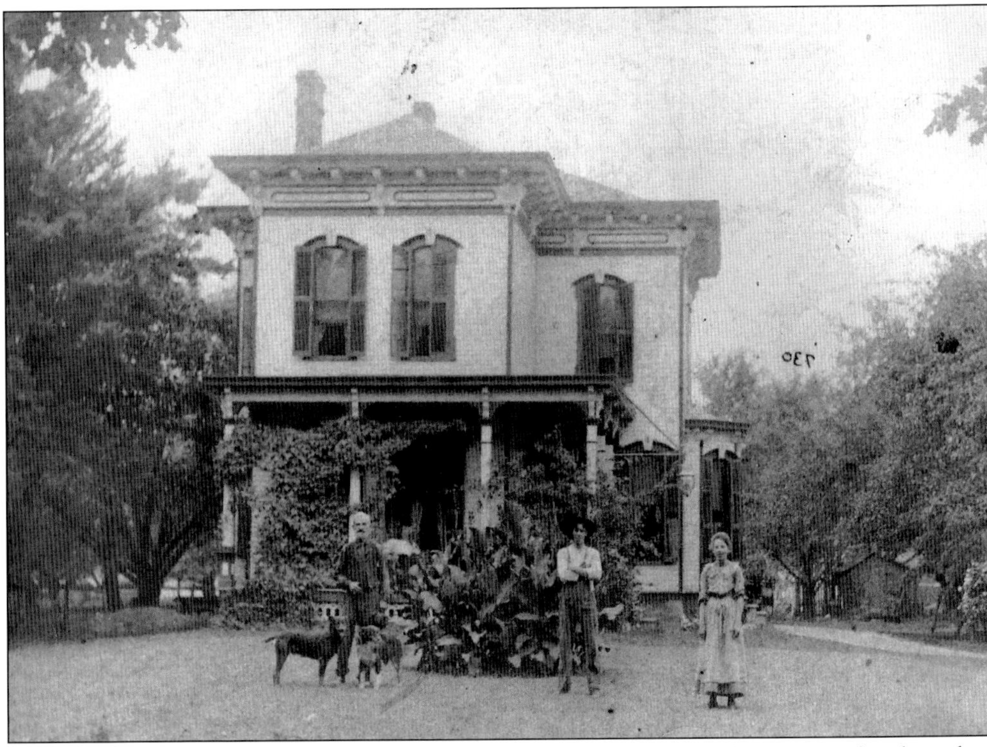

This home at 21566 Mastick Road brought together the Mastick and the Spencer families when Frank Mastick, son of Asahel, married Hannah Spencer, daughter of John Place Spencer. They raised six children in the house, built in 1866. In 1926, the upper half was rebuilt after damage from a fire, hence the less ornate roof. (Fairview Park Historical Society.)

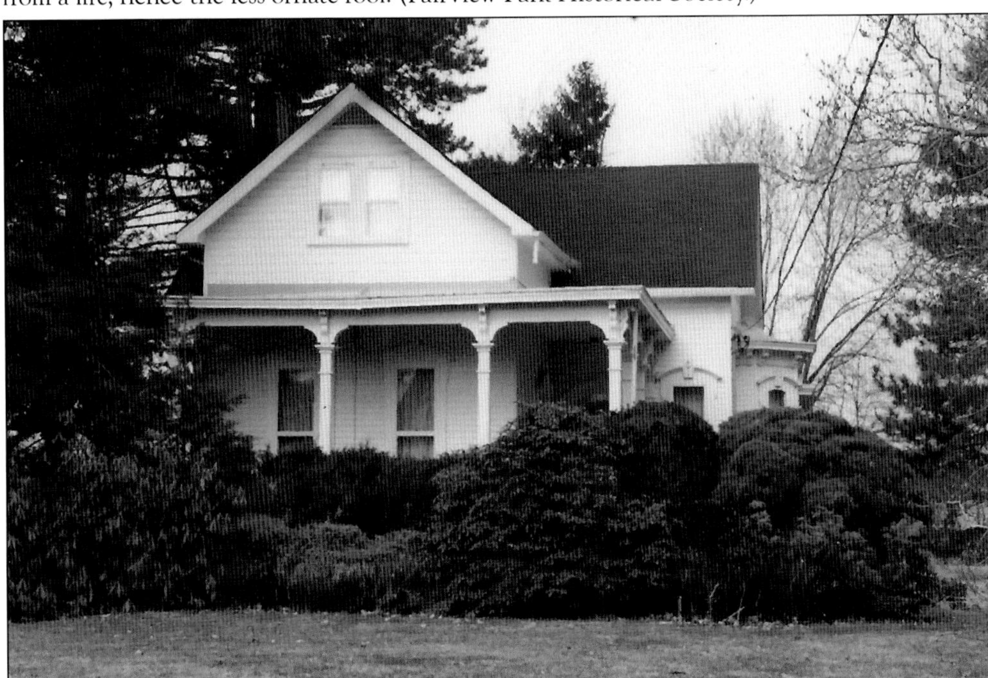

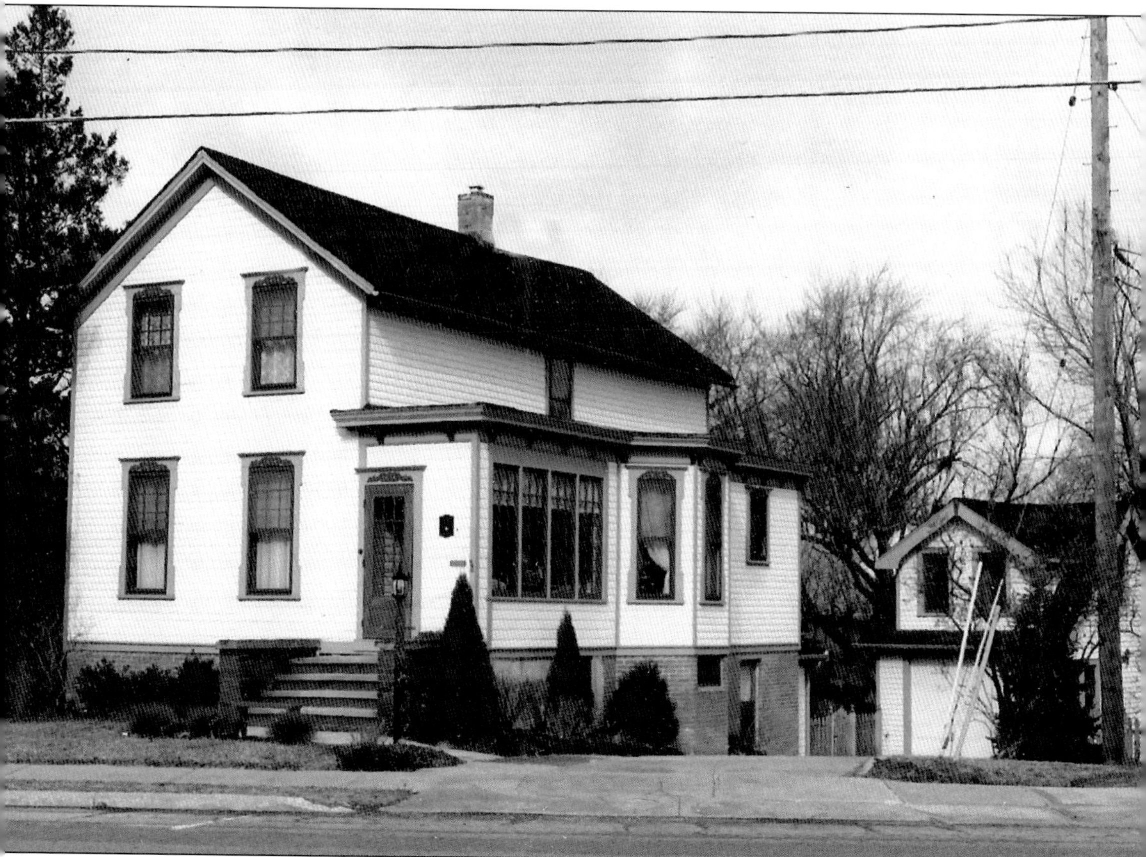

Sometime after marrying and starting a family in their native Germany in 1870, Johann and Maria Frobetier sailed to America. They had not intended the remote country life of Rockport Township, but the family of four children was too large for the planned housing in Cleveland. Johann was referred to George Mastick in Rockport, and so he made the long walk by himself. Speaking no English, he and George managed to agree to the farm work he could do and the house he could live in at 19270 Lorain Road next to the Masticks. This property used to extend all the way into the Coffinberry area before that was developed. Here they grew produce and raised some farm animals. The only change over the years was enclosing the front porch. (Fairview Park Historical Society.)

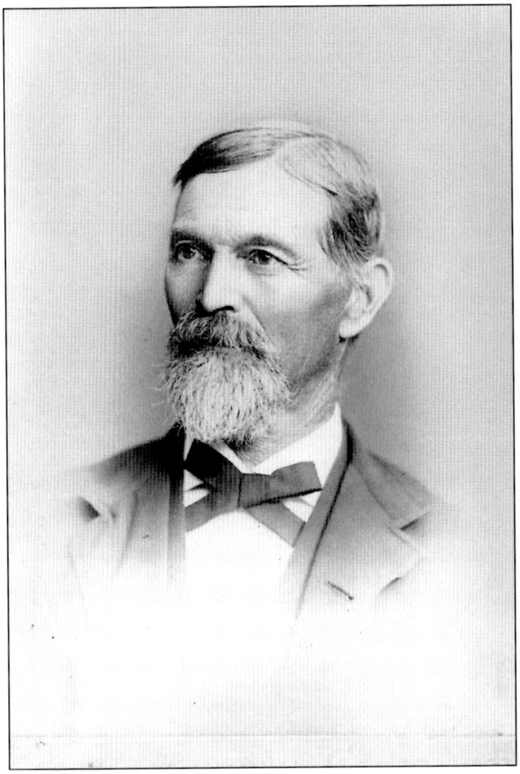

William Caleb Eggleston acquired land in 1846 but did not build a house until 1867 after heading west for gold. Whether it is true or not, the story goes that he finally returned to the site in classic gold rush style, riding a mule and carrying his gold riches to pay for the house. (Fairview Park Historical Society.)

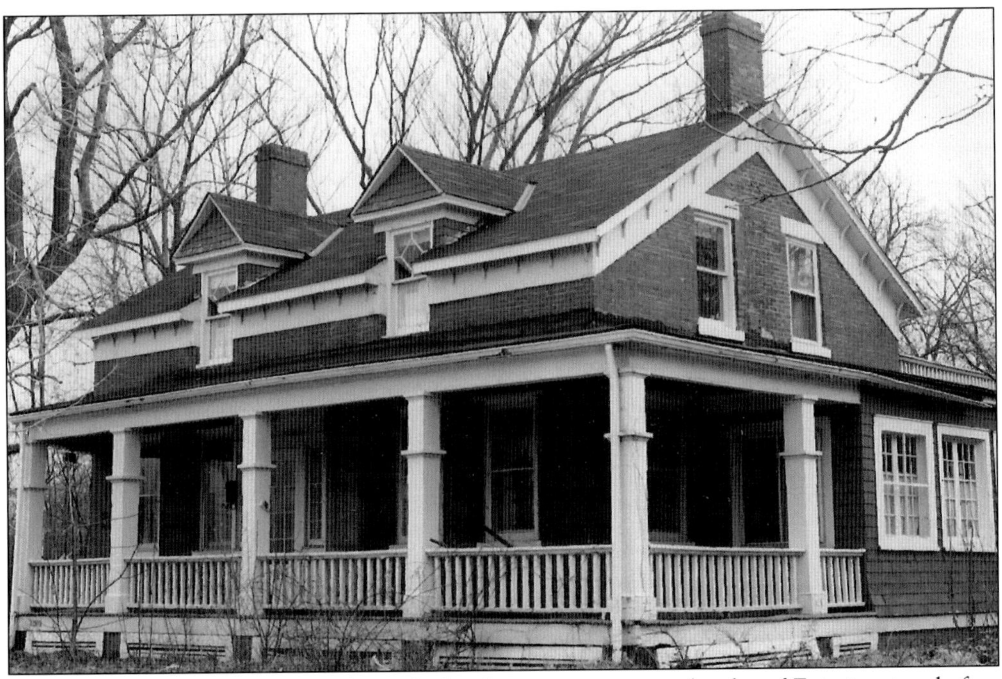

This home at 22915 Lorain Road is right by the current western border of Fairview just before North Olmsted. William Caleb Eggleston built it and was the first of several Egglestons in Fairview history, including one of the early mayors of the village. (Fairview Park Historical Society.)

When James Potter married Mary, another child of John Place Spencer, they combined the land she got from her father with the Potter land. The farm was originally on both sides of Lorain Road, although the northern half was sold when James died in 1911. The remaining land eventually became the Fairview Shopping Center, with the house originally where the Fairview Theater was built. West 217th Street, which ends at Lorain Road across from the shopping center, used to be called Potter Street. (Fairview Park Historical Society.)

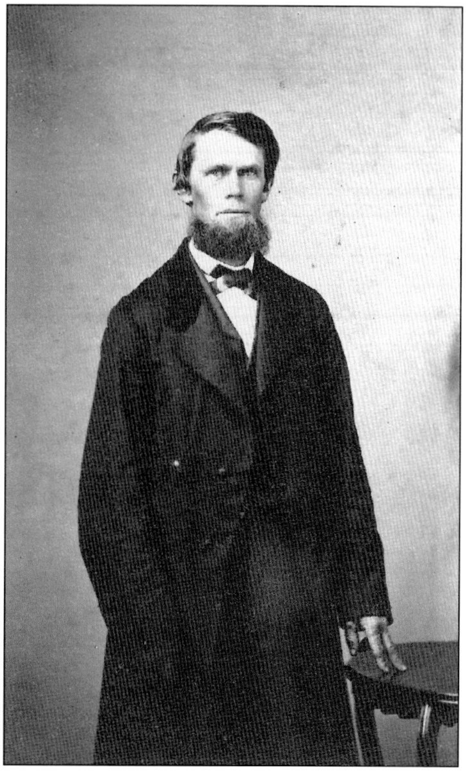

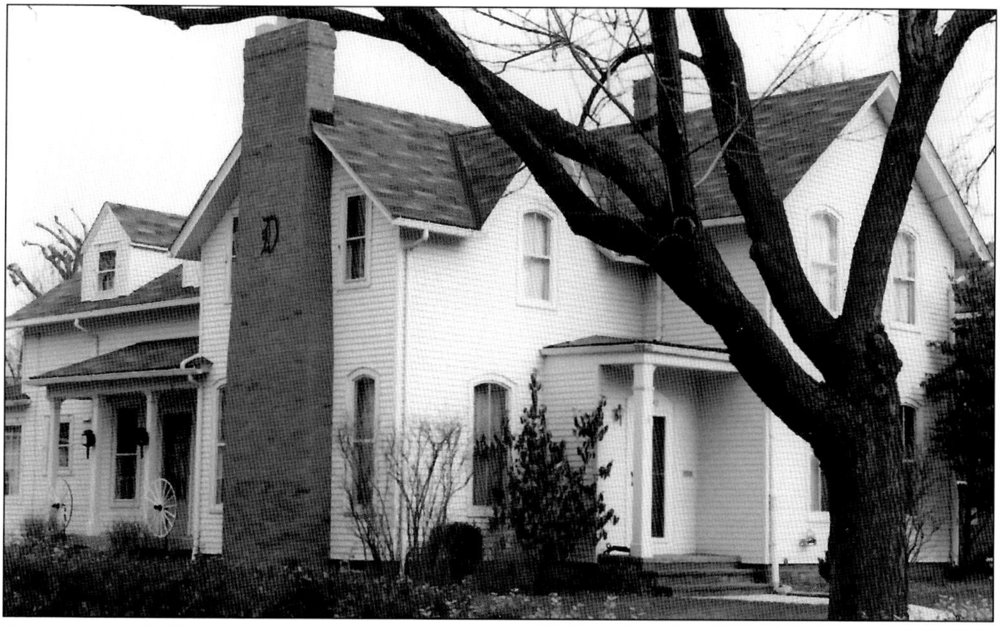

At one time, Willis Potter, heir of his parents' farm had a very popular produce stand on Lorain Road. His success came to an end, losing the land in the Great Depression. Eventually his children repurchased the house and some of the land, moving the structure to what became 21492 Hillsdale Avenue. The farm eventually became the Fairview Shopping Center. (Fairview Park Historical Society.)

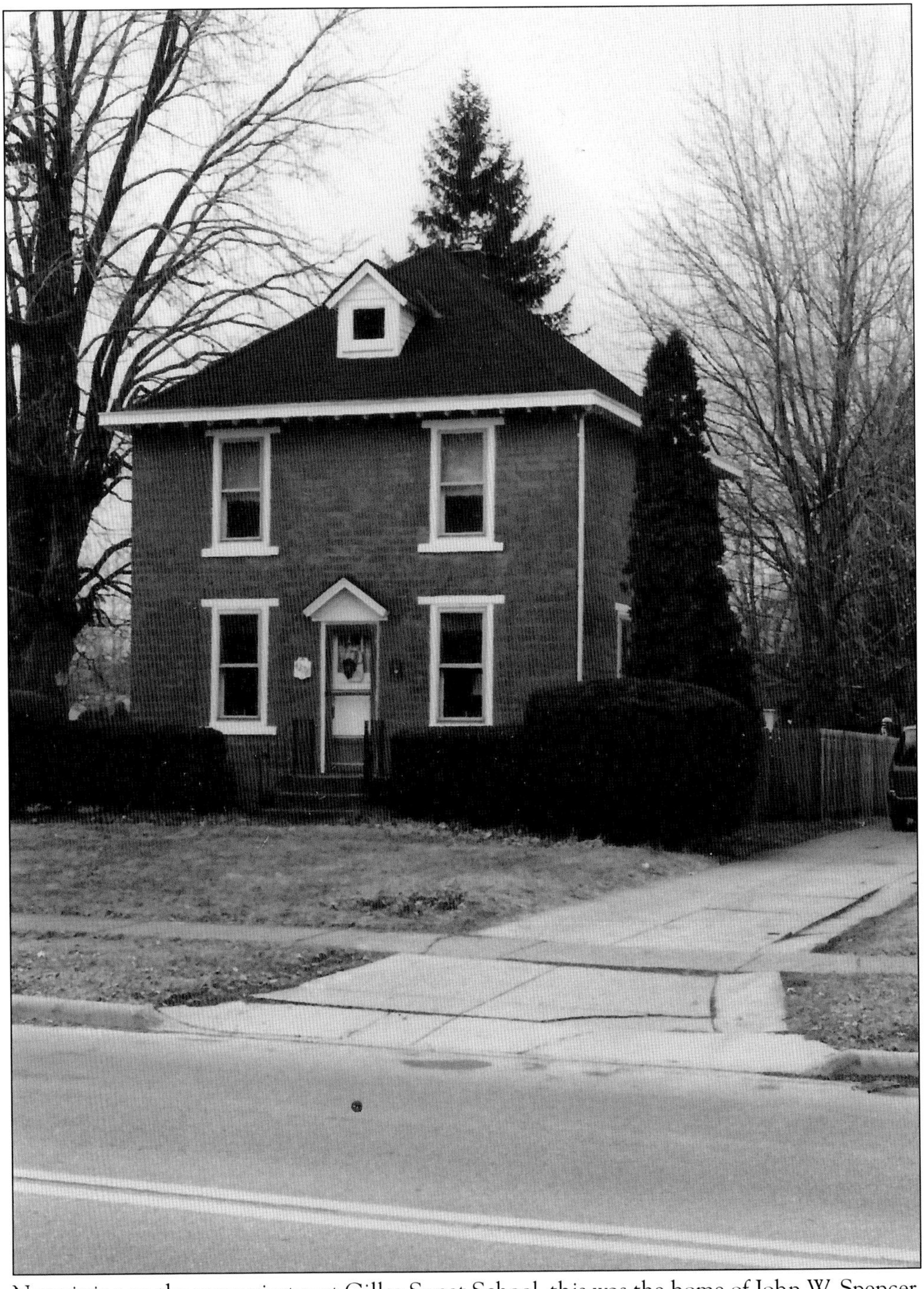

Now sitting on the corner just past Gilles-Sweet School, this was the home of John W. Spencer, son of John Place Spencer, built in 1876 at 4278 West 220th Street. He started a brick-and-tile business nearby, which probably made these clay tiles. Goldwood Township, the short-lived division of Rocky River Village before it further divided into Fairview Village, was named after John's wife, Deborah Goldwood. (Fairview Park Historical Society.)

Four

LIBRARIES AND SCHOOLS

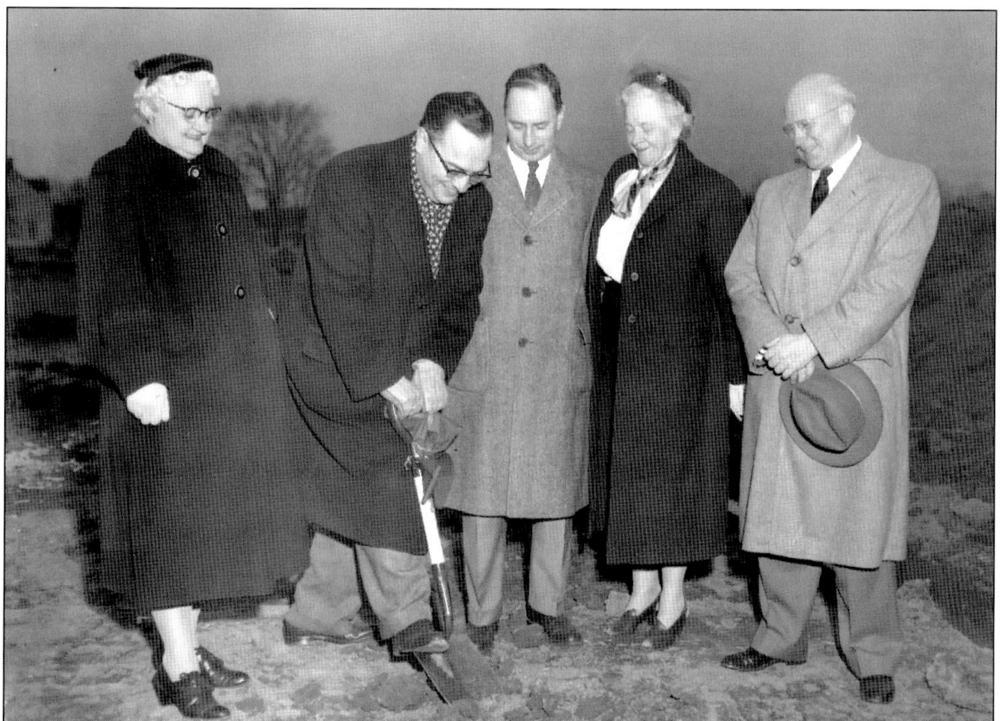

Breaking ground for the new library on November 21, 1955, from left to right are Bernice Happer, Reg Meridew, Theo Hills, Mary Cameron, and school superintendent Lewis F. Mayer. (Cleveland Press Archives, Cleveland State University.)

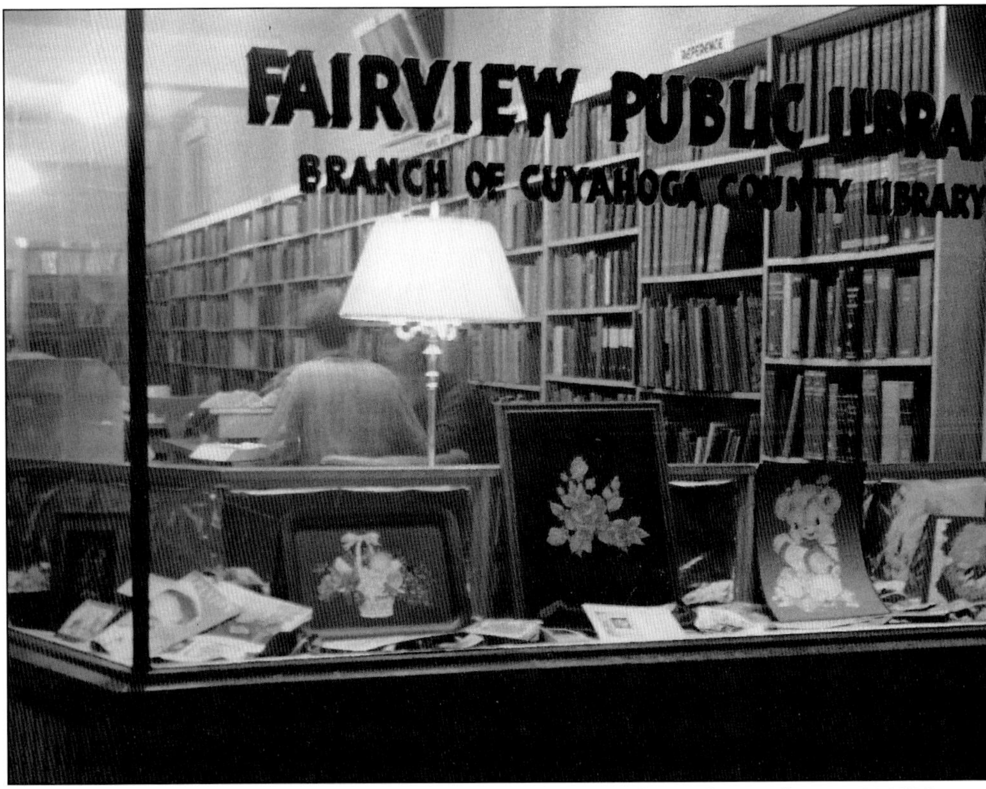

Fairview Park actually outgrew two libraries. This one operated out of a storefront at 21468 Lorain Road from 1942 to 1956. (Fairview Park Historical Society.)

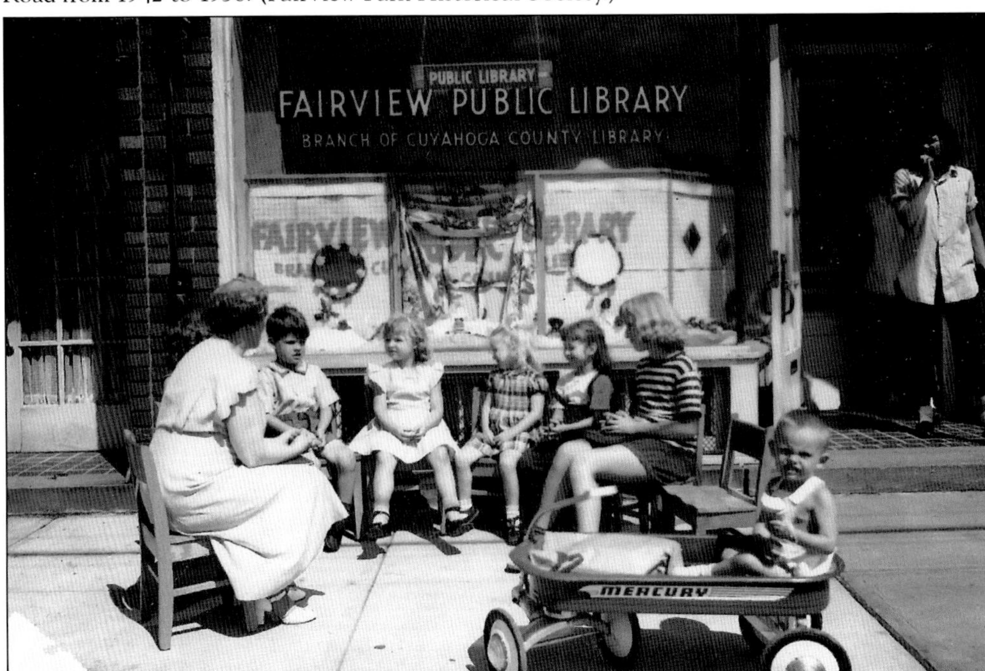

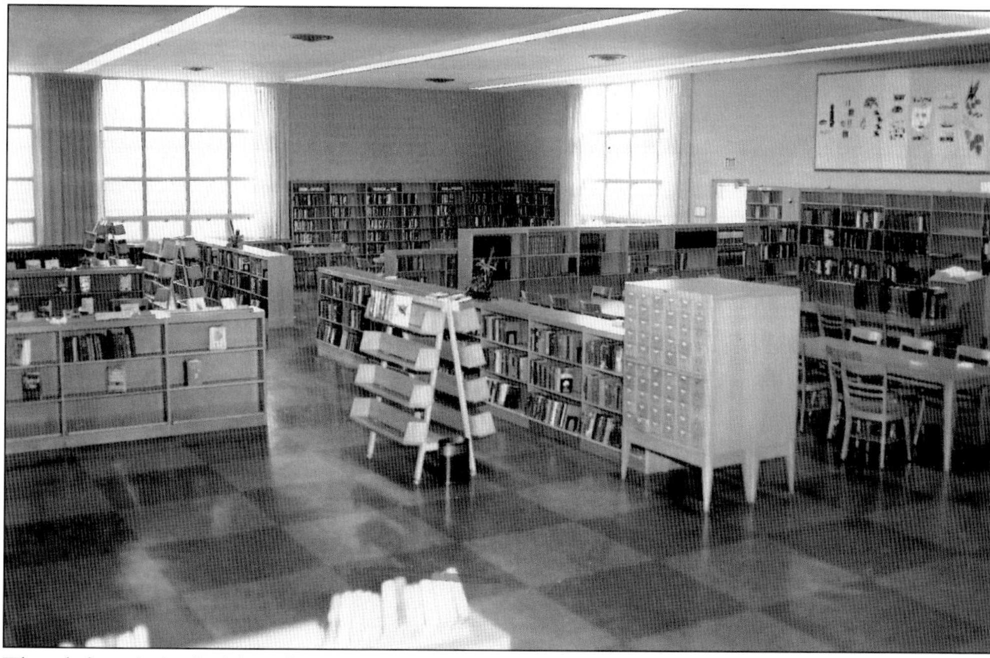

This definitely looks like adequate space for a library in 1957. But longtime users remember the floor space slowly becoming less and less; another rack or bookcase might show up or another table might get moved to storage. Even lounging space to read magazines was slowly shrinking. Eventually, more computer terminals replaced card catalogs. As some of the last open space so vital to libraries for reading and lounging was gobbled up, a much bigger library opened just north of here in 1997. This building sat empty for a few years and for a while was even considered as space for sixth-grade classes. That never happened, and the building was eventually demolished for the recreation center. (Cleveland Press Archives, Cleveland State University.)

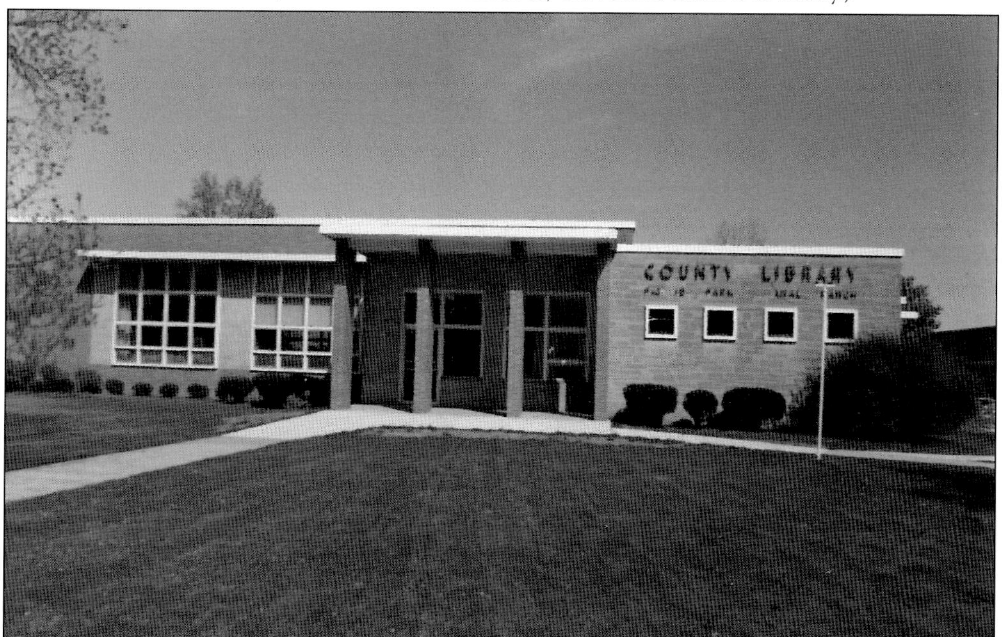

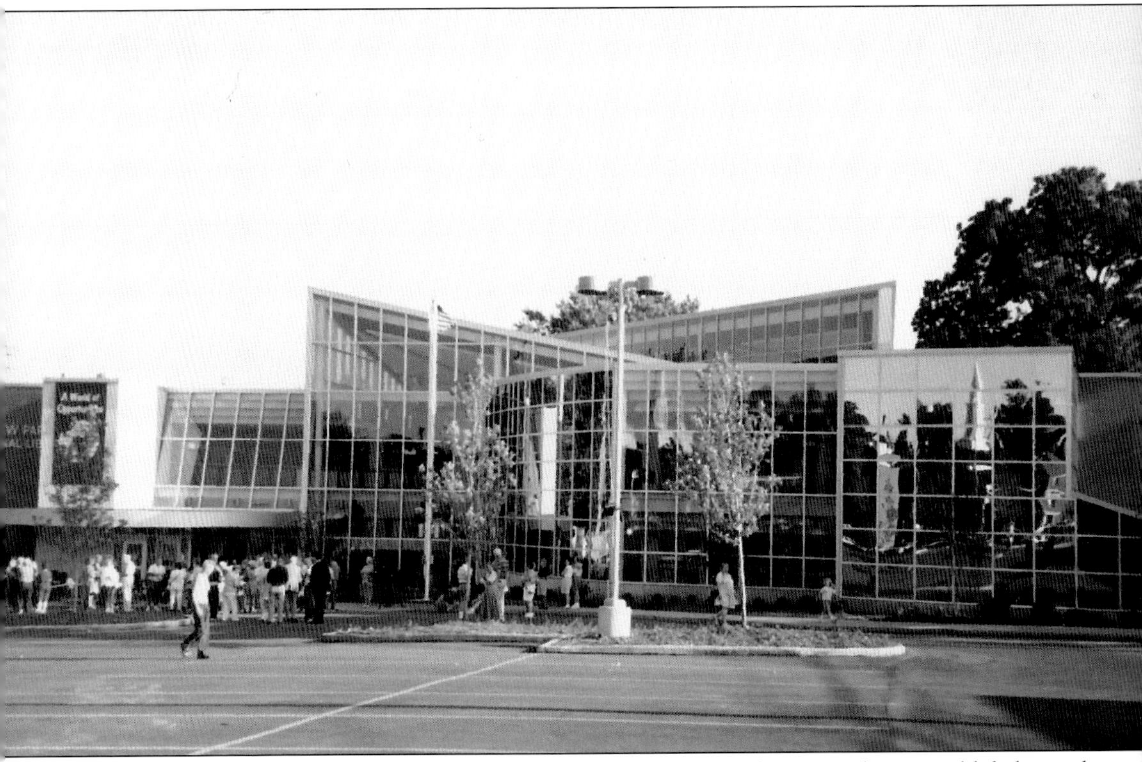

Libraries have struggled against modern technology to prove that something as old fashioned as reading books is still popular. Fairview Park obviously proved that it was when a huge new library was dedicated on August 8, 1997. (Fairview Park Historical Society.)

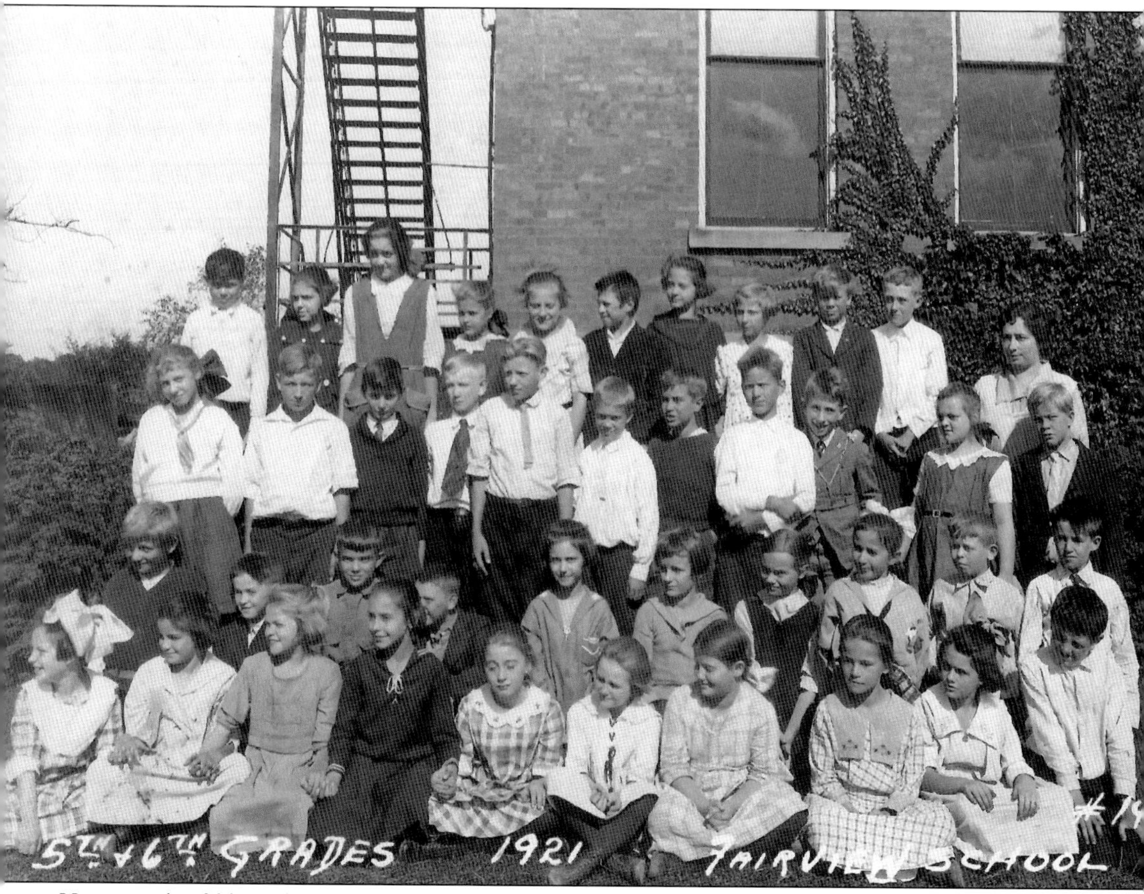

Here are the fifth and sixth grades in 1921 shortly after the school's name changed from State Street School to Fairview Grammar School. The name changed again to Garnett School when the high school was built, to avoid confusion. This was the only school in the village until Gilles-Sweet School was built in 1925. The building was expanded a few times with four rooms and a gymnasium added about the time of this picture. Most of it was demolished in 1968 for the new Garnett School, which stood for almost 40 years, until it came down in 2007 for retail development. One can only speculate why most of the children in this picture are looking off to the right. (Fairview Park Historical Society.)

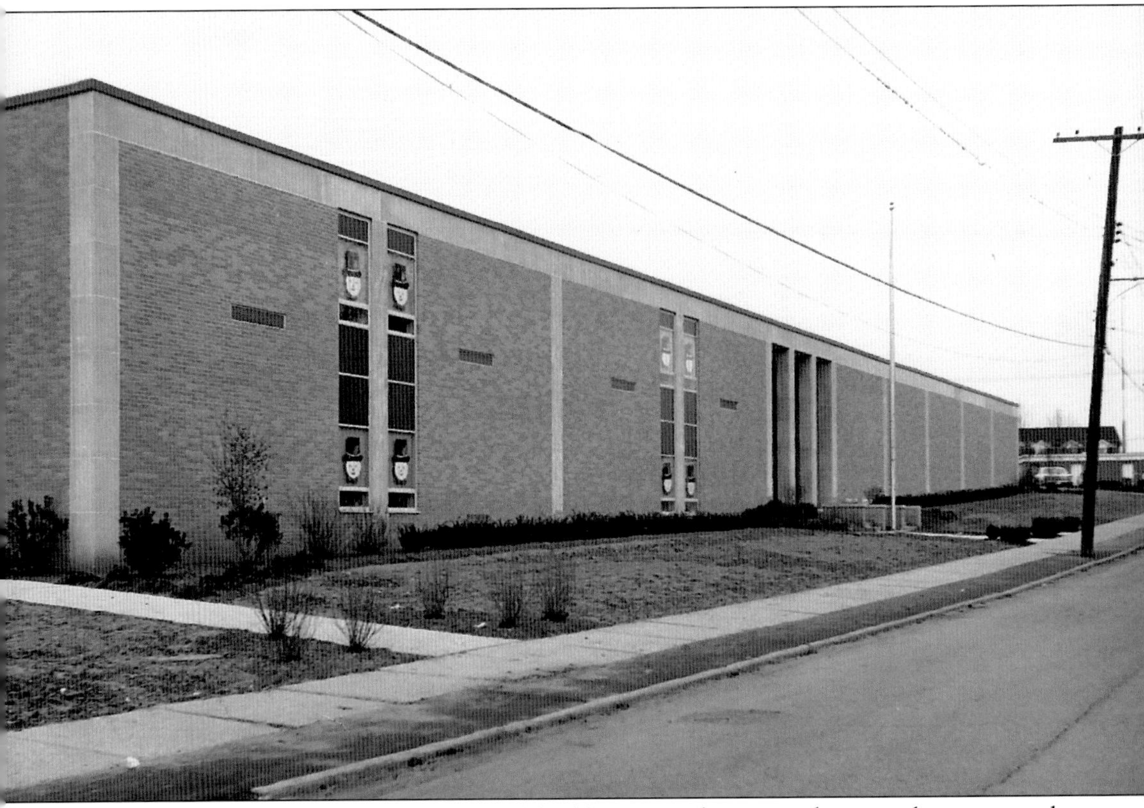

With all the expansions of the original building over the years, this was the most modern updating of Garnett School in 1968. When Fairview Grammar School needed a new name in 1928, the name was chosen to honor Lisle Garnett, who was on the village's first board of education and its president for 15 years. He was married to Hannah, one of the daughters of Johann and Maria Frobetier, whose house was one of the first designated Fairview century homes. After some name changes and several expansions over the years, Garnett School was demolished in 2008. (Fairview Park Historical Society.)

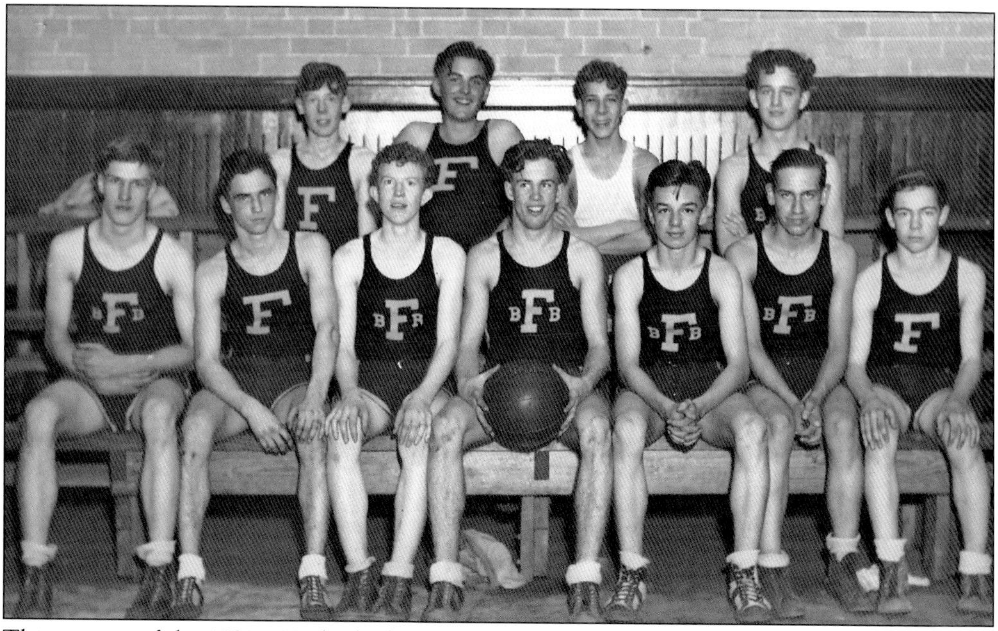

This picture of the 1931–1932 basketball team was in the first Fairview High School yearbook. (Fairview Park Historical Society.)

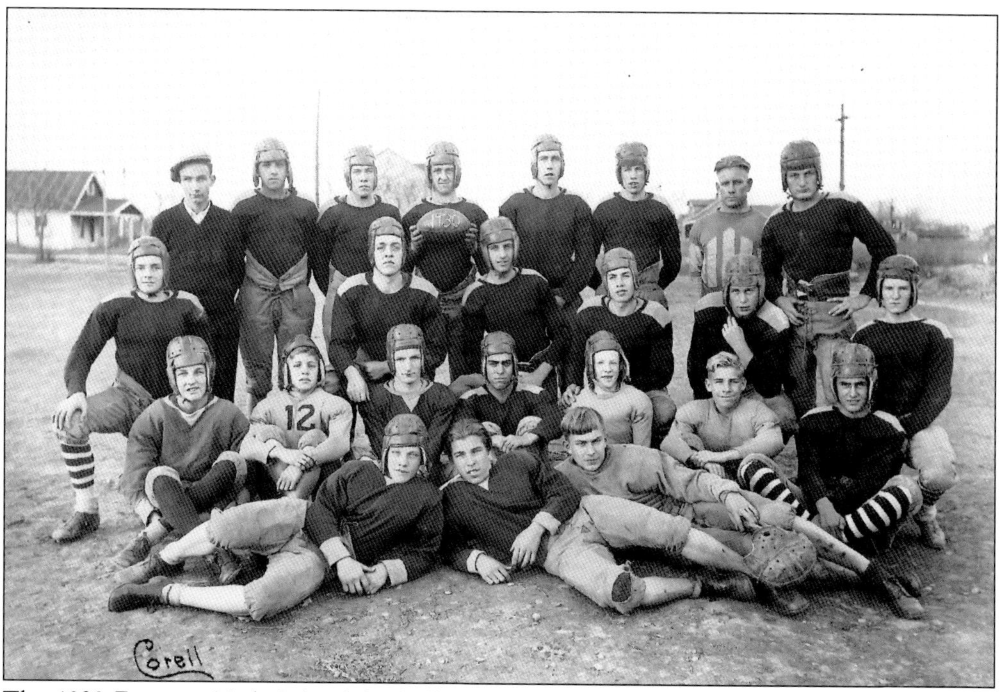

The 1930 Fairview High School football team looks ready to prove that because the village finally had its own high school, these guys were a force to be reckoned with. (Fairview Park Historical Society.)

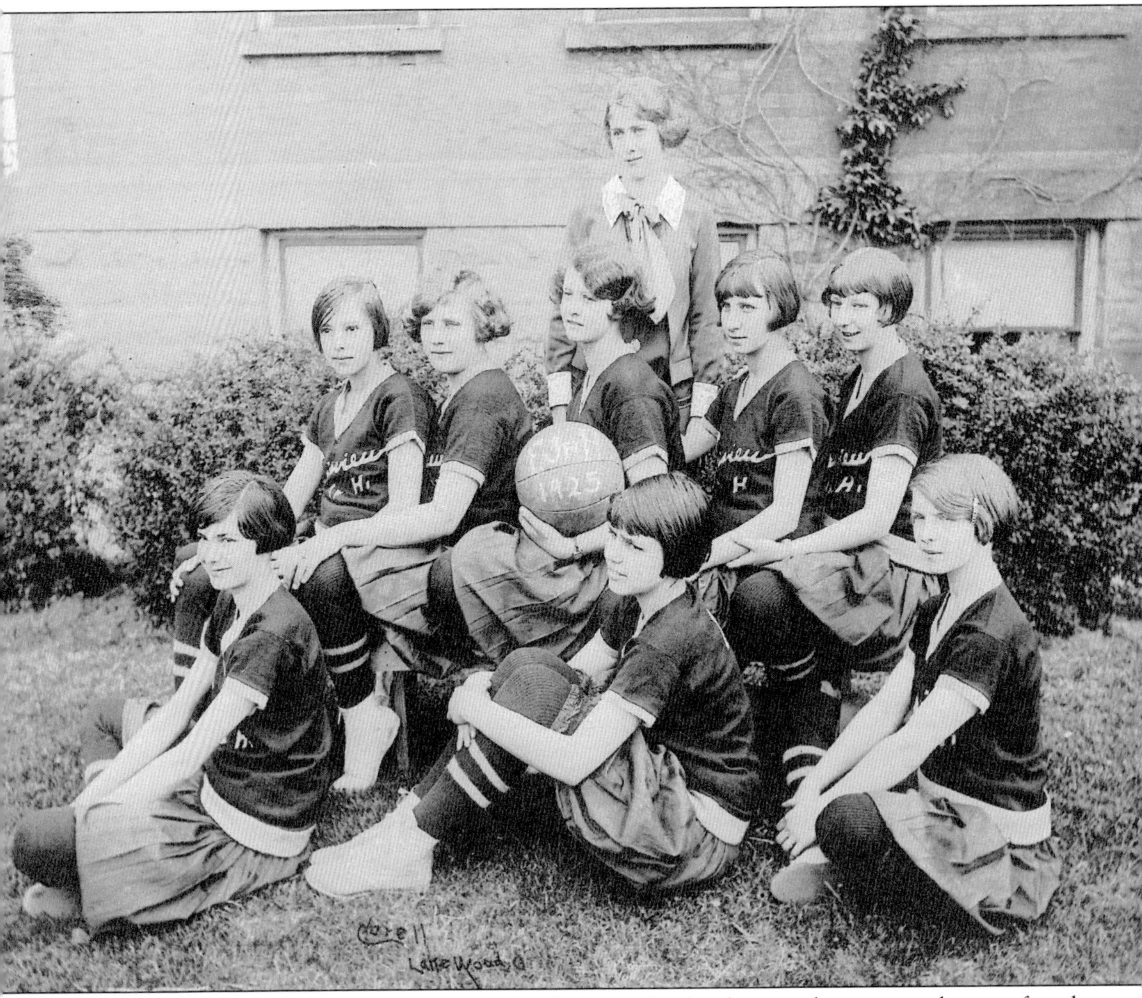

Posing at the usual corner of Garnett School where all school group shots were taken are female athletes from the junior high school around 1925. They were the oldest girls in Fairview Village sports, since no high school had been built yet. (Fairview Park Historical Society.)

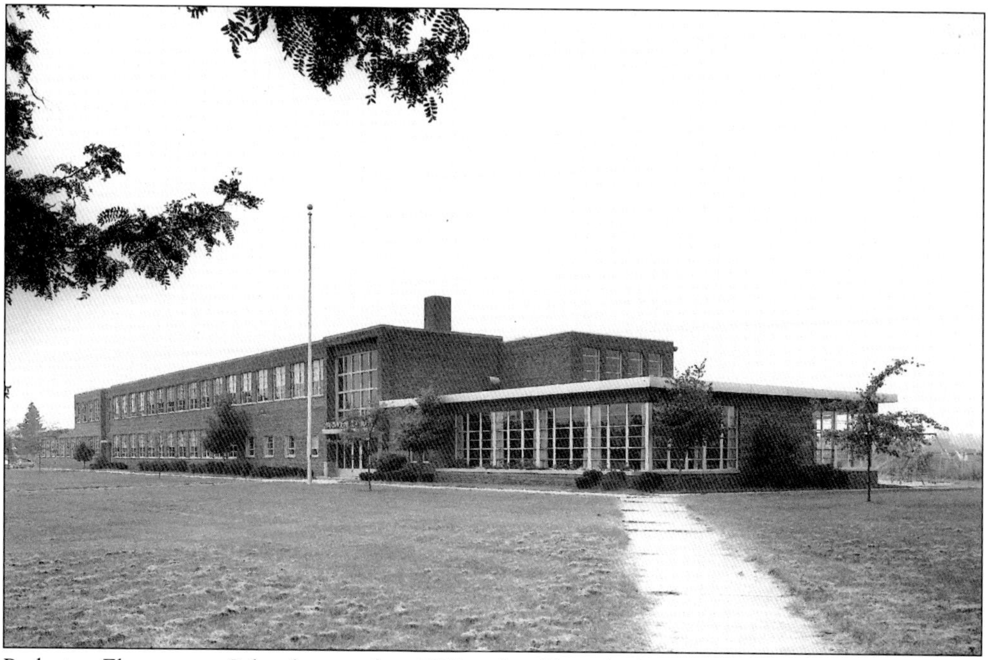

Parkview Elementary School opened in 1955 on land bought from the Spencers in 1926. When it ceased being a grade school, the board of education moved its offices from the Garnett area. For the school's first 10 years, Margaret Schaefer Goebelt was the principal. Ten years after that, she wrote *Fairview Park in Historical Review.* (Fairview Park Historical Society.)

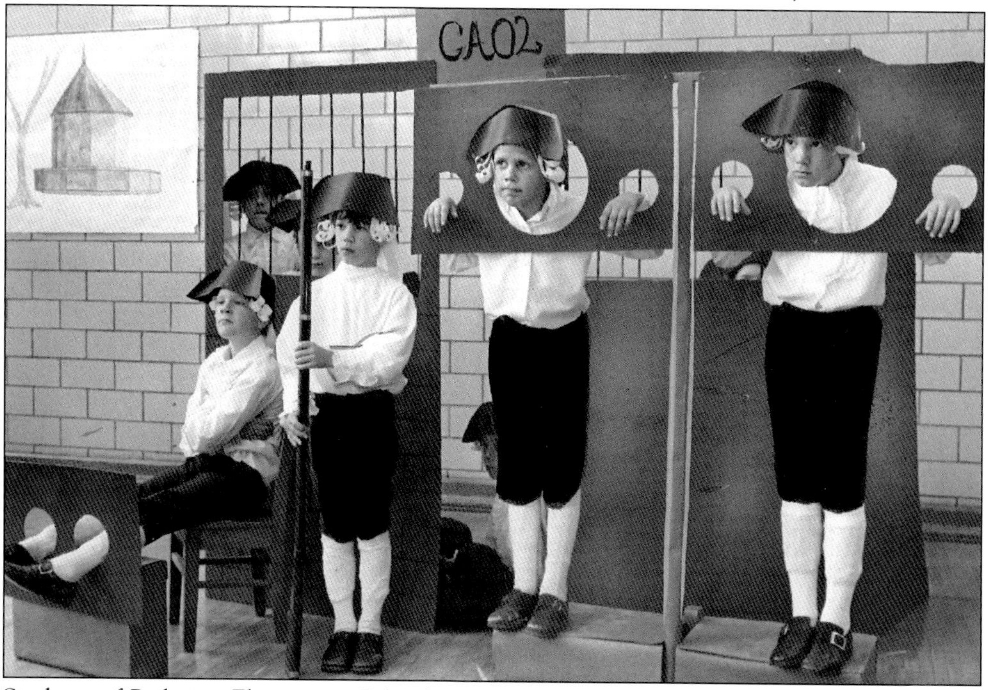

Students of Parkview Elementary School in 1966 are reenacting a Colonial-era penal system. The word *gaol* is old English for jail. From left to right are Jay Burkett, Bill Roemer, Billy Ruffner, and Bobby Mach, all eight years old. (Cleveland Press Archives, Cleveland State University.)

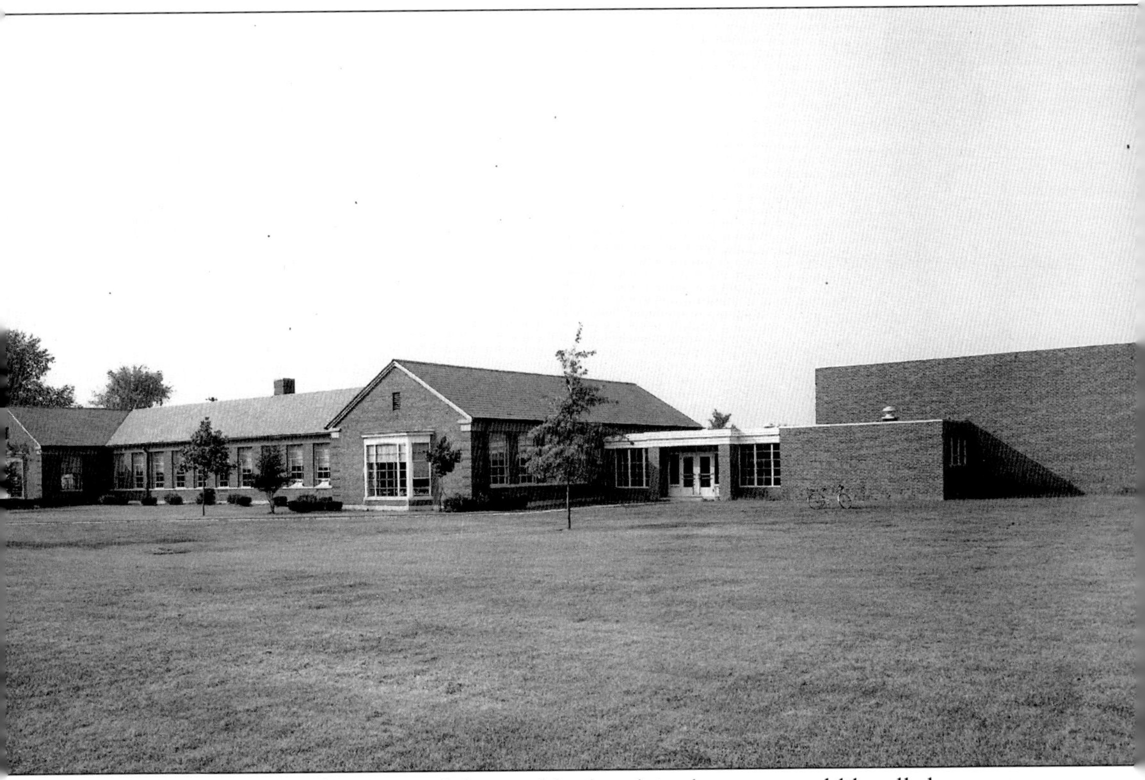

Although not quite the center of the neighborhood, it almost seemed like all the streets were radiating out from Coffinberry School. And yet, the school was not built until 1950. In later years, it got used as a day care until it was demolished in 2008. (Fairview Park Historical Society.)

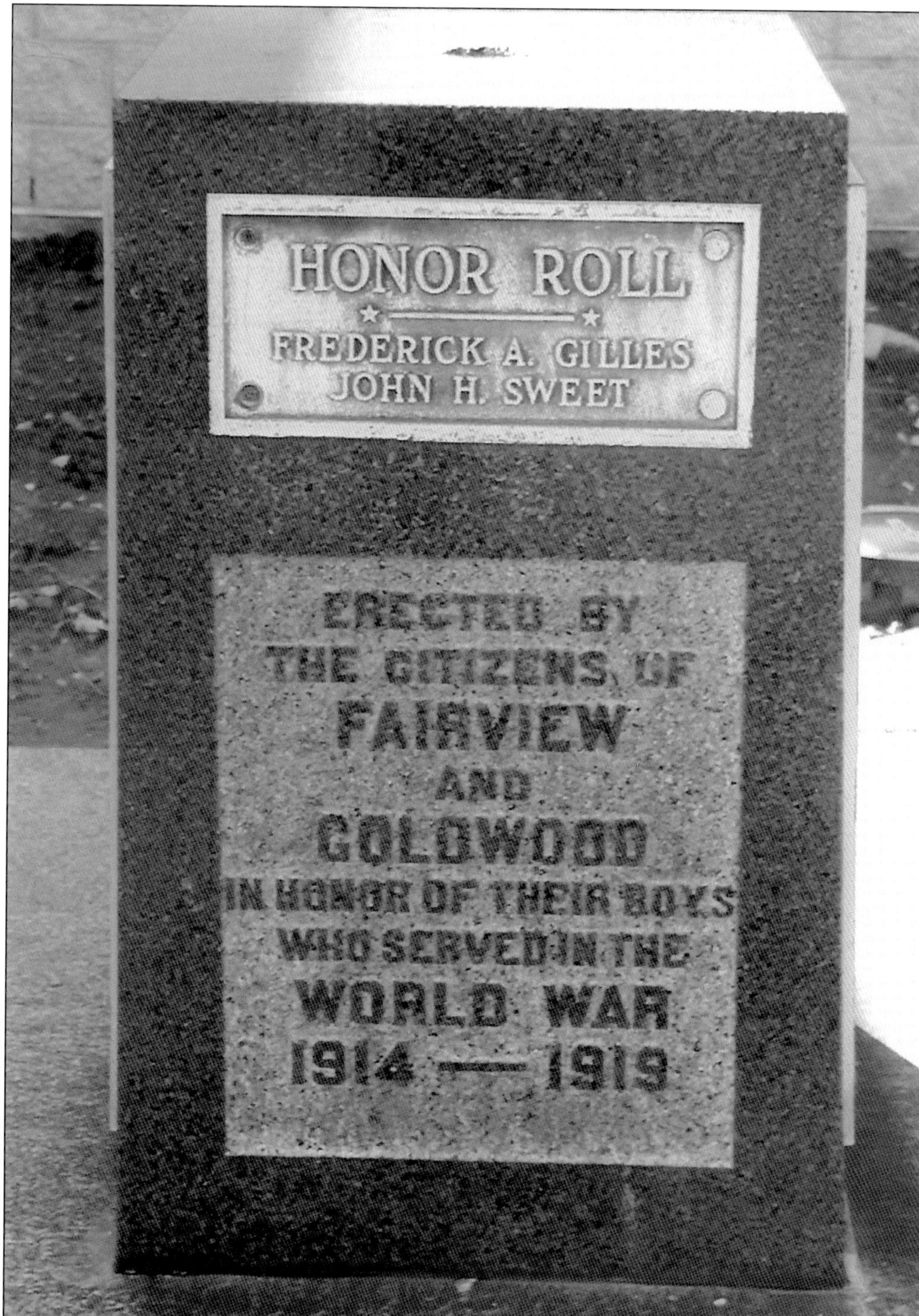

The following is from a John H. Sweet letter dated December 5, 1917: "When Germany finds us out she will assume a different attitude entirely—but when? Well here I am and there I was, and you yourself have seen me and know the change a month or two can produce. Germany is going to get licked, but how soon—after you and I are gone?" (Photograph by the author.)

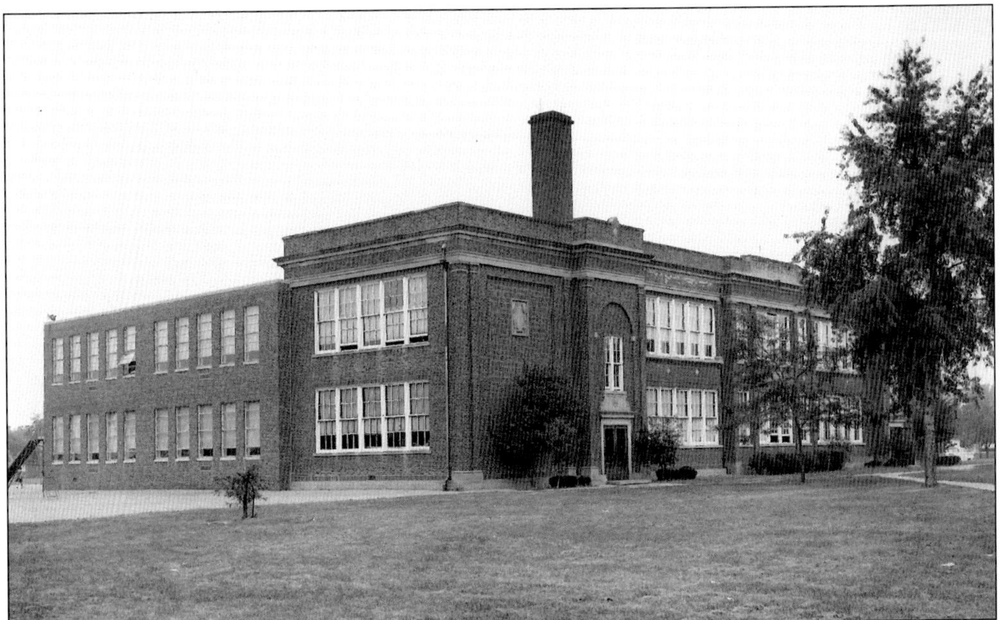

Gilles-Sweet School was named for John H. Sweet and Fred Gilles, both killed in World War I. Standing from 1925 to 2005, the original Gilles-Sweet School first closed in 1982 due to declining enrollment. It then became home to the senior center, the recreation department, the Fairview Park Hunger Center, Youth Challenge, and the Westshore Positive Education Program. (Fairview Park Historical Society.)

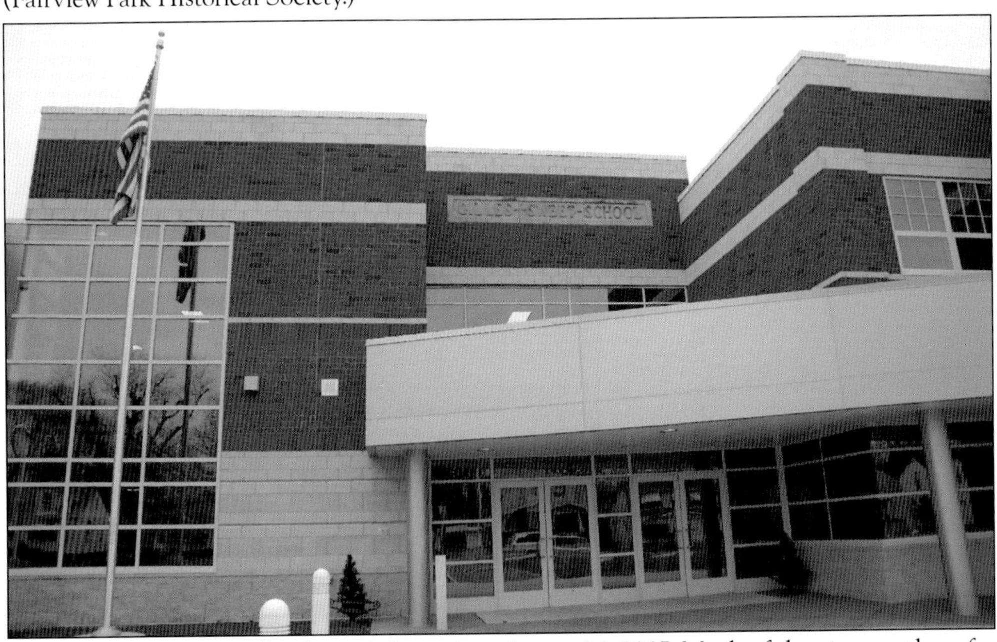

The new Gilles-Sweet School was dedicated on August 26, 2007. Much of the city was there for the grand opening as were a number of descendants of Gilles and Sweet. Particularly noticeable in pictures of the old building is the huge front lawn. The new building made use of this space. Notice that the old stone bearing the name of the school was reinstalled over the new entrance. (Photograph by David Barnett.)

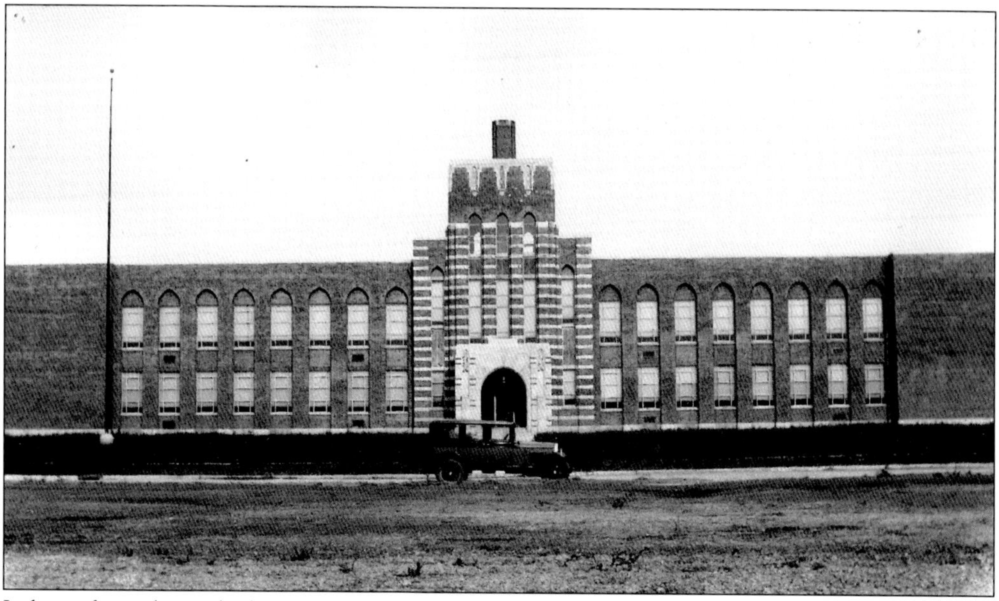

Judging from the parked car, this photograph is probably from the high school's opening. Before the high school was built in 1928, eighth graders had to take the state's Boxwell-Patterson exam. If they passed, they could go to any accredited high school in the state; some went to Cleveland, and some went as far as Elyria. It was similar to the SAT tests that present-day high school seniors take to advance to college. (Fairview Park Historical Society.)

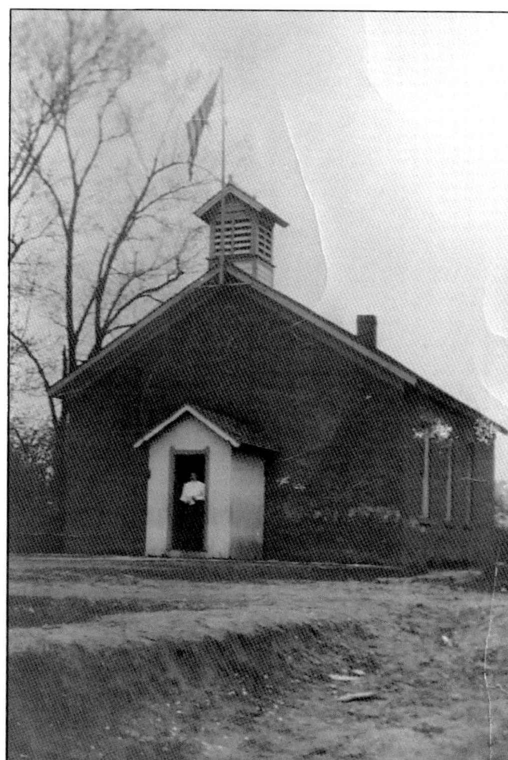

After about 20 years, the first public school in the area was replaced in 1860 by this building, across the street, the one-room State Street School where Garnett School later developed. A two-room school replaced it about 1908, with two more rooms added in 1917 and four more in 1921. It was called Fairview School and State Road School before becoming Garnett School. Teacher Hattie King stands in the doorway. (Fairview Park Historical Society.)

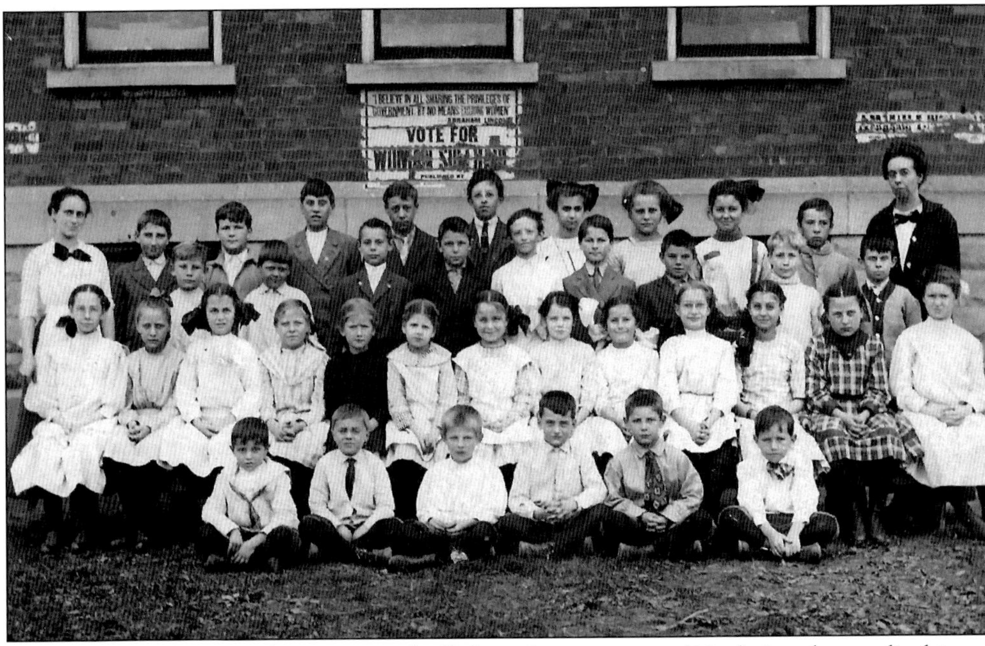

One might wonder in modern times with all the polarization in political views how radical it was having a sign for women's suffrage behind these Fairview Village children in 1907. The teachers are Hattie King (upper left) and Irene Nettleton (upper right). (Fairview Park Historical Society.)

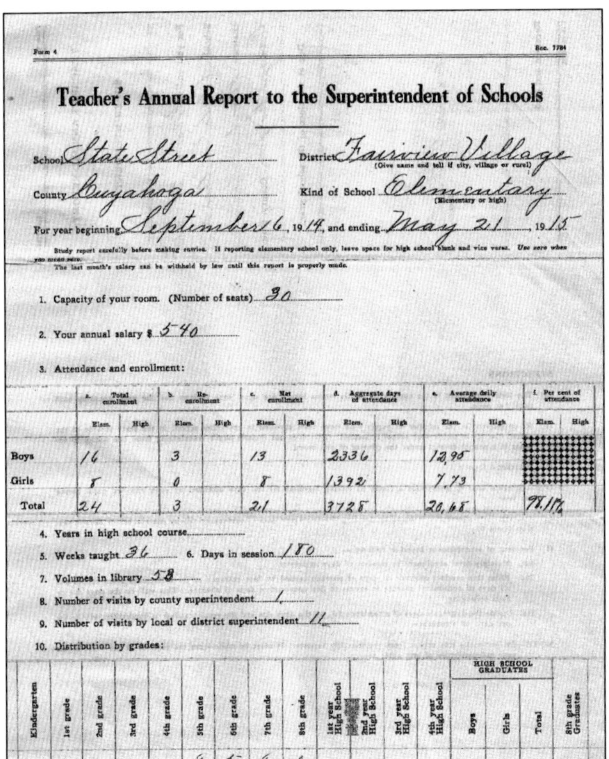

Form 4 Sec. 7784

Teacher's Annual Report to the Superintendent of Schools

School State Street District Fairview Village (Give name and tell if city, village or rural)

County Cuyahoga Kind of School Elementary (Elementary or high)

For year beginning September 6, 19 14, and ending May 21, 19 15

Study report carefully before making entries. If reporting elementary school only, leave space for high school blank and vice versa. Use zero when you mean zero.

The last month's salary can be withheld by law until this report is properly made.

1. Capacity of your room. (Number of seats) 30
2. Your annual salary $ 540
3. Attendance and enrollment:

	a. Total enrollment		b. Re-enrollment		c. Net enrollment		d. Aggregate days of attendance		e. Average daily attendance		f. Per cent of attendance	
	Elem.	High	Elem.	High	Elem.	High	Elem.	High	Elem.	High	Elem.	High
Boys	16		3		13		2336		12.95			
Girls	8		0		8		1392		7.73			
Total	24		3		21		3728		20.68		98.1%	

4. Years in high school course
5. Weeks taught 36 6. Days in session 180
7. Volumes in library 58
8. Number of visits by county superintendent 1
9. Number of visits by local or district superintendent 11
10. Distribution by grades:

Kindergarten	1st grade	2nd grade	3rd grade	4th grade	5th grade	6th grade	7th grade	8th grade	1st year High School	2nd year High School	3rd year High School	4th year High School	High School Graduates: Boys	Girls	Total	8th grade Graduates
					8	5	8	0								

Here in 1915, Anna Baker is reporting that she makes $540 a year teaching in the two-room State Street School. Margaret Schaefer Goebelt wrote, "Teachers were required to sweep the schoolroom daily, scrub the floor once a week, start a fire in the stove an hour before class time, and supervise that the water bucket was filled and the dipper clean. No drinking fountains or paper cups then—everyone drank from the same long-handled dipper." (Fairview Park Historical Society.)

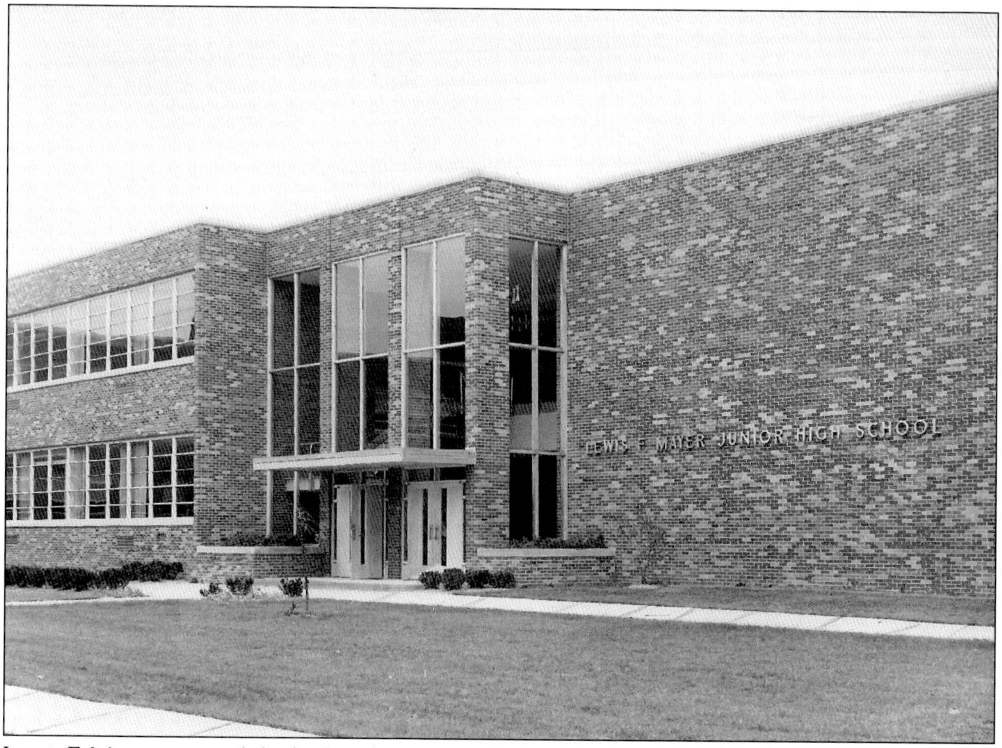

Lewis F. Mayer received the highest honor an educator can get, a school in his name, in 1960. He was recognized for his years of teaching and 43 years as the first superintendent. The only thing that changed about the entrance to Mayer Junior High School is when the name was changed to Mayer Middle School. (Fairview Park Historical Society.)

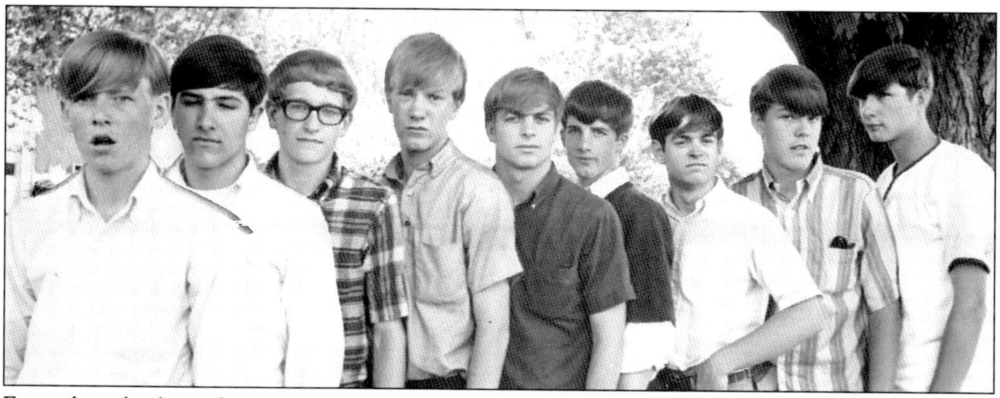

Even though about five years later the dress code would be liberalized to allow blue jeans and long hair on boys, these guys in May 1965 were ordered by Fairview High School principal Jack Moore to get their hair cut because he said they looked "ridiculous." (Cleveland Press Archives, Cleveland State University.)

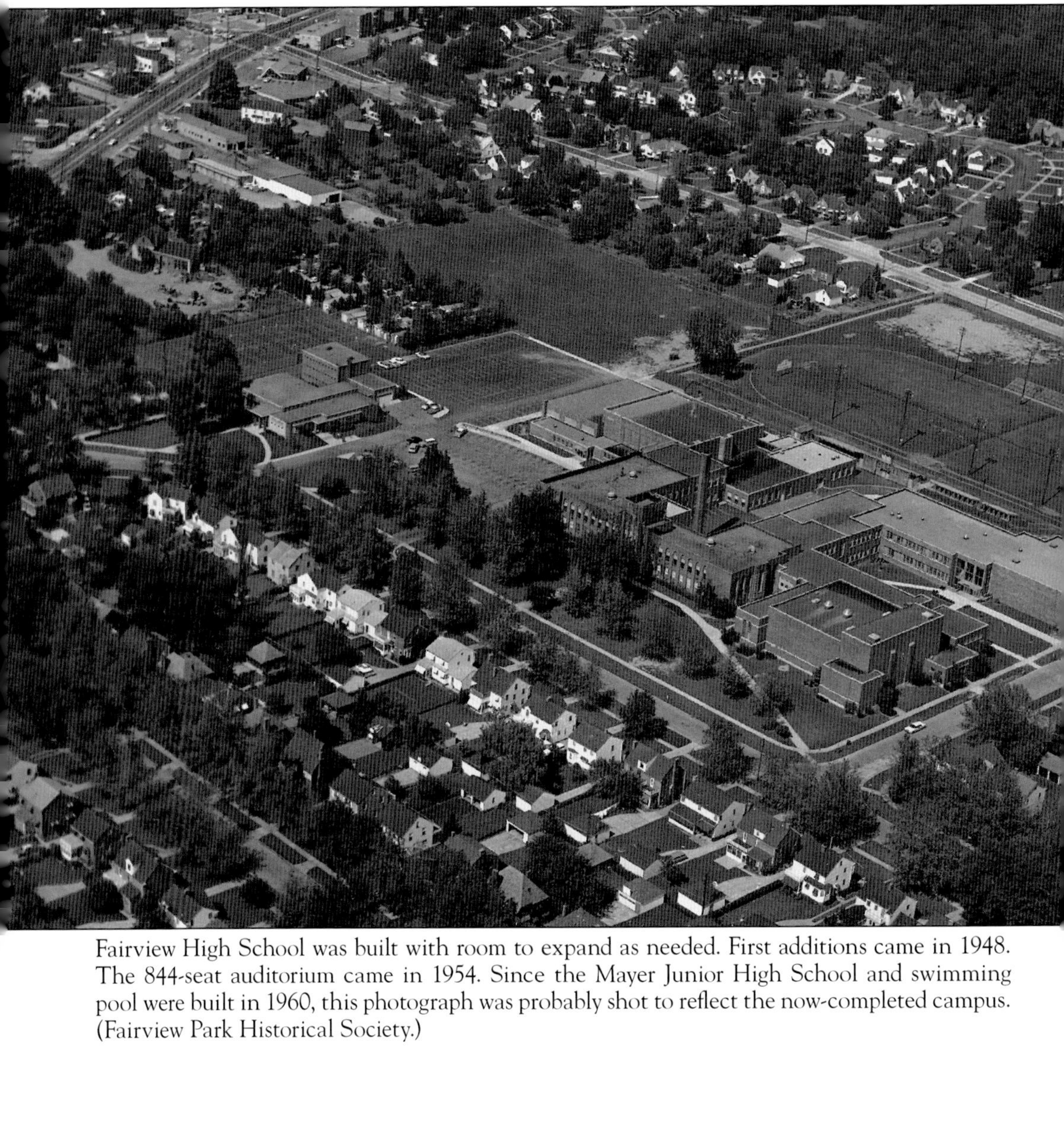

Fairview High School was built with room to expand as needed. First additions came in 1948. The 844-seat auditorium came in 1954. Since the Mayer Junior High School and swimming pool were built in 1960, this photograph was probably shot to reflect the now-completed campus. (Fairview Park Historical Society.)

Five

CHURCHES

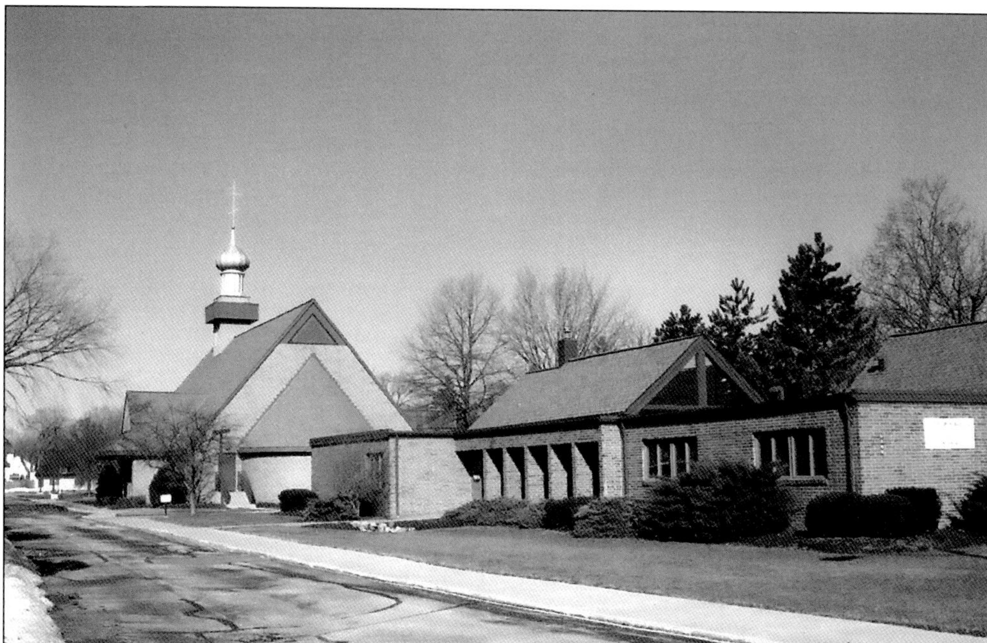

St. Mary Magdalene Byzantine Catholic Church does not take up a lot of frontage on West 220th Street, so it might not catch one's attention when driving by. But the facility is long and reaches back into the parking lot. Between its organization in 1966 and the new church in 1993, a beautiful, modern facility evolved with a couple large meeting rooms as well as the church itself. Before building began in 1969, services were held in either nearby Parkview Elementary School or the brick house on the property that was made into a rectory. (St. Mary Magdalene Byzantine Catholic Church.)

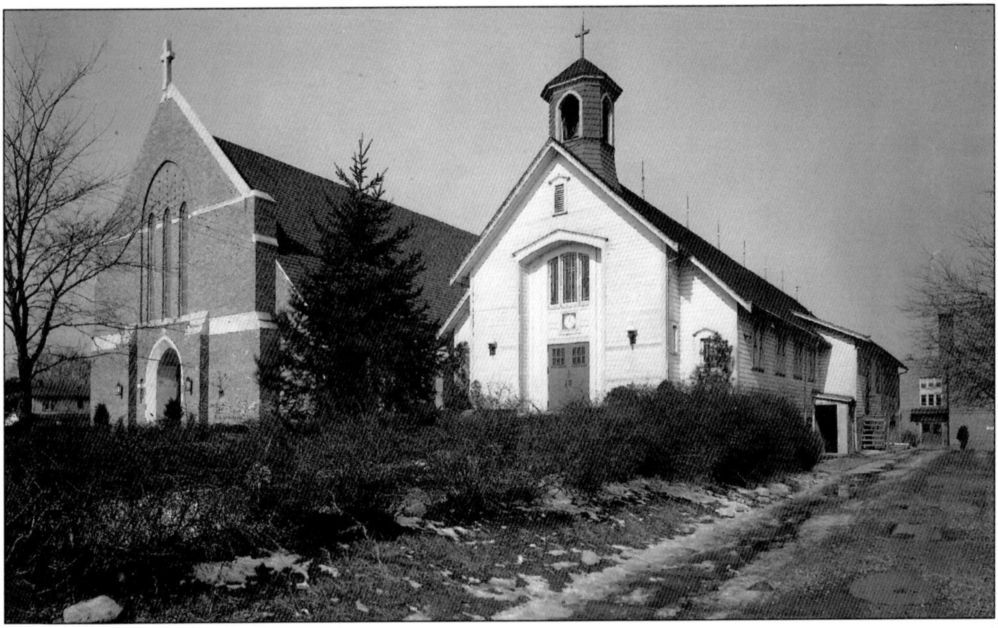

The original 1923 St. Angela Merici remained standing until the new church was completed in 1948. The entire building was then hauled to the side, opening a main driveway back to the school. For almost 40 years, the old church was used as a convent until it became the administrative center in 1988. These two buildings show how much the area was growing. This was also reflected in other area churches that expanded in the 1940s, despite limitations of the Depression and war years. (St. Angela Merici.)

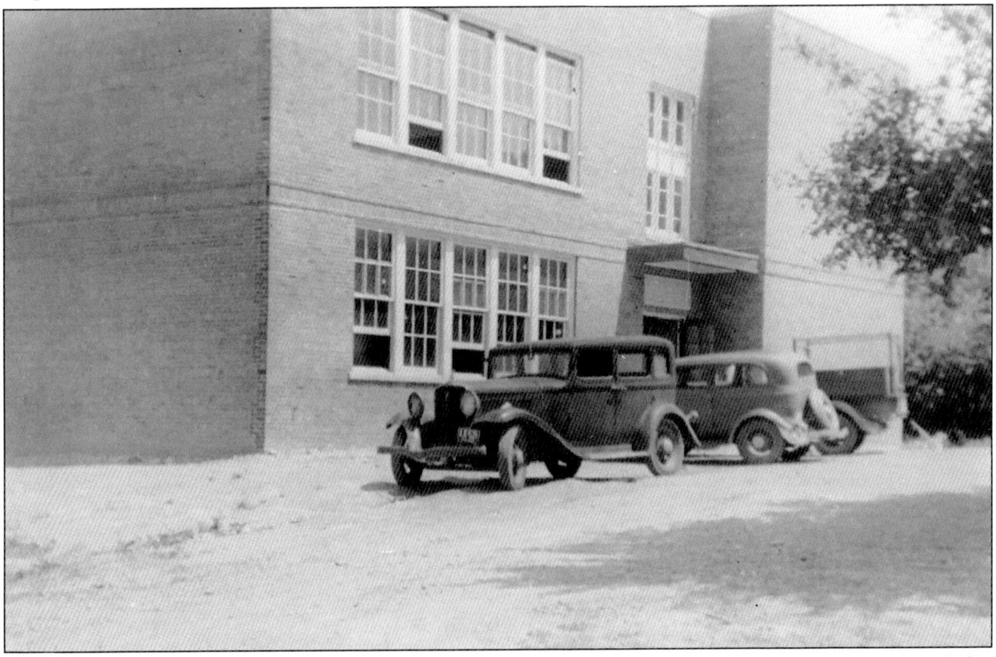

While the other end of St. Angela's School expanded over the years, the south side of the building in the early 1940s looks the same, except of course for the look of the automobiles. (St. Angela Merici.)

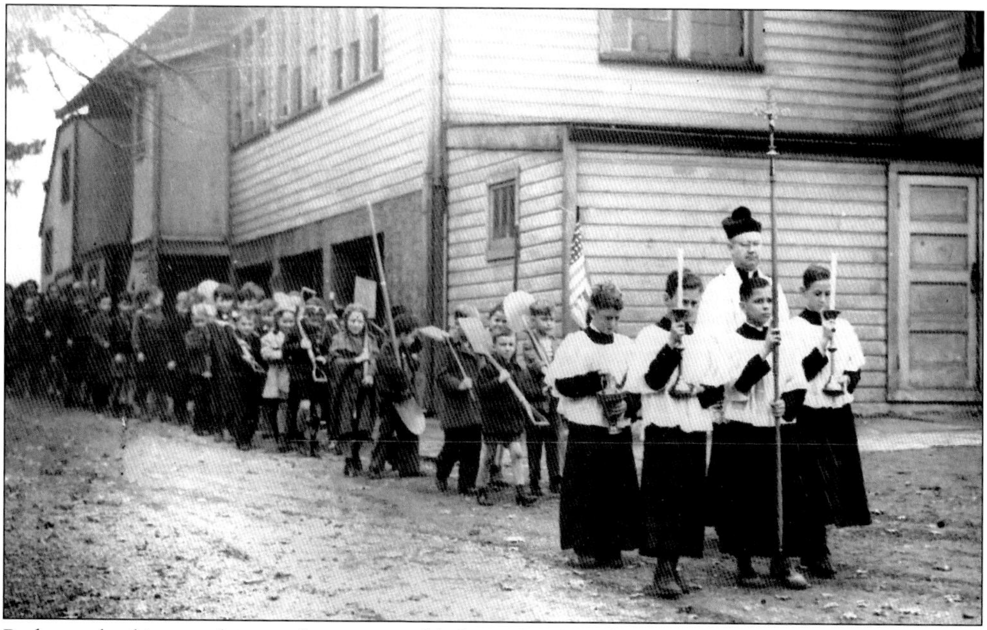

Perhaps the biggest driving force to establishing St. Angela's School in 1923 was providing a strong Catholic education for the children. Classes were conducted in the church when it first opened, but in 1939, ground was broken on a six-room school building north of the church, which expanded over the years. Fr. Michael Stevenson, who served from 1937 to 1954, leads parish children to the groundbreaking site. (St. Angela Merici.)

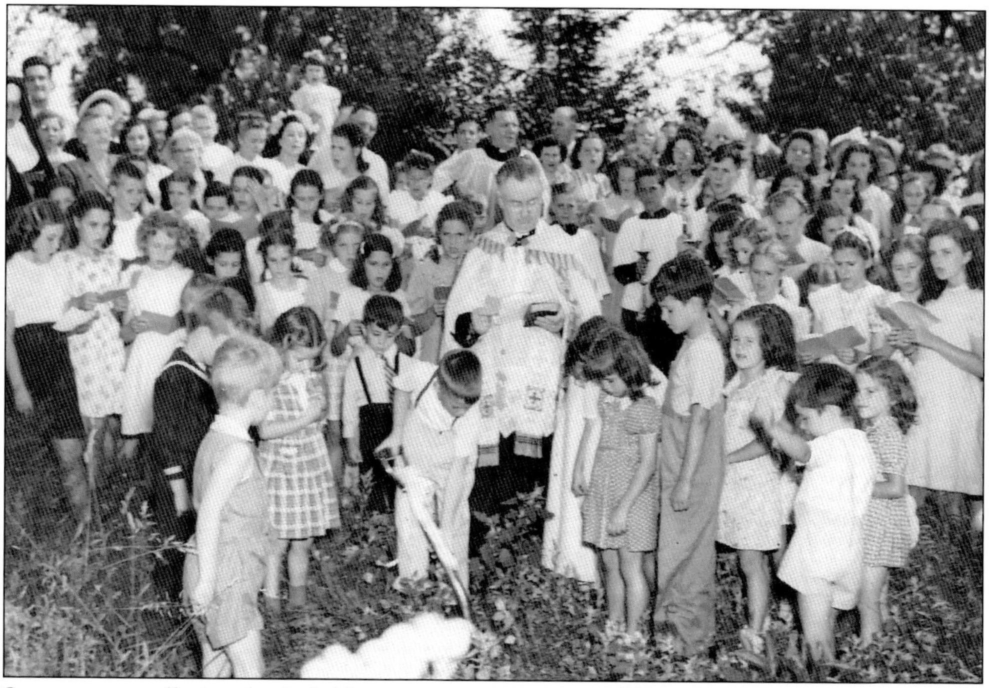

Stevenson usually involved children in activities, presumably to leave them with memories. In October 1939, first graders were chosen to break ground on the building that was dedicated two years later on September 4, 1941. (St. Angela Merici.)

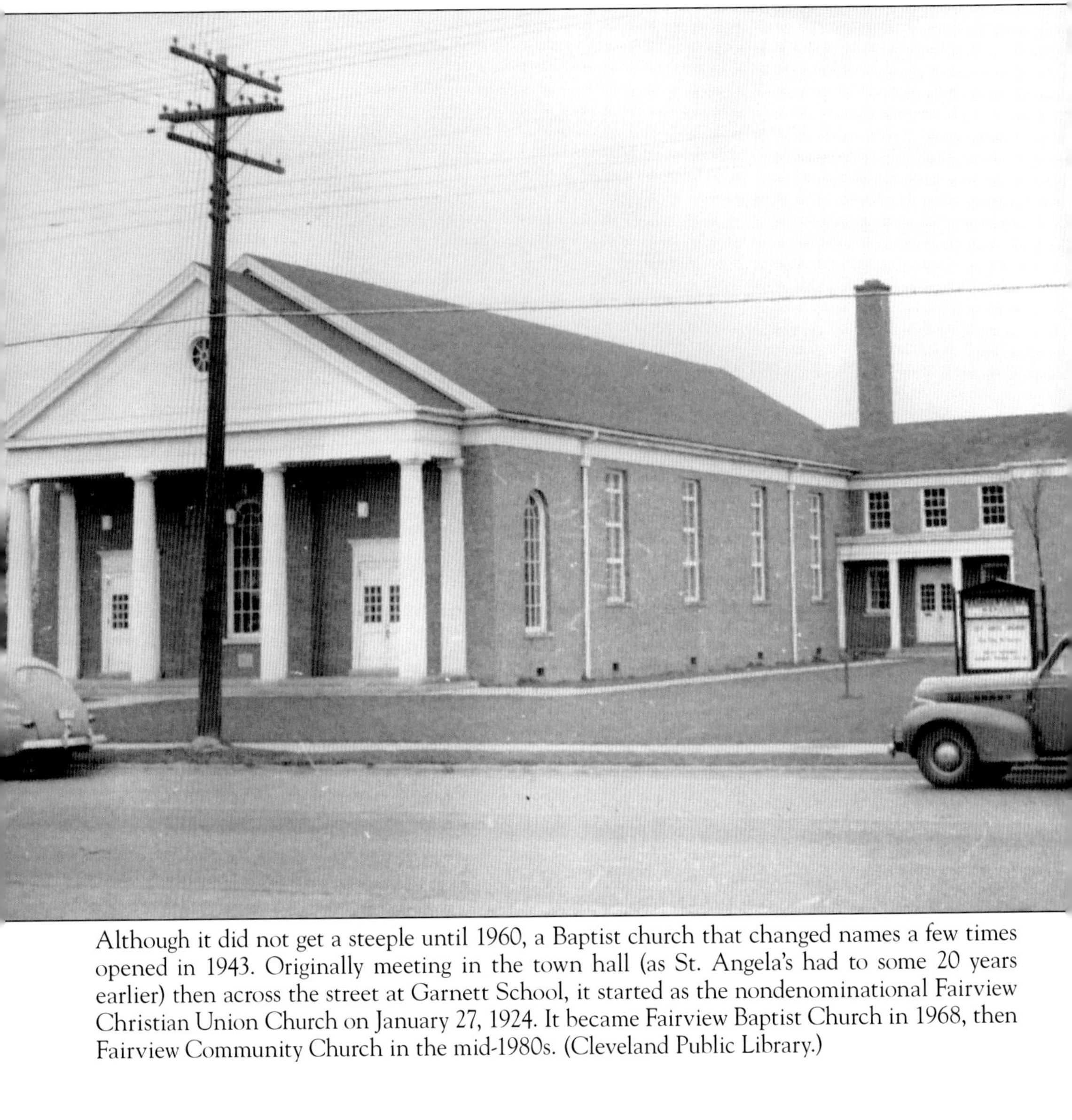

Although it did not get a steeple until 1960, a Baptist church that changed names a few times opened in 1943. Originally meeting in the town hall (as St. Angela's had to some 20 years earlier) then across the street at Garnett School, it started as the nondenominational Fairview Christian Union Church on January 27, 1924. It became Fairview Baptist Church in 1968, then Fairview Community Church in the mid-1980s. (Cleveland Public Library.)

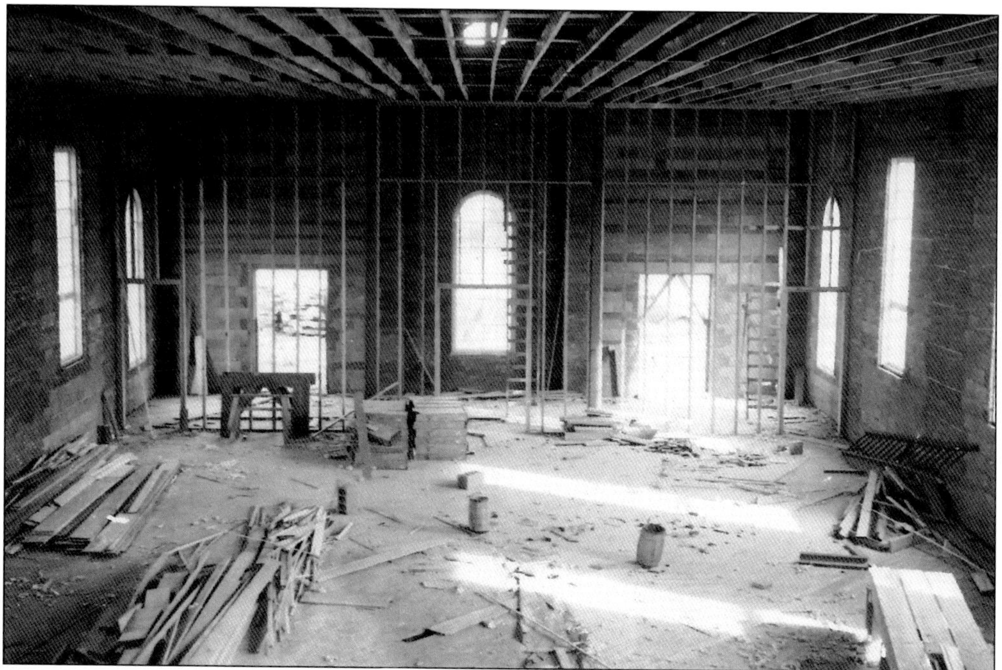

Comparing this picture to an exterior shot of the Baptist church, one will recognize this is the front door from the inside. It is the winter of 1942–1943. (Fairview Community Church.)

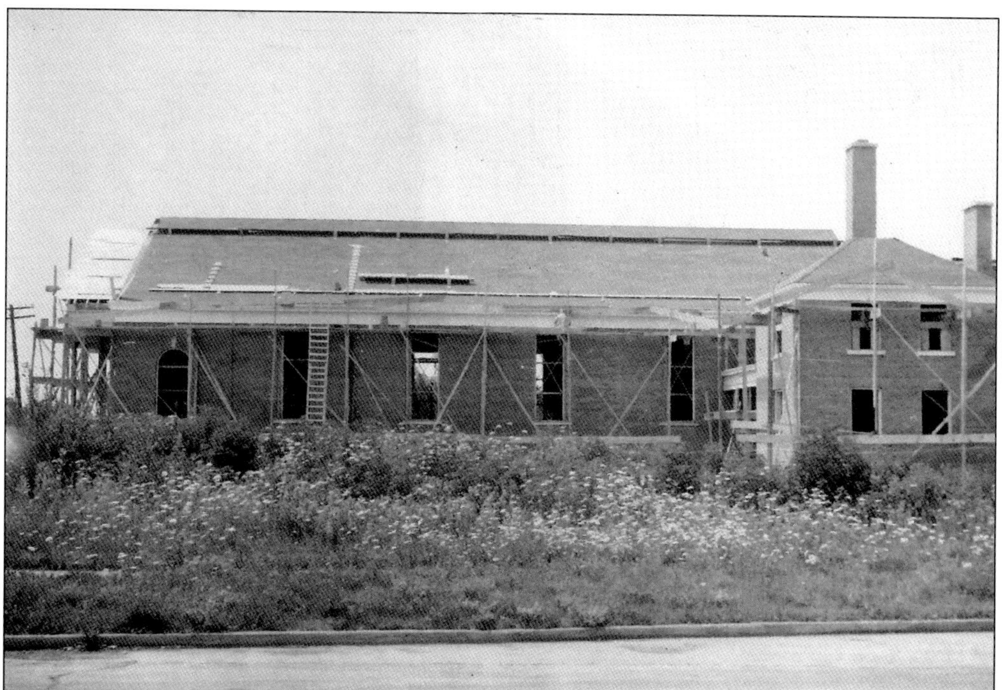

The familiar L-shaped building is being constructed in the fall of 1942. (Fairview Community Church.)

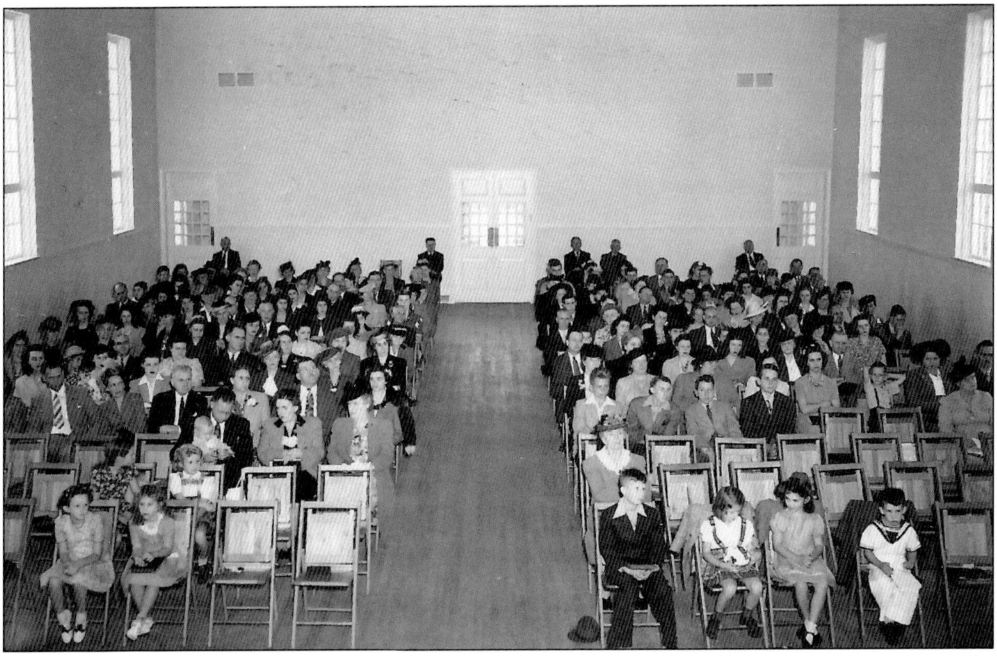

This is an early interior shot from 1944 of what was later named Fairview Community Church. (Fairview Community Church.)

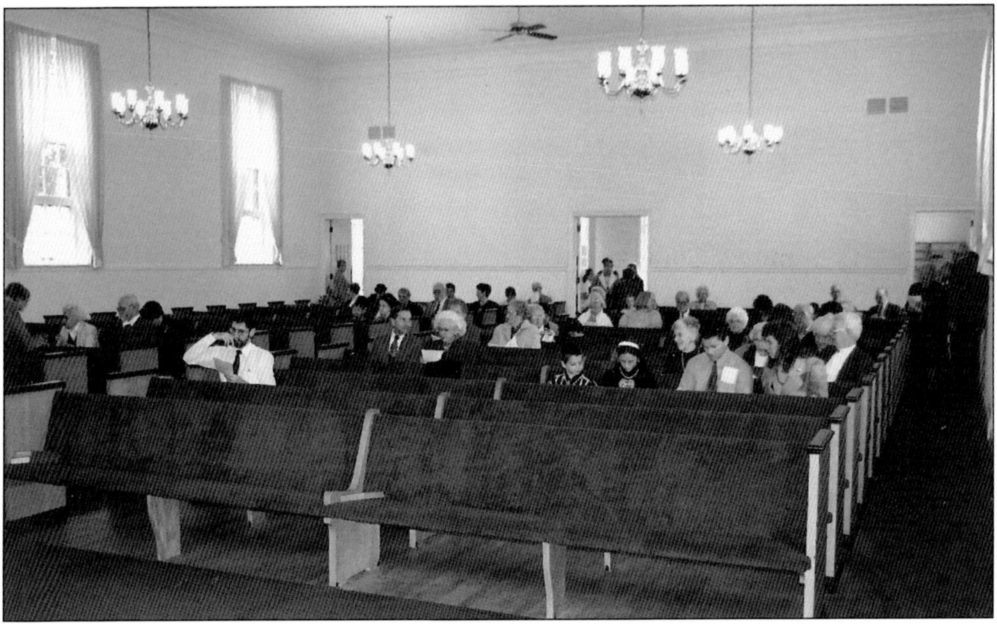

Not much changed in 50 years, other than the seating. Here is the same interior in 1998. (Fairview Community Church.)

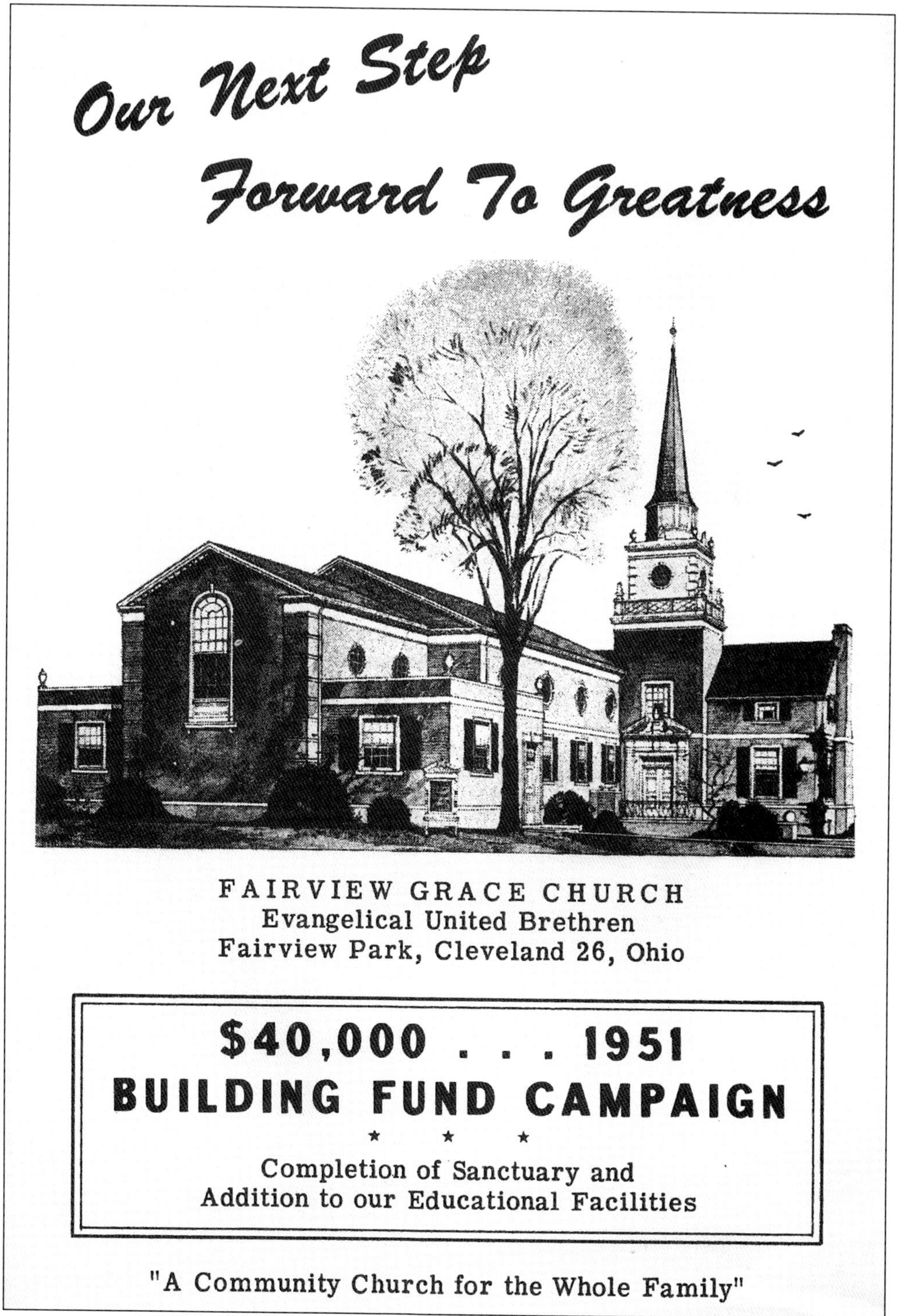

This drawing of the completed Grace Church was not fully realized until 1957, but they were determined to raise what now seems like a very modest $40,000. (Grace United Methodist Church.)

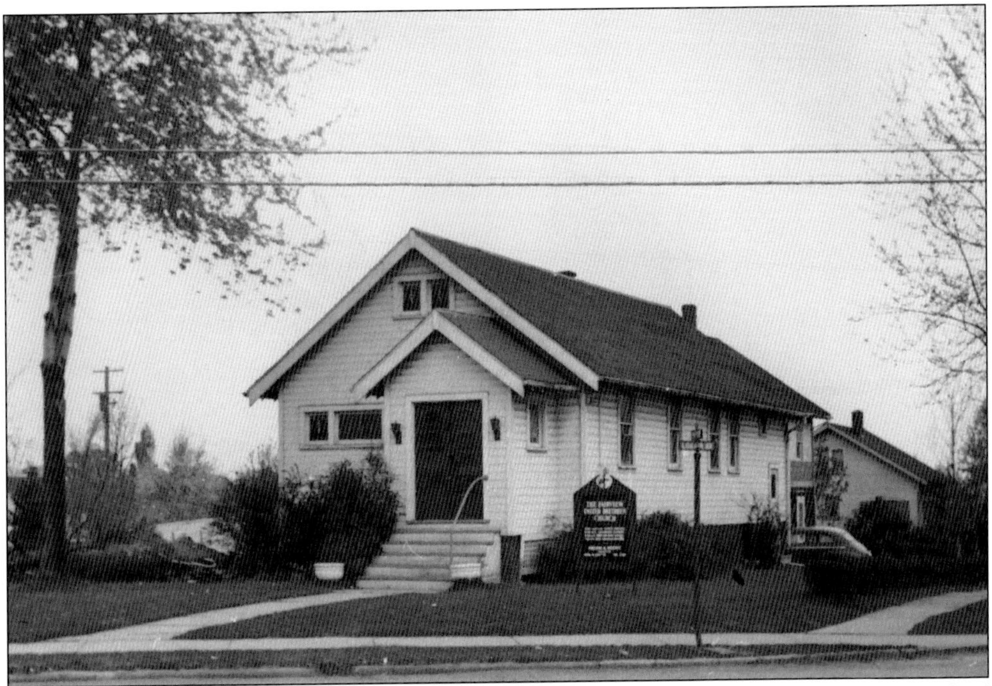

The Lutherans first built this church in 1919 at Lorain Road and West 224th Street but soon had to leave it for financial reasons. It became the Grace United Brethren Church in 1939 before the Brethrens merged with the Methodists. (Cleveland Public Library.)

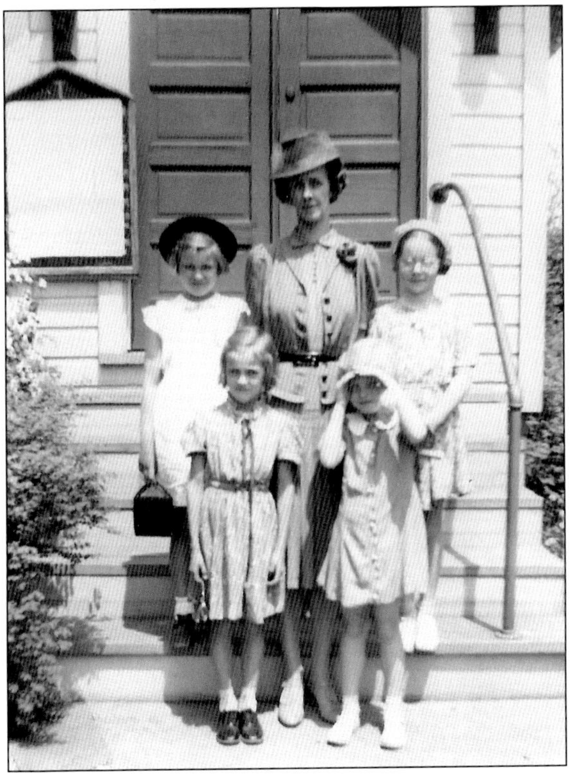

This family stands outside what was the Grace United Brethren Church in 1939. In 1948, a brand new church opened at this location. And 20 years after that, the national Brethren and Methodist churches merged, making this the Fairview Grace United Methodist Church in 1968. (Grace United Methodist Church.)

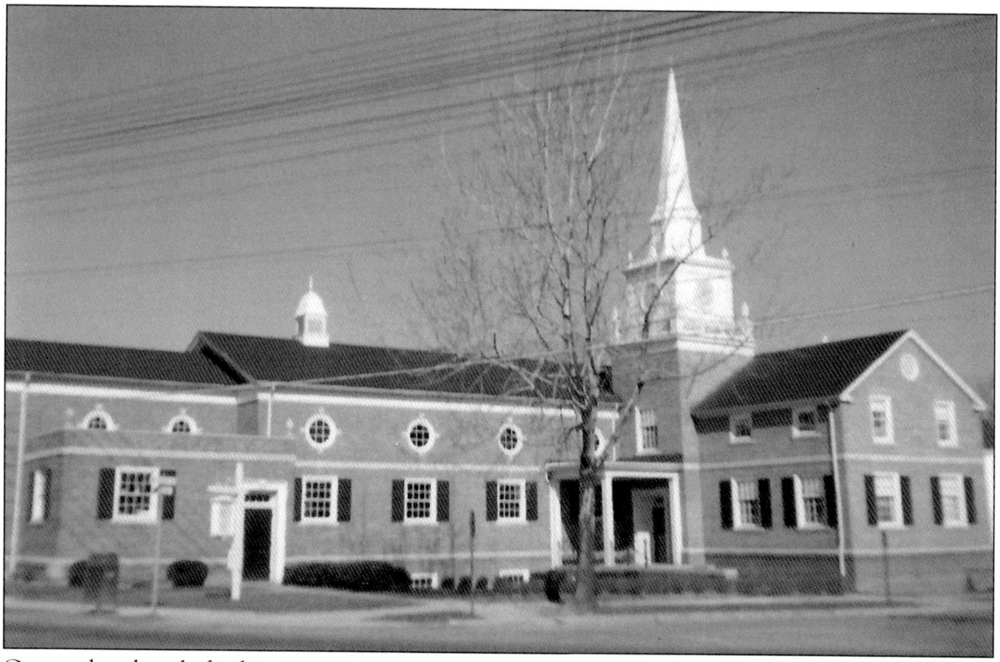

Grace, the church farthest west in Fairview Park, was built in three phases between 1948 and 1958. (Grace United Methodist Church.)

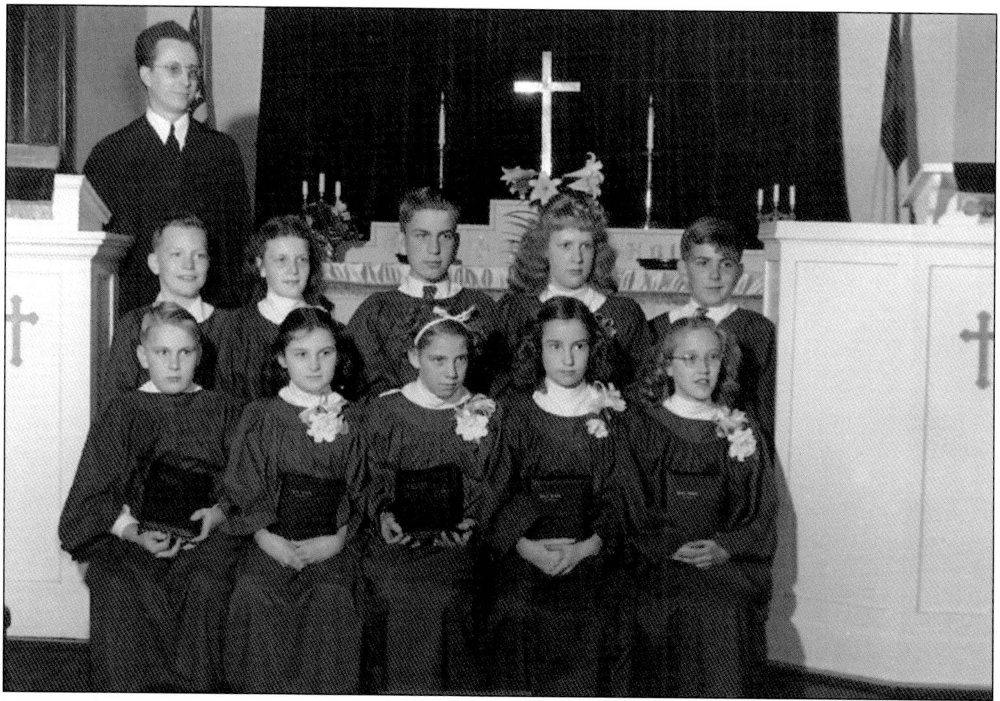

Here is the 1948 Grace Church confirmation class with Rev. Richard Rodes. From left to right are (first row) Clifford Bade, Jackie Allen, Marguerite Wessel, Carol Hartman, and Judy Gillam; (second row) Charles Morton, Carolyn Weihl, Ronald Bade, Carolyn Hammond, and Dick Kinkoph. (Grace United Methodist Church.)

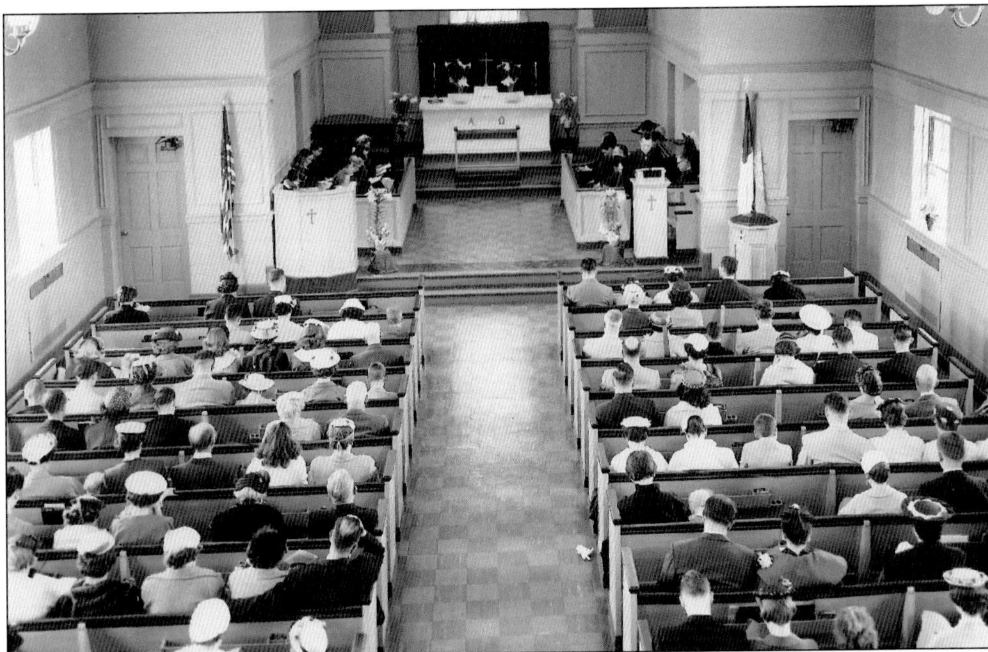

The new Grace Church chapel did not change much over the years from this mid-1950s photograph, except for the addition of stained-glass windows. (Grace United Methodist Church.)

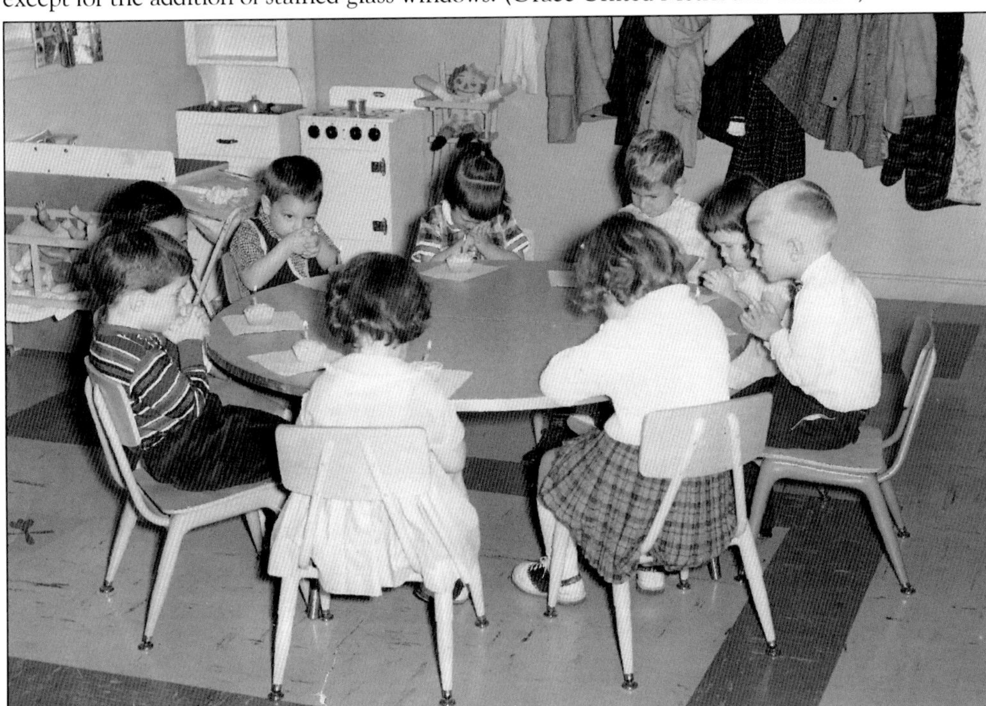

Grace Church nursery school children are pictured about 1960 or 1961. Clockwise from the lower left are Allen Hoffmeister, Tommy Ohmura (half hidden), Brian Herwick, Polly Crews, Danny Wenner, Carol Everett, Jeff Hutton, Debbie Shores, and Janet Wissmer. (Grace United Methodist Church.)

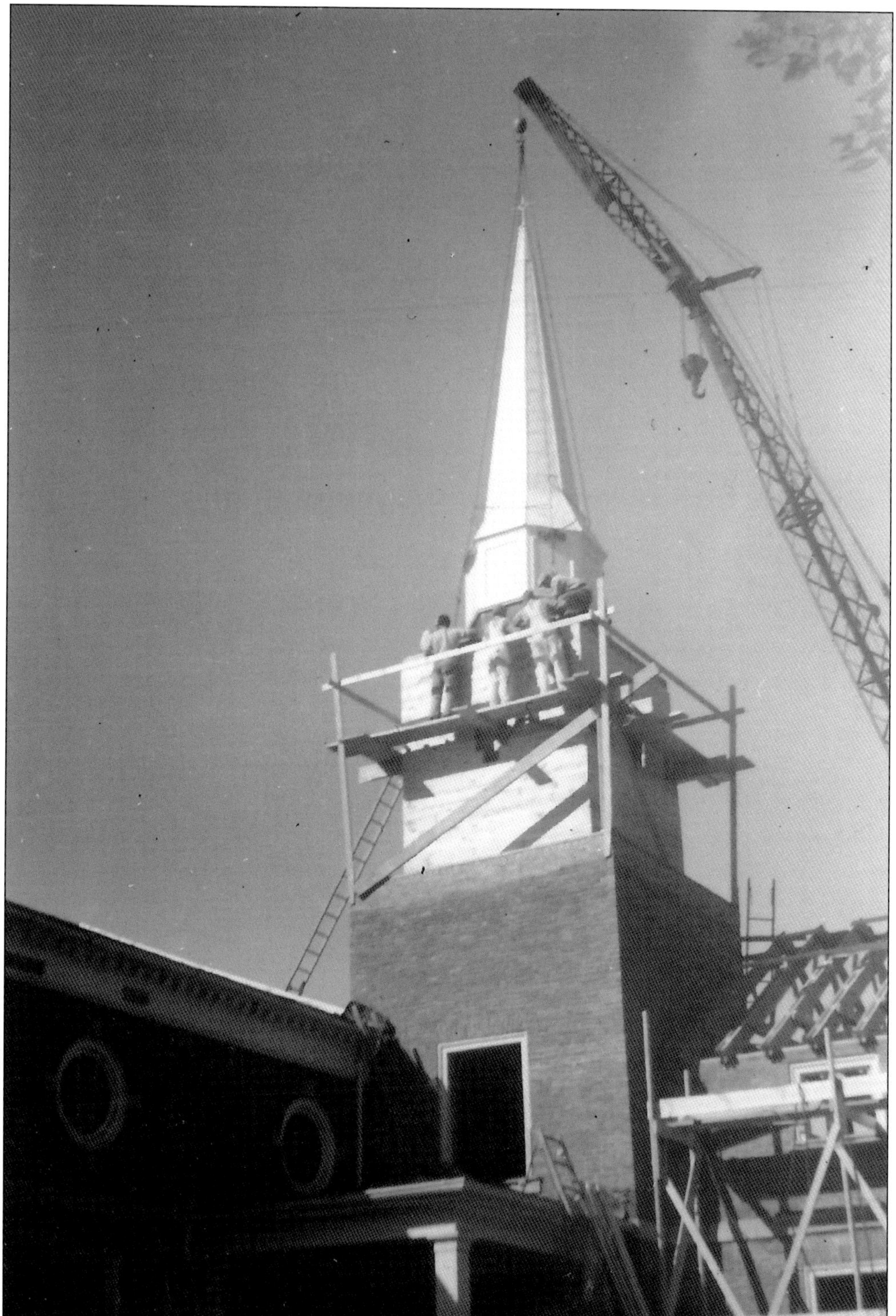

Congregants moved into the new Grace Church chapel in late 1949, but it was not complete until the steeple was finally hauled into place in the fall of 1957. (Grace United Methodist Church.)

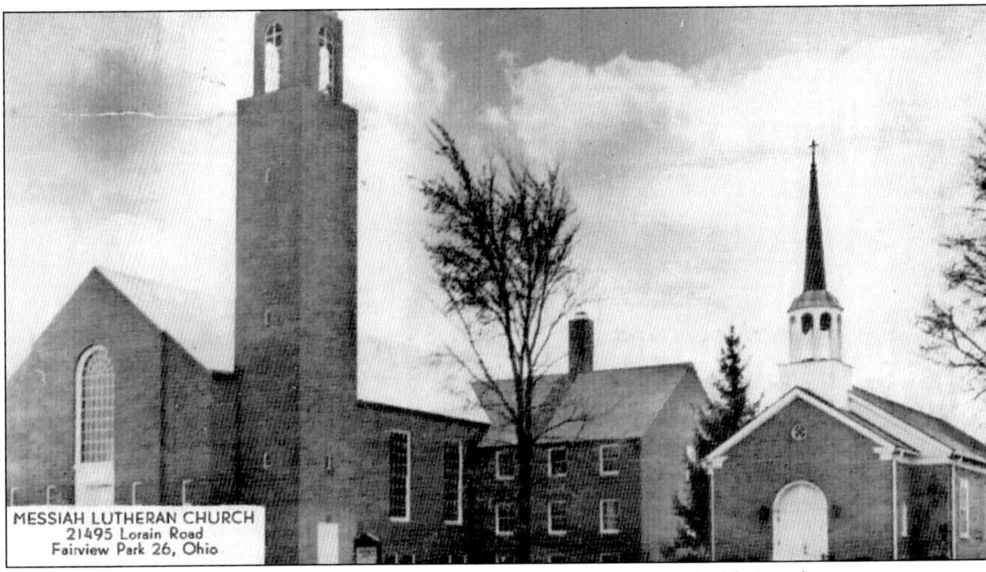

September 1929 services at Messiah Lutheran Church were held in the gymnasium of Gilles-Sweet School. Prior to that, the Luther Society of Fairview Village built a church at West 224th Street and Lorain Road, but due to financial problems, it was not there long. The building remained unused until Grace Church purchased it in the 1930s. The current facility at West 215th Street and Lorain Road opened in 1953, with a school for kindergarten through eighth grade following in 1954. (Gordon Kramp postcard collection.)

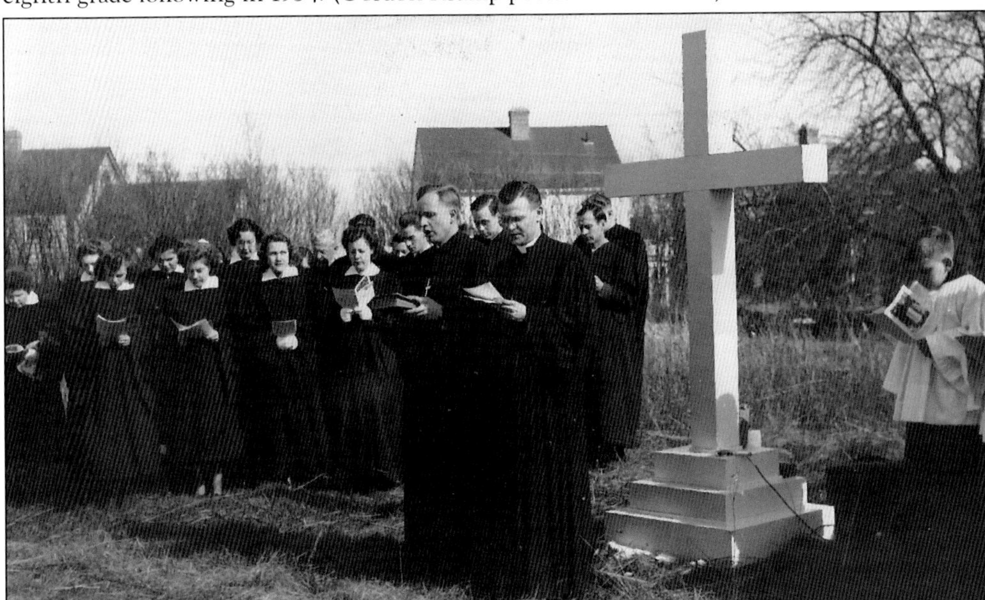

Pictured in 1948, Rev. Wilbert Fields (front right) of Chicago joins Rev. Frederick Kemper, Messiah's second pastor from 1942 to 1957, in the groundbreaking ceremony of the current sanctuary. The first service of Messiah Lutheran was held at Gilles-Sweet School in 1929, as plans were made for the first chapel, which opened in 1936. After a few years, more room was needed, as the village population continued to grow. (Messiah Lutheran Church.)

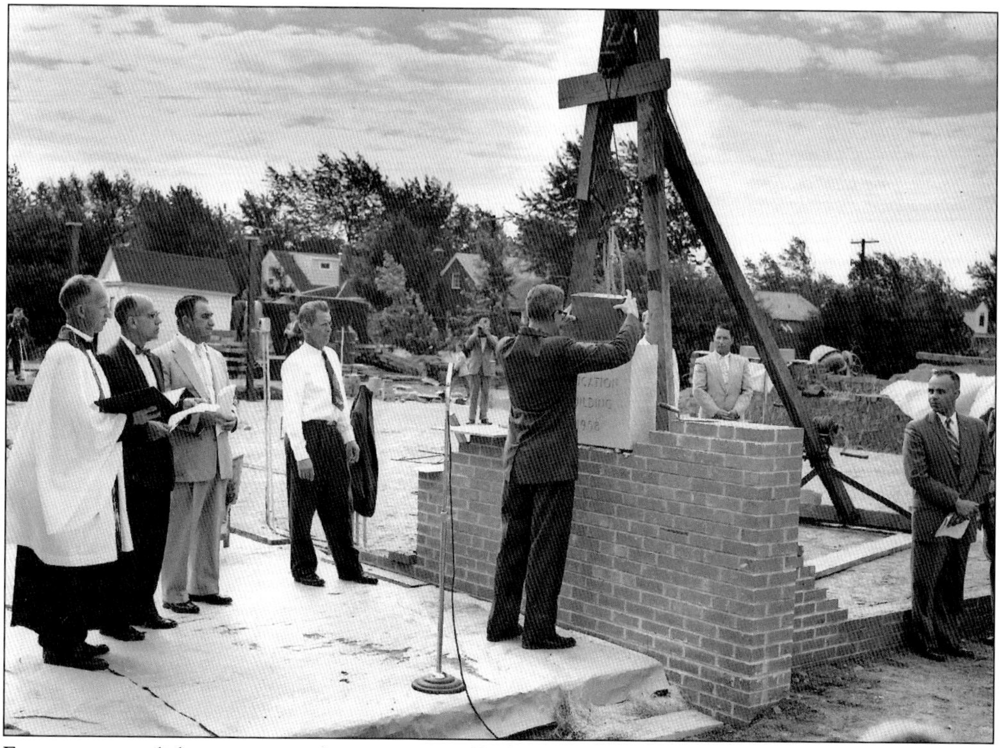

Even a very solid cornerstone has to originally be set into place like a jigsaw puzzle. (Messiah Lutheran Church.)

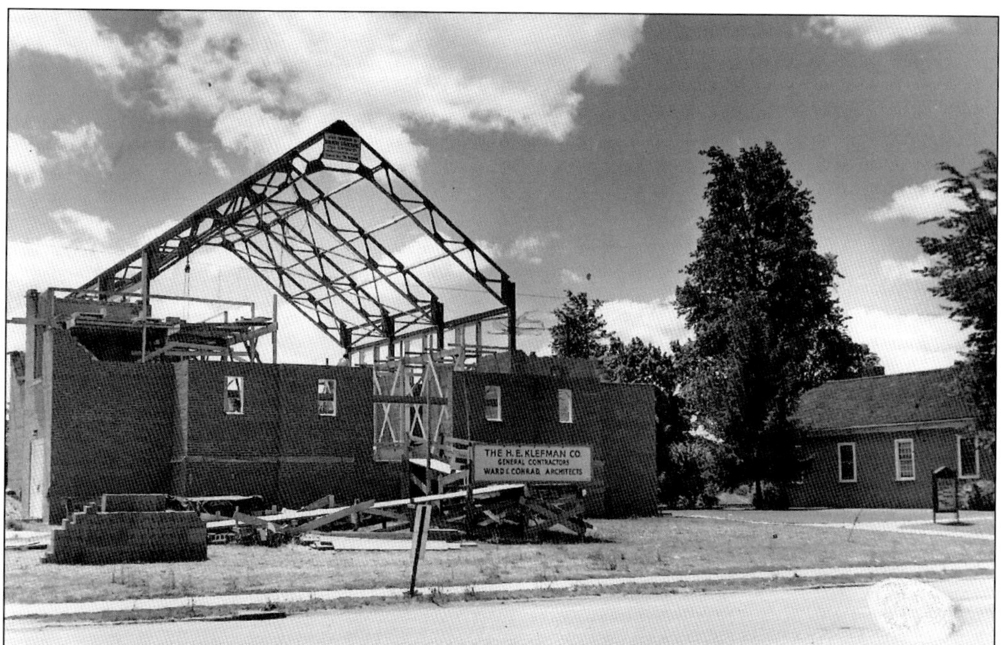

The roof of Messiah Lutheran, a prominent feature of this well-known building, was at one time so much like a skeleton that one could see the clouds through it. (Messiah Lutheran Church.)

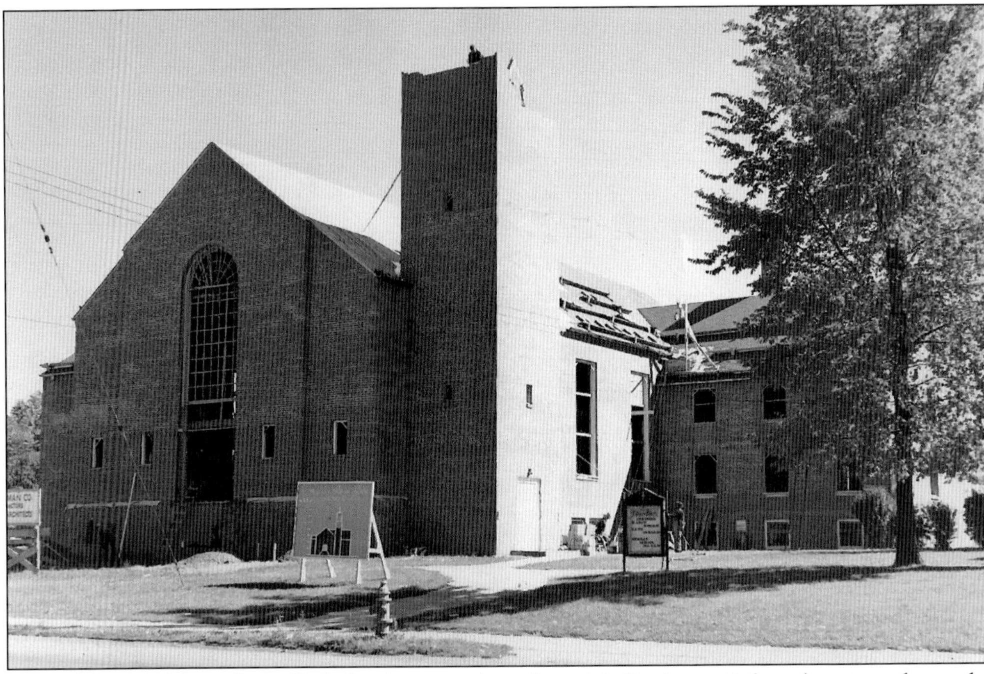

This photograph can be called the "pre-windows Messiah Lutheran," for what is perhaps the most noticeably missing feature. (Messiah Lutheran Church.)

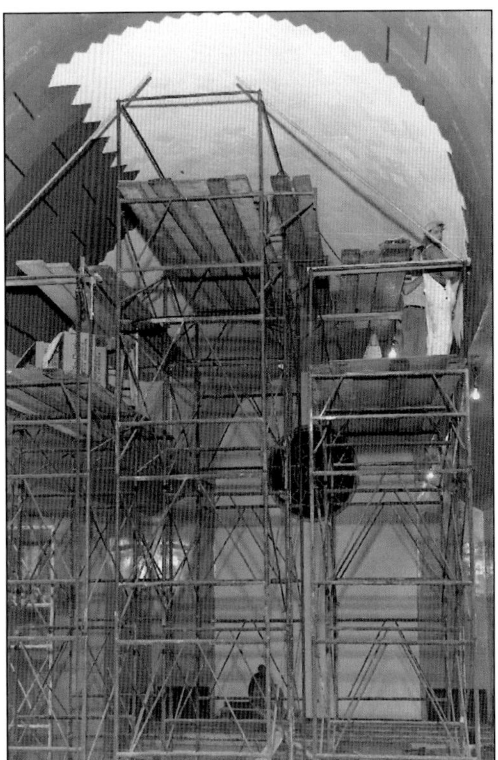

The interior of Messiah Lutheran's chapel begins to take shape in 1953. (Messiah Lutheran Church.)

Artist Willard Combes creates the dynamic mural in Messiah Lutheran's chapel. (Messiah Lutheran Church.)

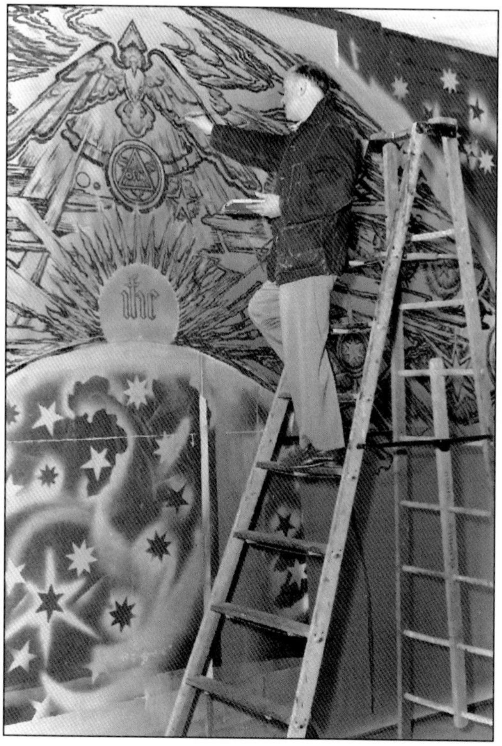

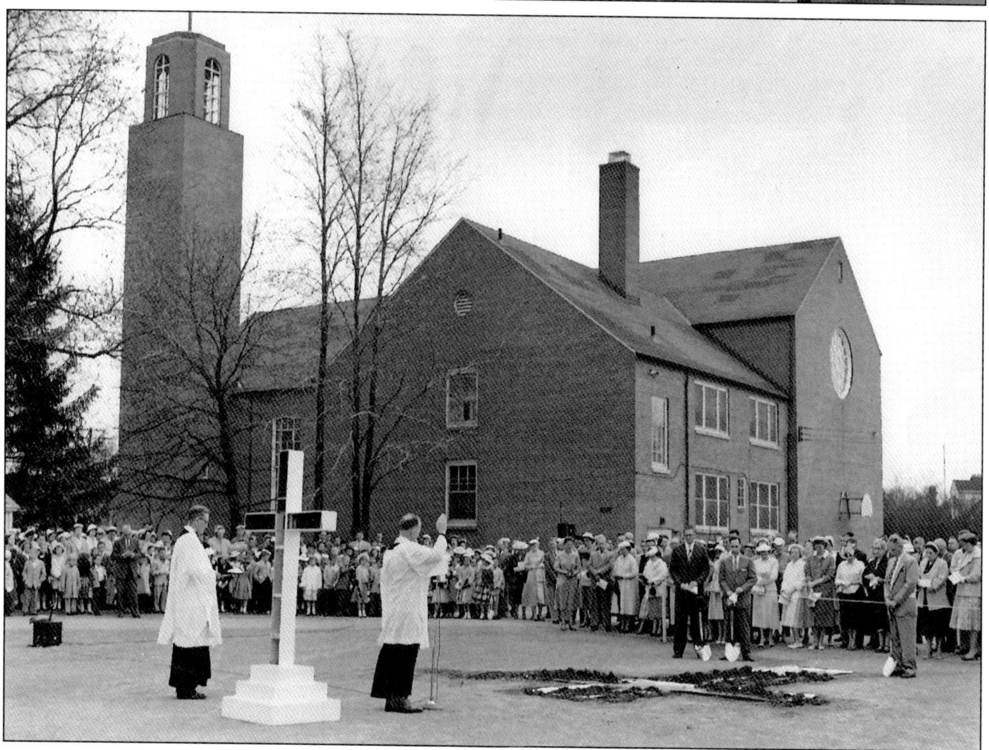

The Messiah Lutheran campus continued to expand as this ample crowd arrives for the August 1958 groundbreaking of the expanded school, which first opened in 1954. (Messiah Lutheran Church.)

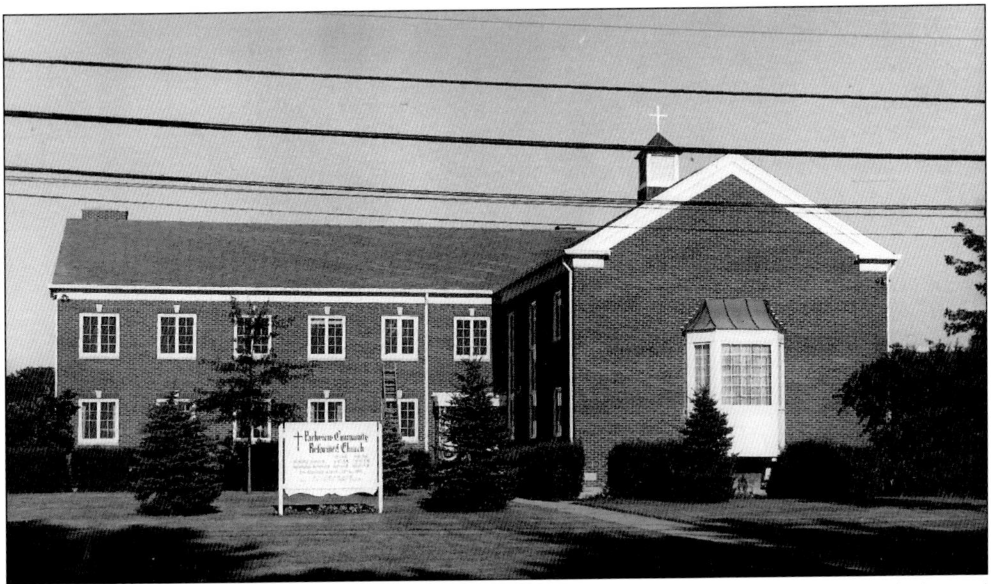

New Hope Church was originally built as Parkview Community Reformed Church and dedicated on April 29, 1960, when Parkview Village was still separate from Fairview Park. Before it was built, services were held in the Parkview Town Hall in 1954, until Parkview School opened in 1955. When Cleveland's Riverside Church closed, it merged with Parkview to become New Hope Church in March 1992. (Fairview Park Historical Society.)

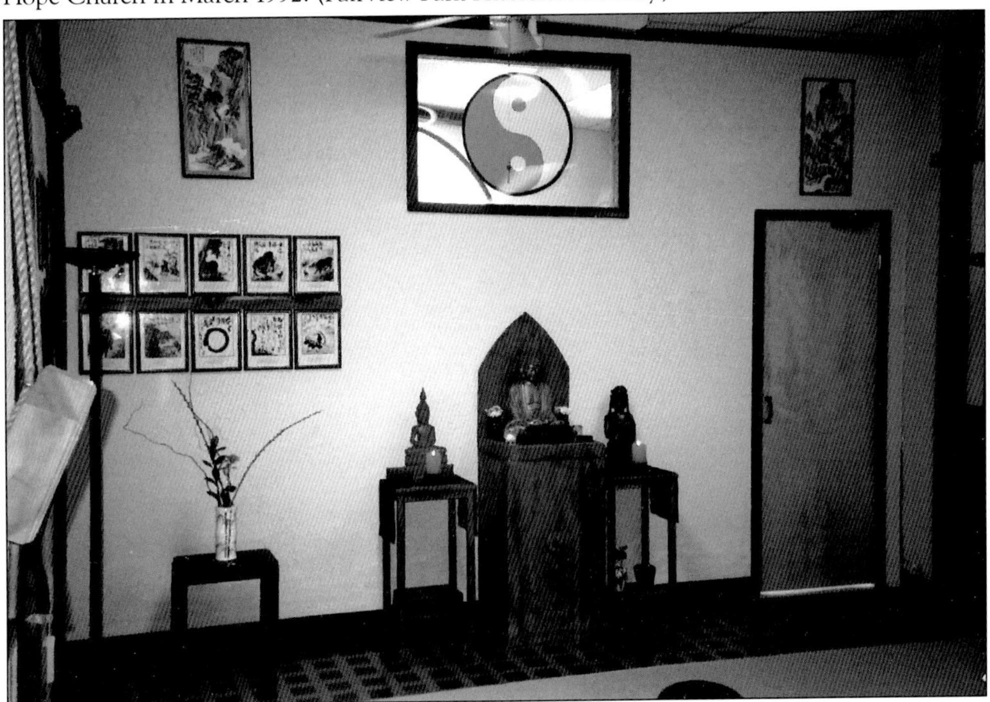

Fairview Park had a Buddhist temple for a few years in the late 1990s. Cloud Water Zendo was started by an American with the spiritual name of Ven. Shih Ying-Fa and grew into one of the most-respected centers of Buddhist thought in the Greater Cleveland area. The dawn of the 21st century brought a change in location to the West Park area. (Cloud Water Zendo.)

Six

Civic

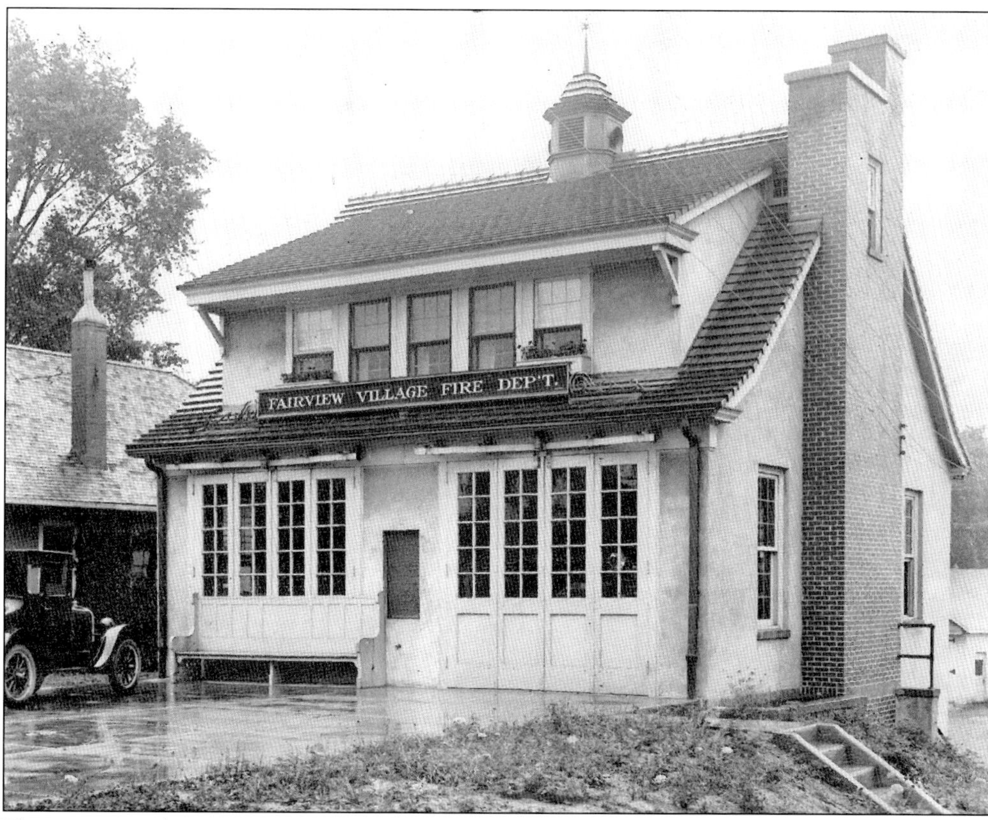

This picture is from January 1926, a few months after Fairview Village Fire Department opened. There were not a lot of emergencies at the time, but Prohibition gave them something to enforce and made for a lot of seized liquor, and this is where it was stored. Reportedly, because of this history, a liquor bottle was placed inside the cornerstone of the new fire department in the mid-1960s. (Cleveland Press Archives, Cleveland State University.)

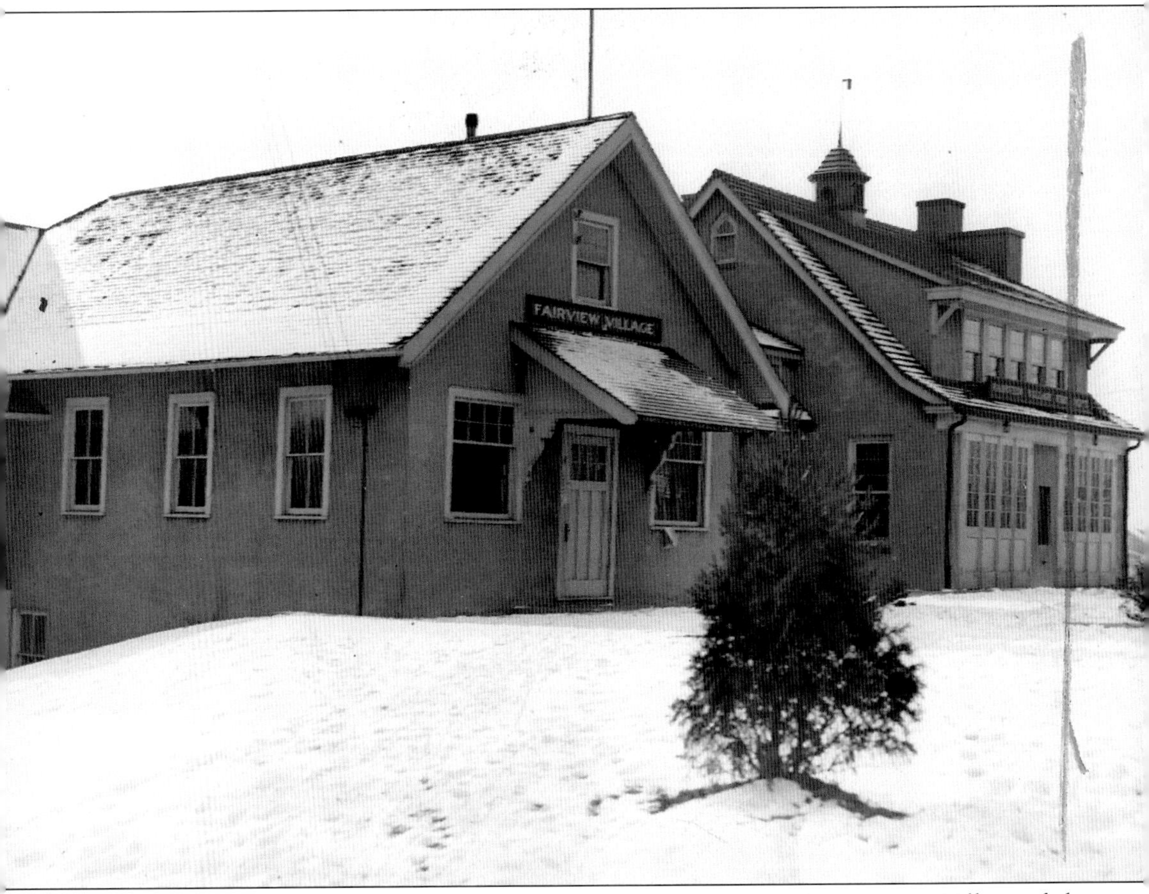

A simple administrative center like this was quite sufficient for the Fairview Village of the mid-1920s. But by the mid-1960s, the population grew considerably, and after more than 10 years as a city, a larger, more modern facility was long overdue. (Cleveland Press Archives, Cleveland State University.)

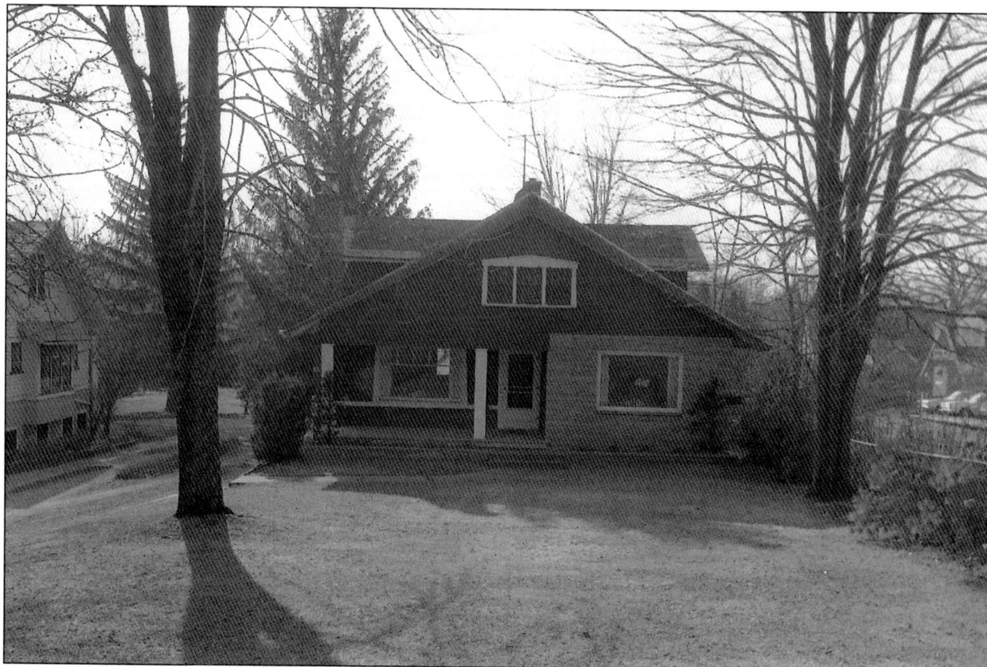

Needing more room for a bigger building to replace the old town hall required the demolition of two houses to the east. (Fairview Park Historical Society.)

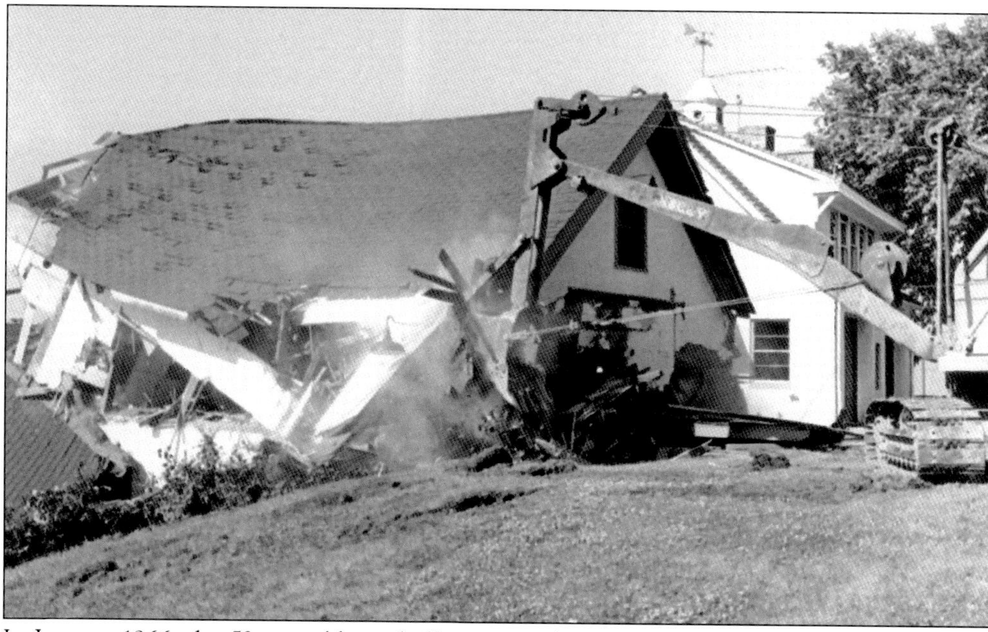

In January 1966, the 53-year-old city hall was torn down. The modern building that replaced it cost $810,000. The old village fire department behind it stayed in place for another year until its replacement could be built. This signaled that the city had come of age, shedding the last of its connections to the little old village government. Still some critics at the time complained the new building was an opulent Taj Mahal. (Cleveland Press Archives, Cleveland State University.)

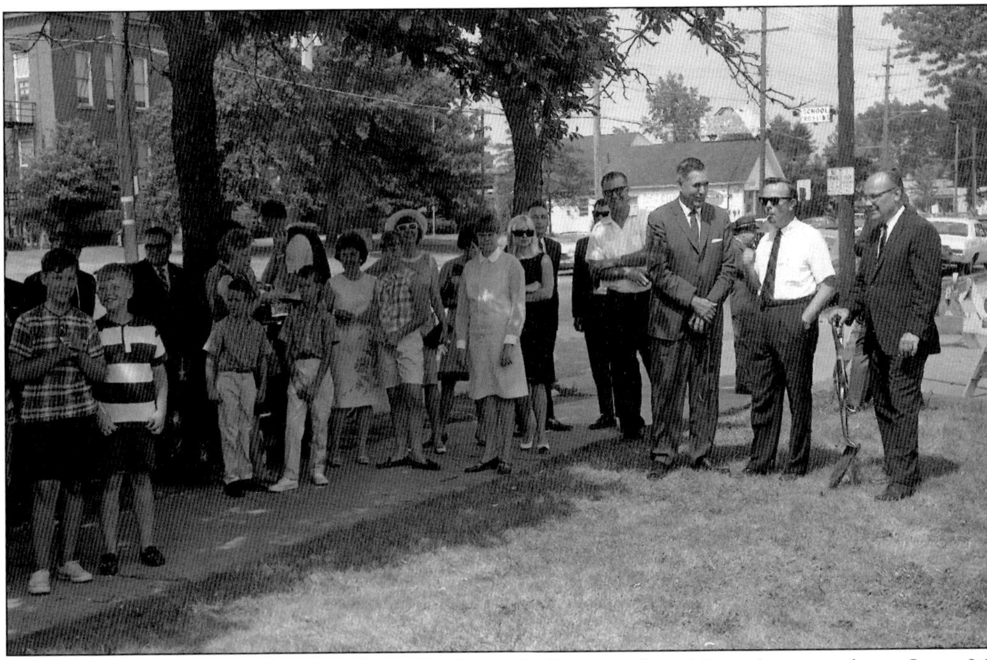

Before the dignitaries gather for the official city hall groundbreaking photograph on June 26, 1966, random spectators make up this unofficial shot. Appropriately enough, across the street and along the left side of this photograph is the familiar corner of Garnett School, the backdrop of many group pictures in the early 20th century. (Fairview Park Historical Society.)

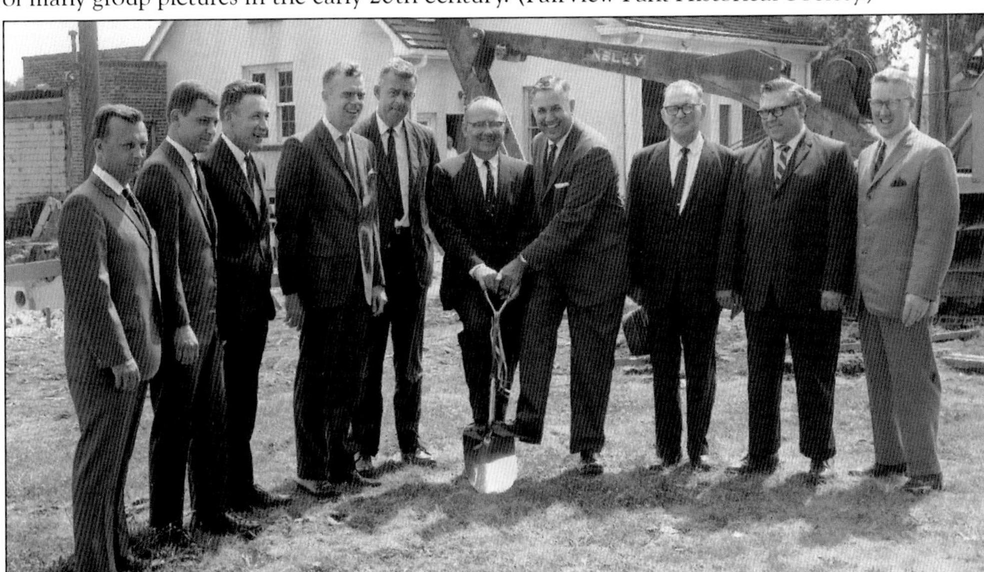

Here is a typical groundbreaking photograph. Mayor James A. Dunson is in the center, holding the shovel with councilman Marvin Schatz (right). The proud architects, Peter and Mark Steigerwald, stand fourth and fifth from the left, respectively. On the far right stands councilman Joseph M. Gaul, who later served as mayor. Next to him is councilman William Kunkle, who was married to Georgia Kunkle, a very well respected fourth-grade teacher at Gilles-Sweet School. (Cleveland Press Archives, Cleveland State University.)

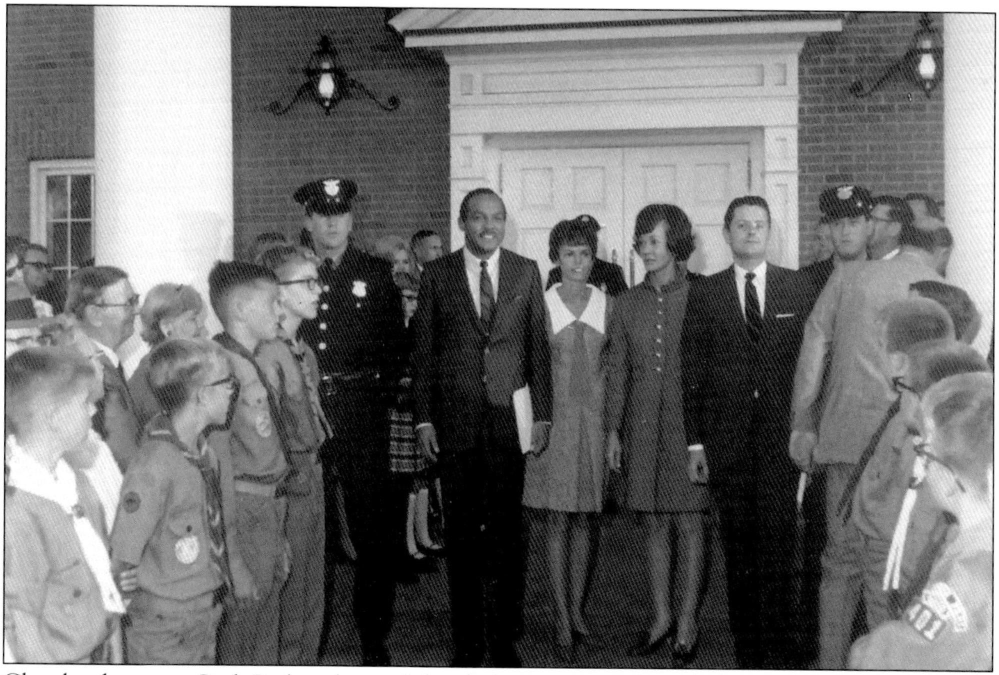

Cleveland mayor Carl Stokes (center) headed west in 1967 to help Fairview Park open its beautiful new, expanded city hall. To the right of Stokes are his wife, Shirley, Laurie Mooney, and new Fairview Park mayor Charles Mooney. (Fairview Park Historical Society.)

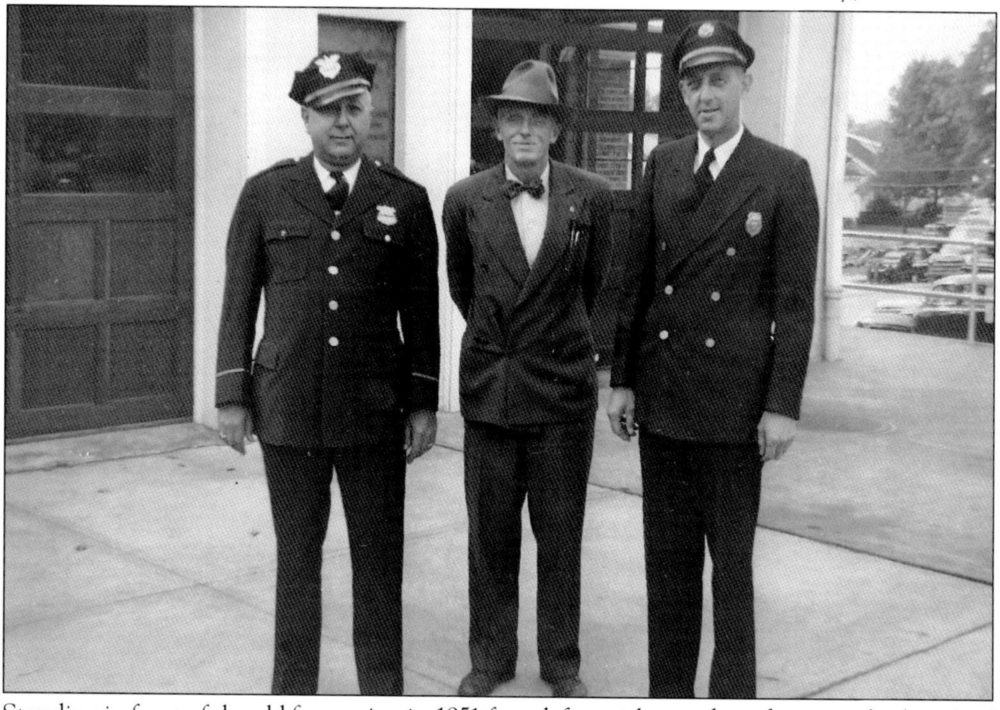

Standing in front of the old fire station in 1951 from left to right are the safety trio of police chief Edward Elliott, safety director James Russell, and fire chief J. Orrie Baumgardner. (Fairview Park Historical Society.)

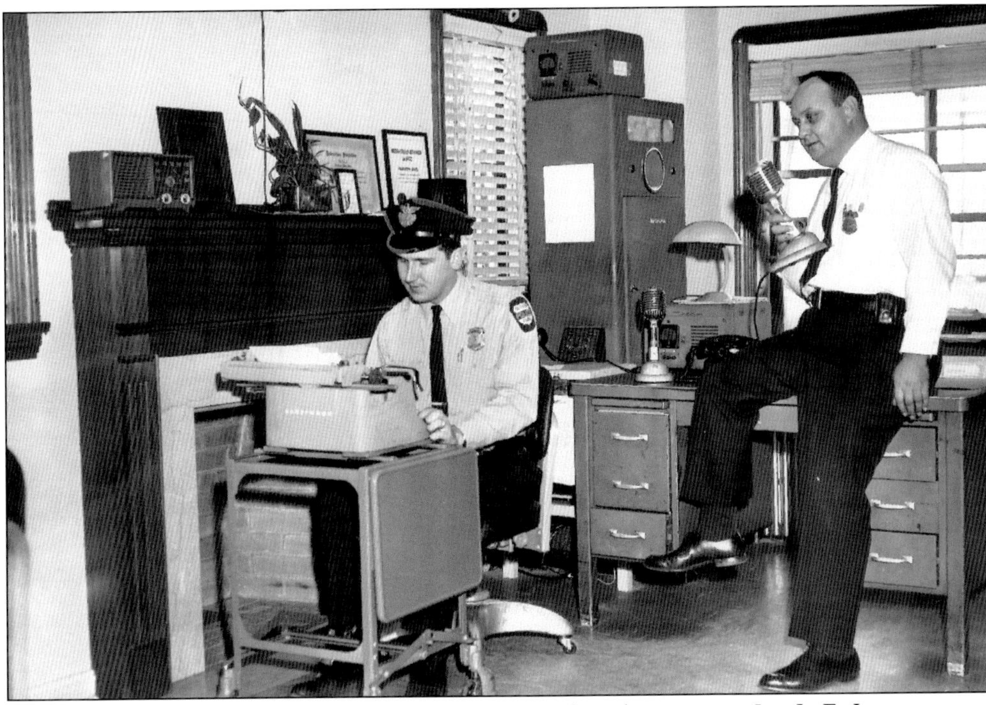

In 1962, police officer Ronald Kuty does some predigital typing as Lt. J. F. Jayson uses a microphone. Apparently these were new police quarters at the time, although an entirely new facility was to come a few years later. (Cleveland Press Archives, Cleveland State University.)

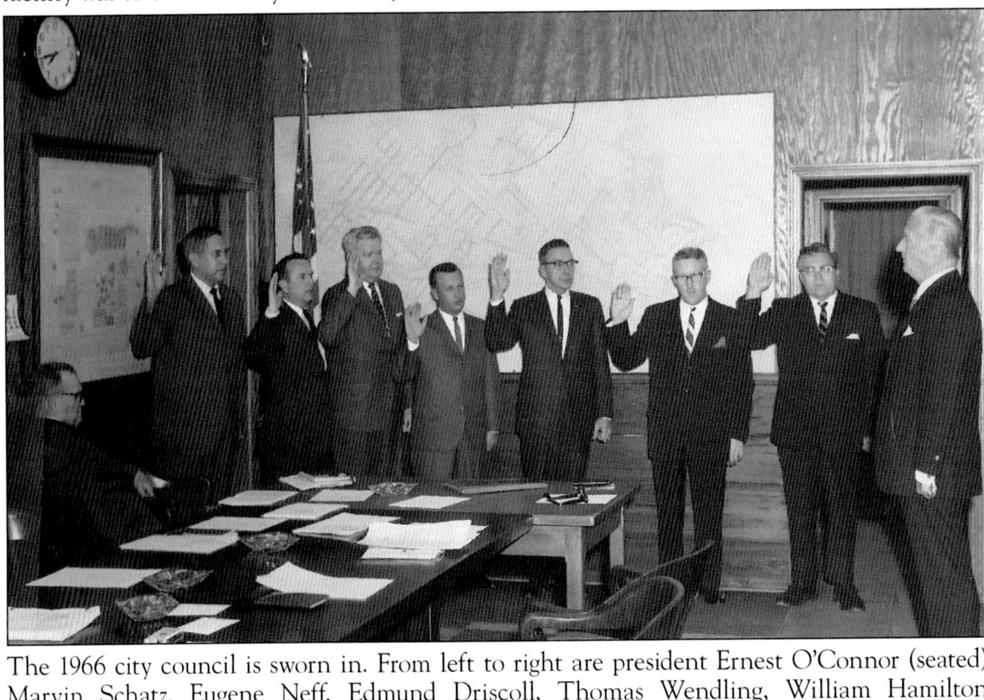

The 1966 city council is sworn in. From left to right are president Ernest O'Connor (seated), Marvin Schatz, Eugene Neff, Edmund Driscoll, Thomas Wendling, William Hamilton, Joseph M. Gaul, William Kunkle, and Ohio Supreme Court judge J. J. P. Corrigan. (Fairview Park Historical Society.)

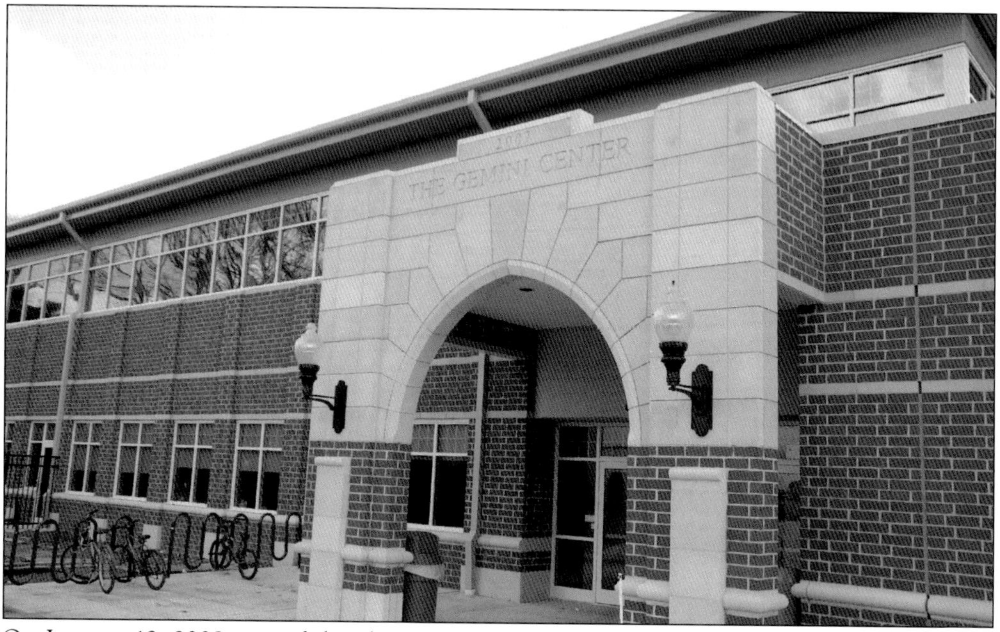

On January 12, 2008, one of the elements of the Gemini Project, a state-of-the-art recreation center called Gemini Center, was opened. The center also provides modern rooms for city meetings and special events. The Gemini Project was a massive urban renewal project just barely passed by the voters. It ambitiously aimed to not only build a recreation center but to also rebuild or renovate the existing school buildings. (Photograph by David Barnett.)

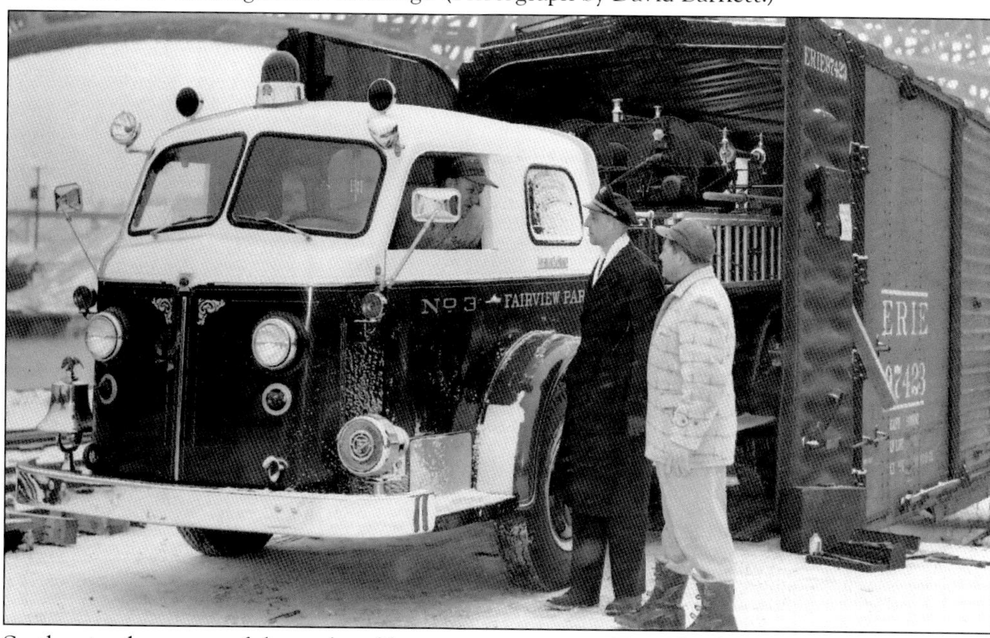

So that is what some of those closed boxcars are carrying. Fire Chief J. Orrie Baumgardner and councilman Arthur Reitz went to a rail yard to see their new $28,000 fire truck. It supposedly received 14 coats of paint, meant to last 25 years. It was ordered in July but did not arrive until a winter day near zero degrees in January 1955. (Cleveland Press Archives, Cleveland State University.)

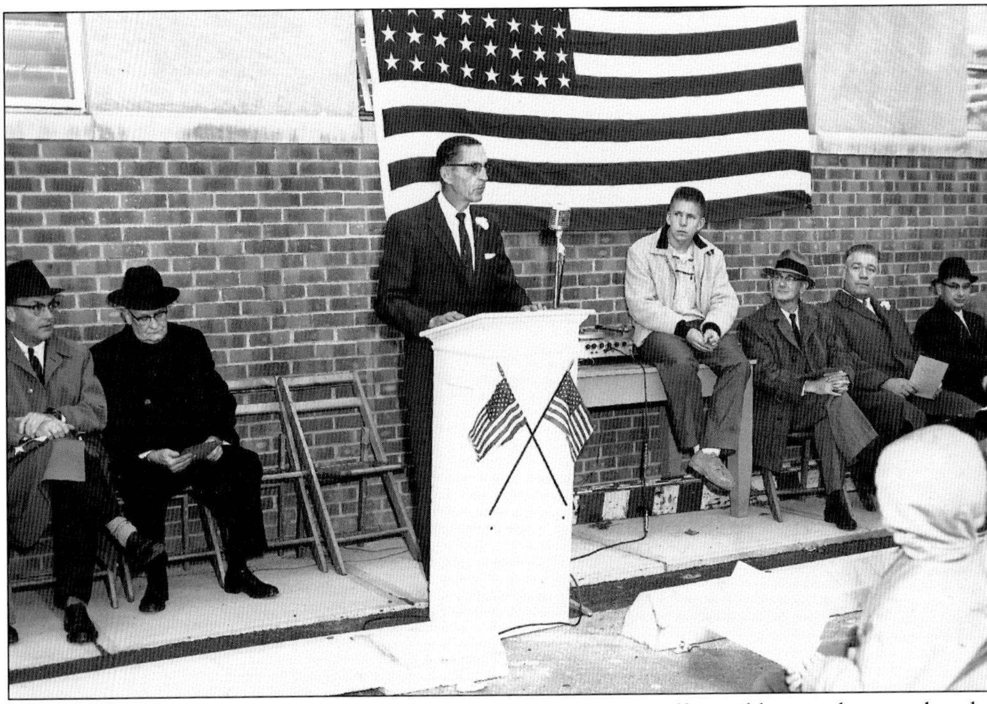

Warren Christopher, superintendent of the Fairview Park Post Office, addresses the crowd at the dedication of the new building on November 1, 1960. (Fairview Park Historical Society.)

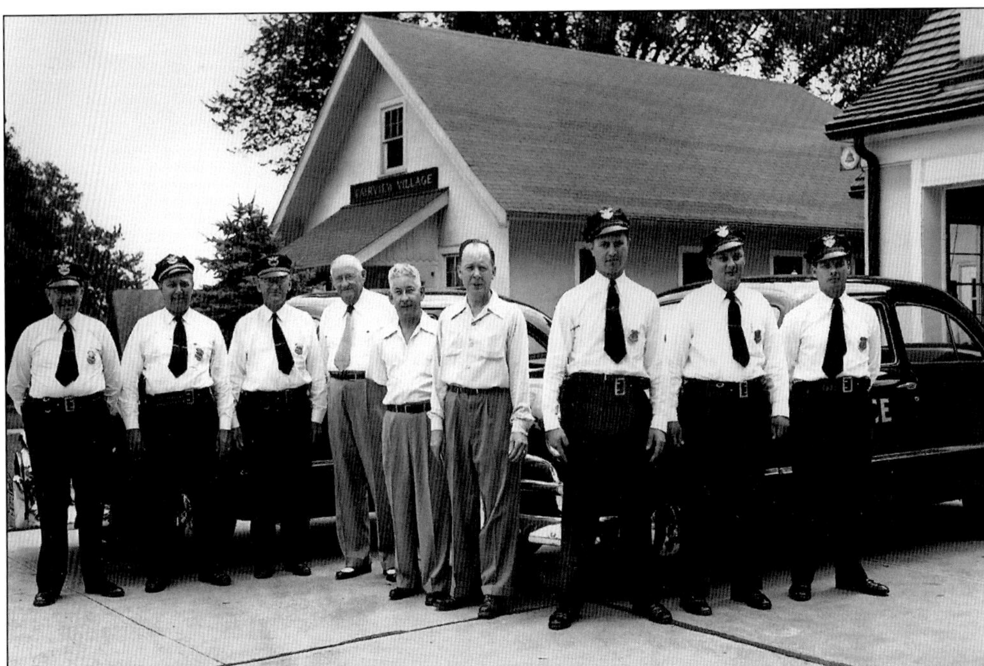

Flanked by Fairview Park's finest in 1949, the nonuniformed are, from left to right, Mayor Karl A. Bohlken, councilman L. Owens, and council president Taylor von Allen. (Fairview Park Historical Society.)

Seven

The Mayors

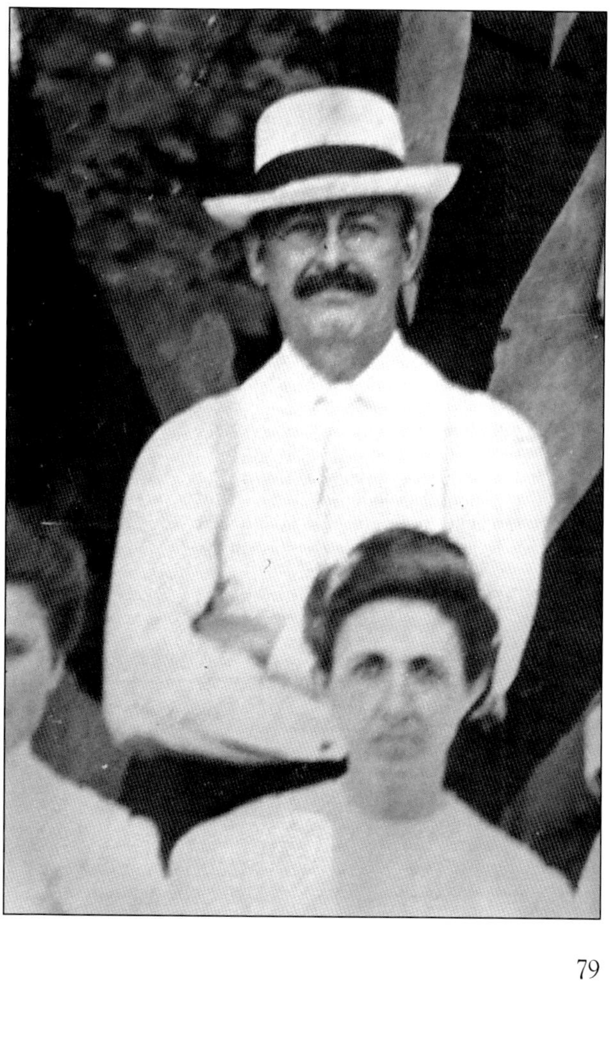

Someone was needed to run Fairview Village when it was started in 1910, and George B. Sweet fulfilled that need sufficiently because he held the job for 10 years until he resigned. In addition to starting a village government from scratch, he was one of the farsighted leaders who helped start the Cleveland Metroparks, assuring that, despite developing new villages like Fairview, some land needed to remain as wooded trails so people could enjoy the serenity of nature. (Fairview Park Historical Society.)

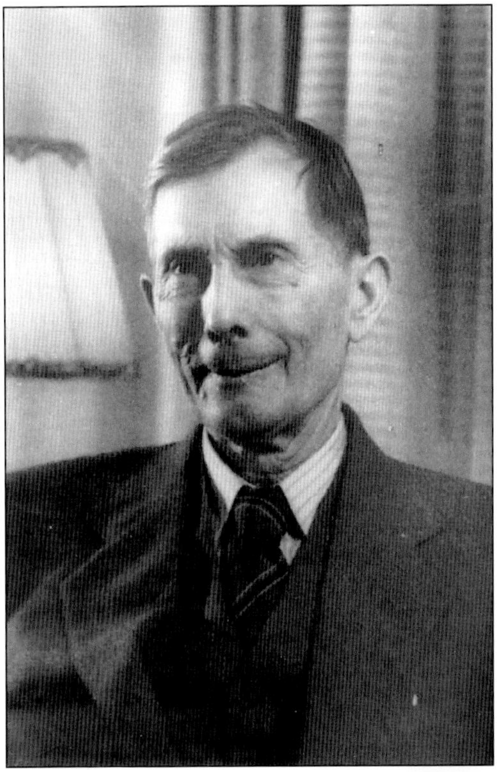

Arthur H. Eggleston was only mayor for one year from 1920 to 1921 but remained active in the village until his death in 1943. His final 12 years were spent as the village's building inspector. His father built the century home at 22915 Lorain Road, and West 228th Street used to be called Eggleston Avenue. (Fairview Park Historical Society.)

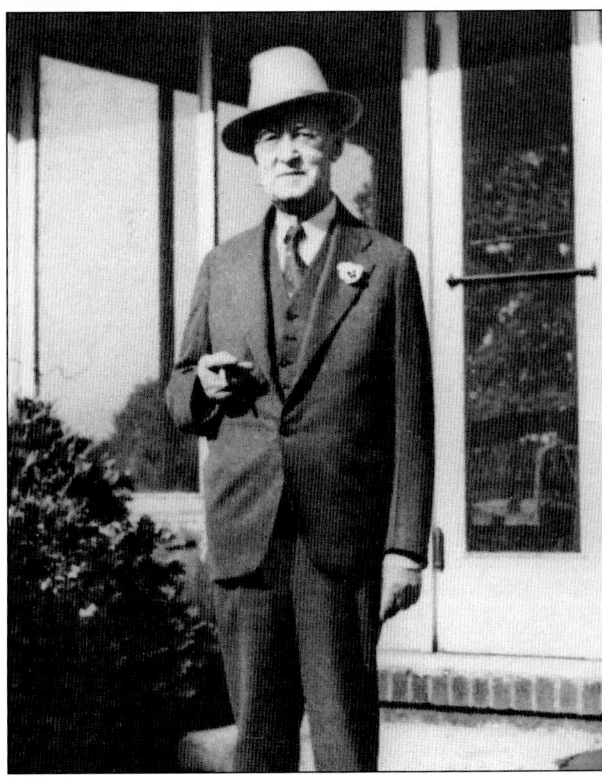

Before serving as mayor from 1922 to 1927, David J. Zinner was on the Cleveland City Council from 1905 to 1913. He also chaired the Cuyahoga County Tax Commission. (Fairview Park Historical Society.)

Joseph Daugherty was mayor from 1928 to 1931. His two biggest problems originated beyond the village borders. The Depression slowed down village projects for a few years, and West Park decided to annex to Cleveland in 1925. Many in Fairview were confident becoming part of Cleveland would be beneficial, but ultimately it was not annexed, leaving the Rocky River Valley the well-defined eastern borderline that it is. (Fairview Park Historical Society.)

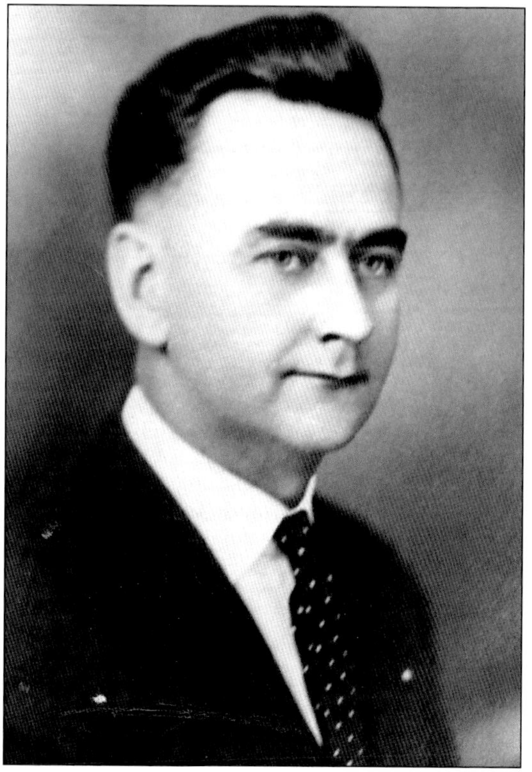

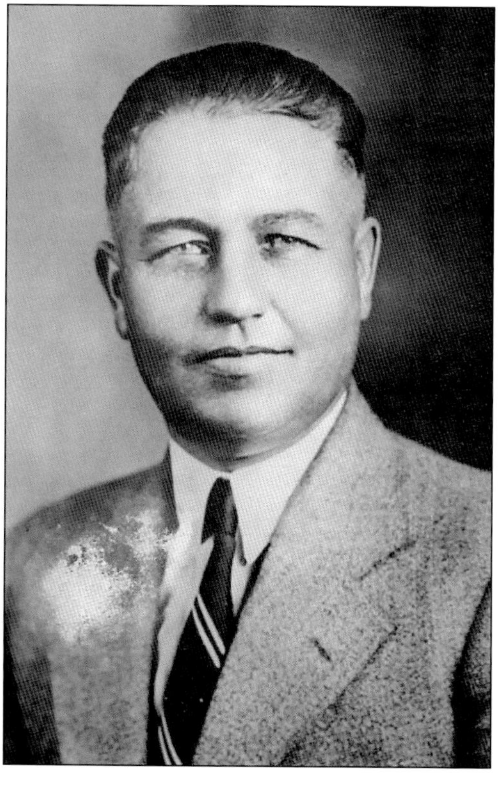

Mayor from 1932 to 1943, David Bain accomplished much despite the Depression and the resulting budgetary restraints. With the end of the interurban railway, he helped start the first municipally owned bus line in Ohio. He also had Lorain Road designated a state highway, which brought funding to build a new steel bridge in 1934. After his death in 1953, the park named Fairview Park became Bain Park, and the Community Cabin became Bain Park Cabin. (Fairview Park Historical Society.)

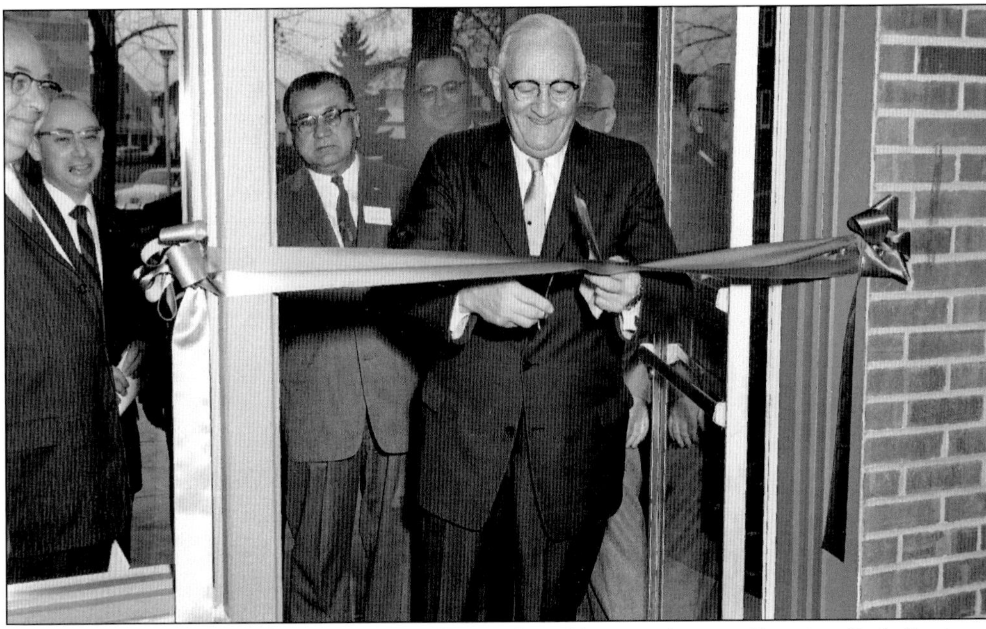

Karl A. Bohlken, mayor from 1944 to 1957, cut the ribbon to the new Fairview Park Regional Library in February 1957. During his tenure, the shopping center and Westgate developments were built, the village's name was changed to Fairview Park, and later the village's status of village was changed to city. Bohlken helped acquire the land next to Westgate, which was turned into Bohlken Park. (Cleveland Press Archives, Cleveland State University.)

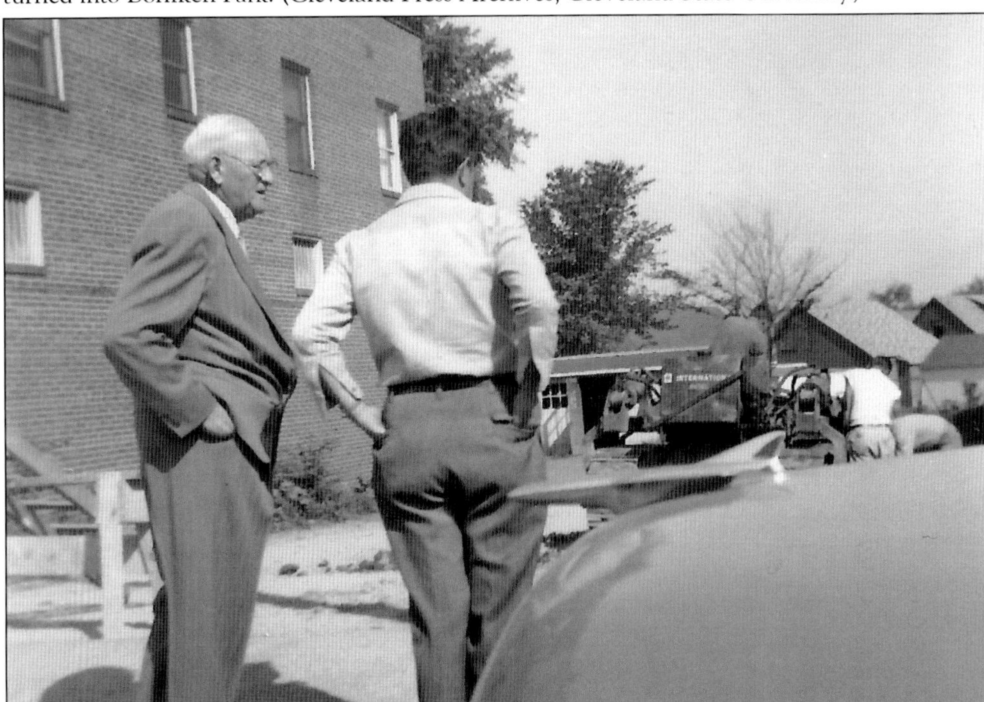

Bohlken inspects an apartment building being built on Lorain Road in the mid-1950s. The Lakios family, who ran nearby Stephens Lunch, built it. (Photograph by Joy Gdovin.)

James A. Dunson was mayor from 1958 to 1967 and had lived in Fairview since he was in the ninth grade in 1931. Having lived in Lakewood and Columbus, he was well aware how rural the area was as he grew up, seeing it grow from village into a city. Preceding his term as mayor, he spent some time on the city council and a couple of terms as law director in the early 1950s. (Fairview Park Historical Society.)

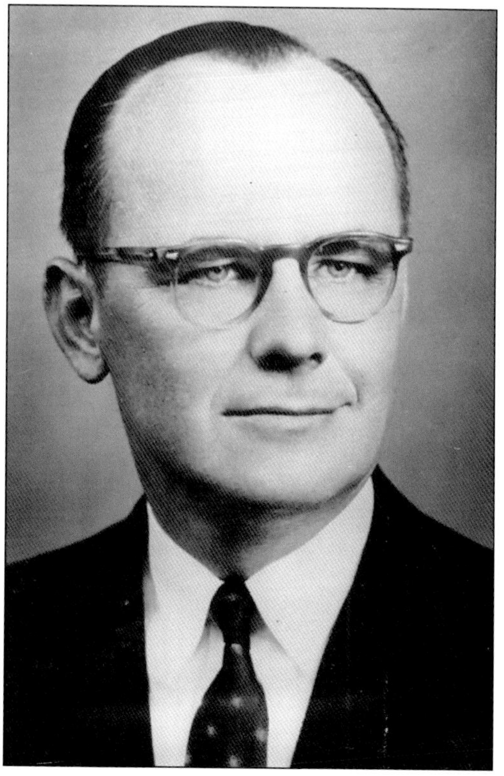

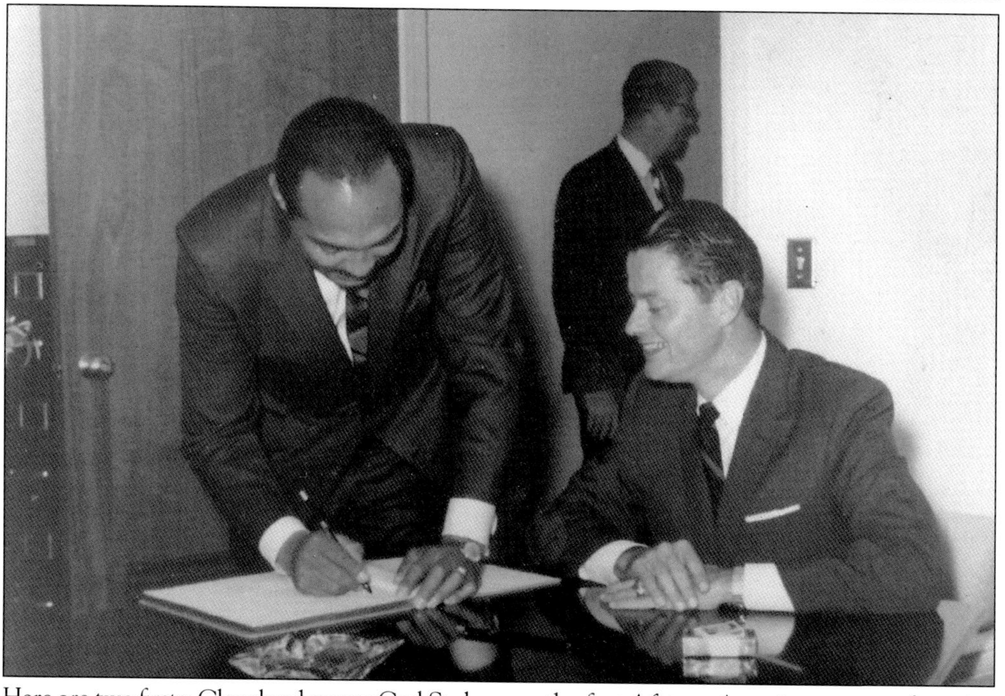

Here are two firsts: Cleveland mayor Carl Stokes was the first African American mayor of a major American city, and Charles Mooney was, at the time of his tenure, Fairview's youngest (until Mayor Richard G. Anter II) and first Democratic mayor. (Fairview Park Historical Society.)

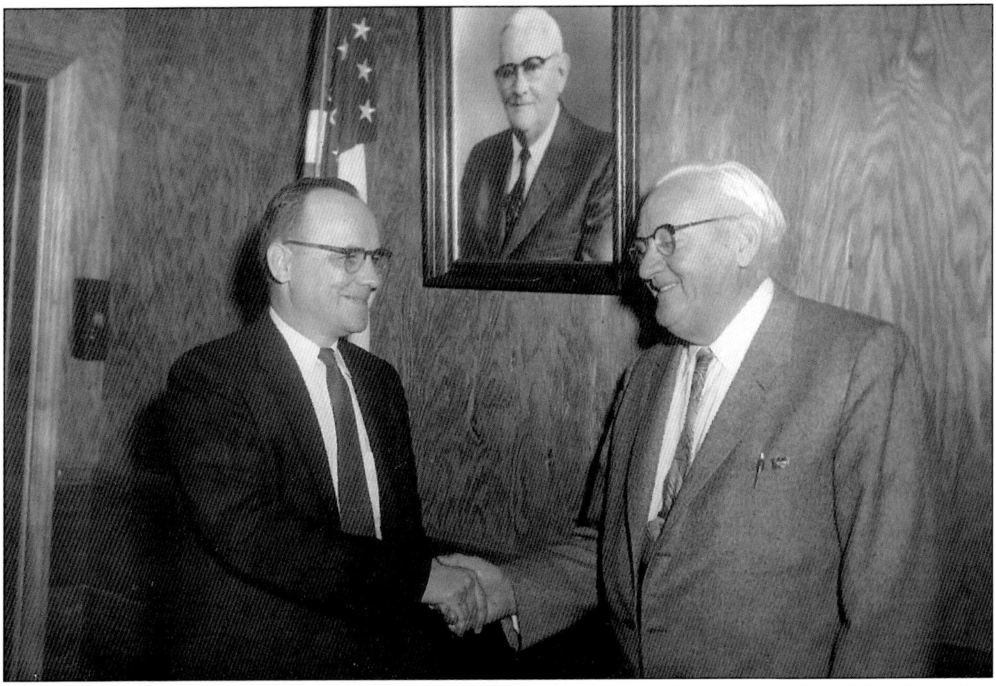

The two pictures on this page bookend Mayor James A. Dunson's term in office. Here he takes over from Karl A. Bohlken in 1958. Bohlken ran the city for 14 years, but Dunson defeated him in the Republican primary. (Fairview Park Historical Society.)

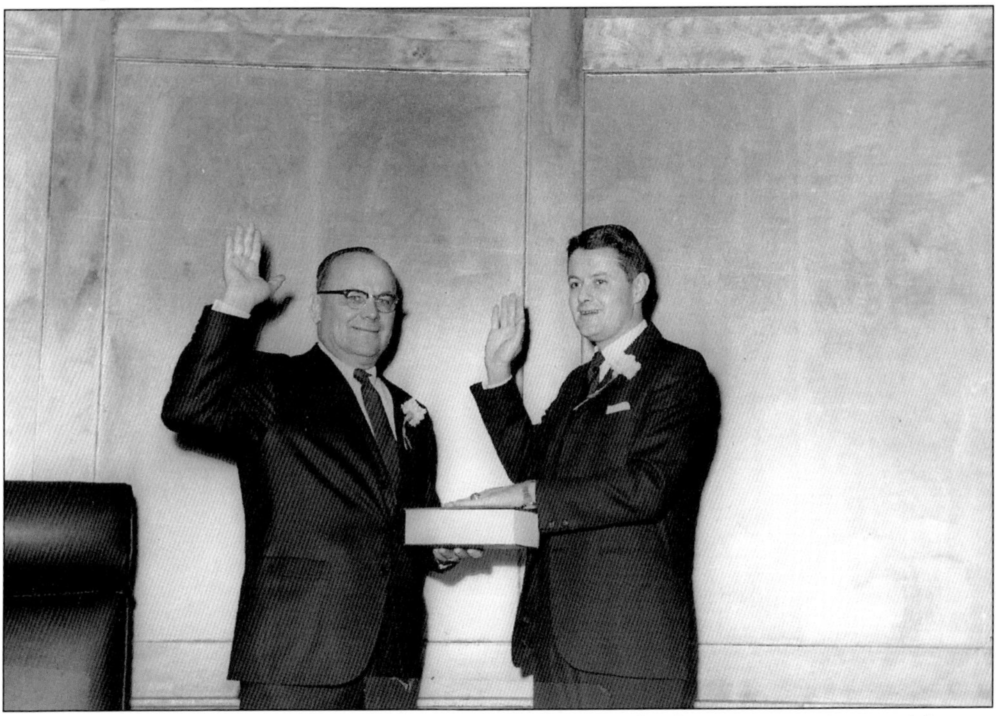

On the last day of 1967, Dunson passes the torch to Mayor Charles A. "Pete" Mooney. Mooney served until 1975. (Fairview Park Historical Society.)

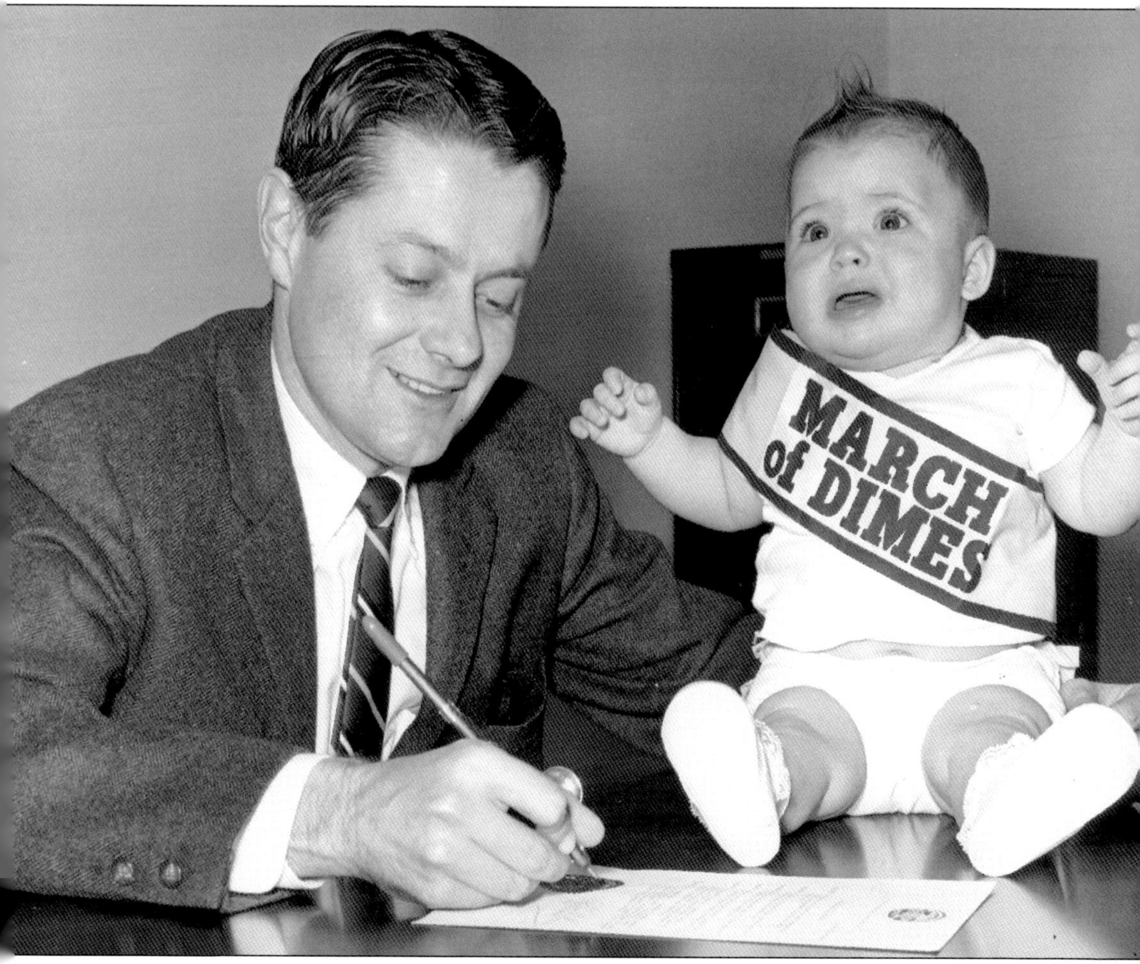

This spokes baby for the March of Dimes does not appreciate what a photo opportunity is as much as a politician does. Mooney signs a proclamation, as Christine Neidering feels a little vulnerable. (Cleveland Press Archives, Cleveland State University.)

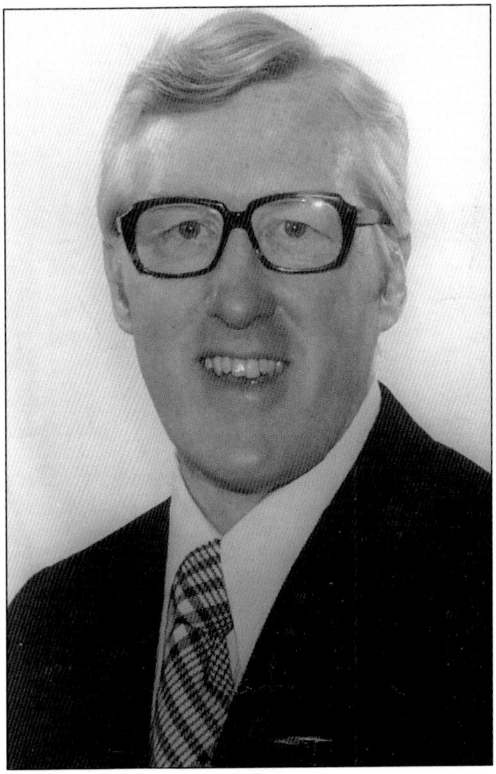

Joseph M. Gaul served as mayor before and after Richard G. Anter II's term. First assuming the position in 1976, he had already served on the council. Gaul carried a paging unit that he could be called on if he was needed at city hall. He helped develop the Bain Park Historical Landmark Commission and helped get the funding for the Willowood Manor Senior Housing Center. (Fairview Park Historical Society.)

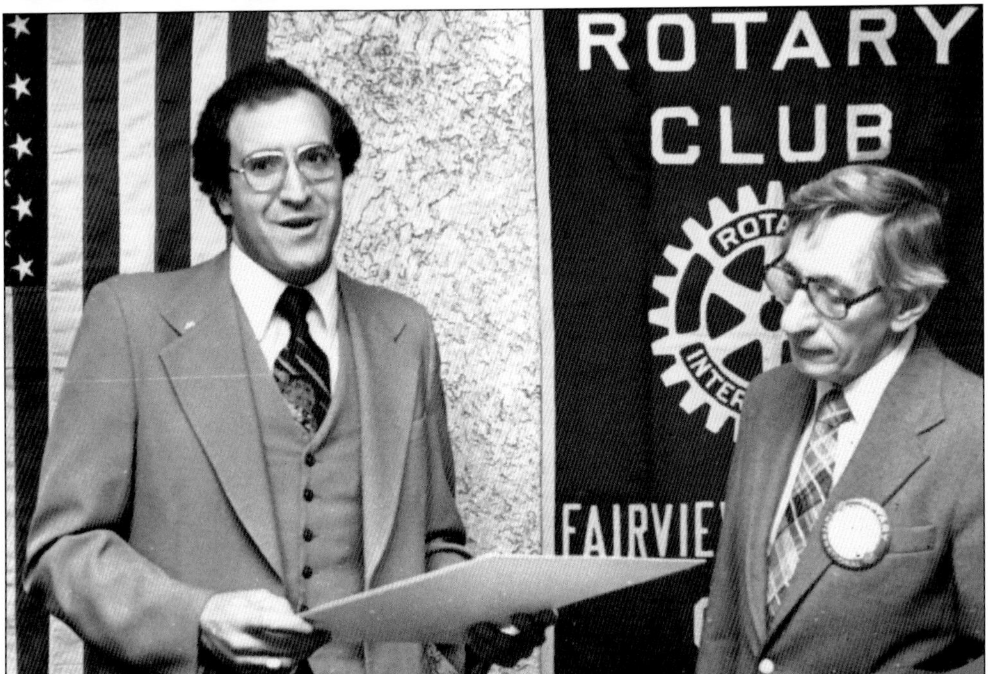

Anter is pictured here presenting a proclamation to Rotary Club president Al Heller in February 1980. Anter served as mayor from 1980 to 1983. Years later, he moved to Rocky River and made an unsuccessful run for that mayor seat. (Cleveland Press Archives, Cleveland State University.)

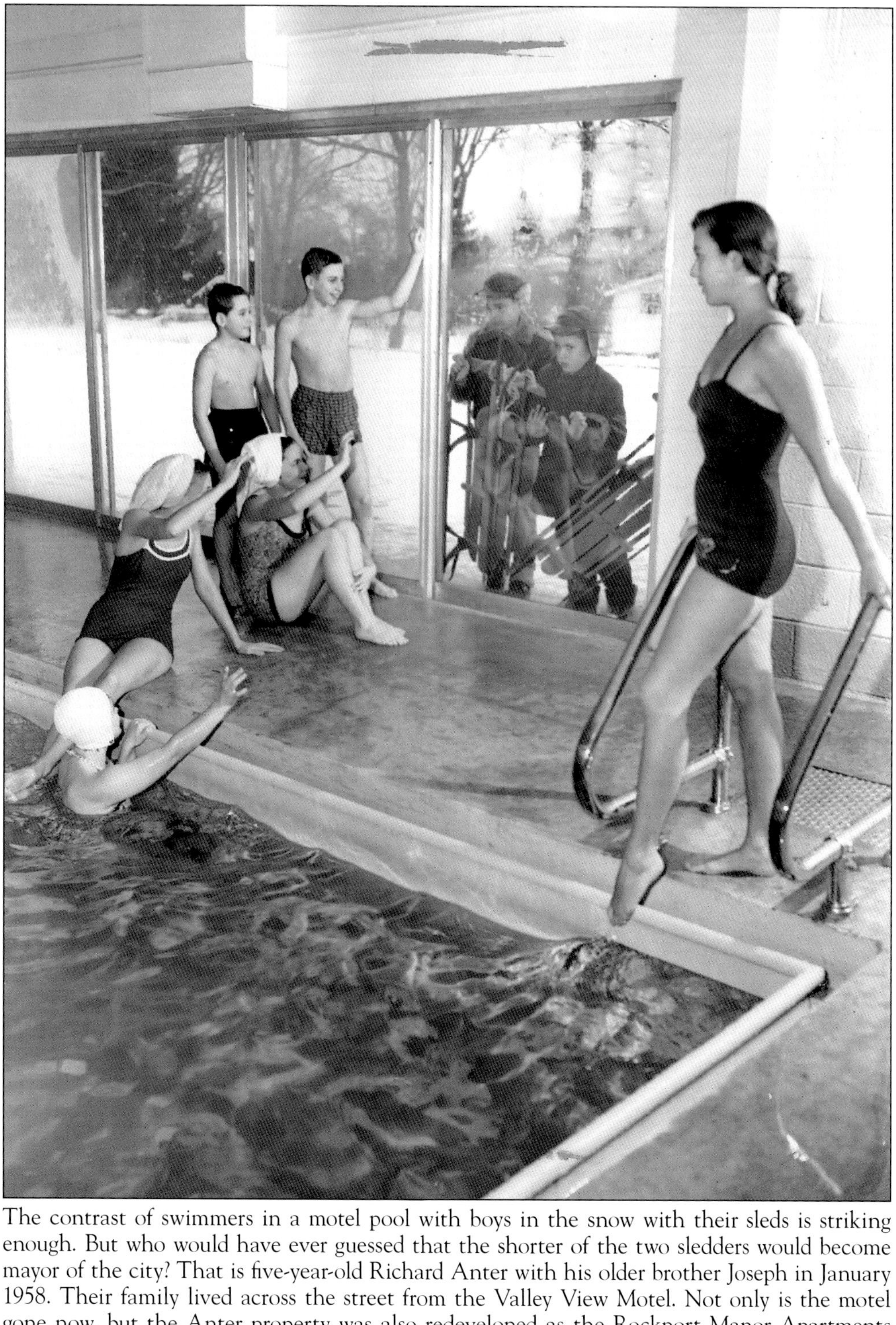

The contrast of swimmers in a motel pool with boys in the snow with their sleds is striking enough. But who would have ever guessed that the shorter of the two sledders would become mayor of the city? That is five-year-old Richard Anter with his older brother Joseph in January 1958. Their family lived across the street from the Valley View Motel. Not only is the motel gone now, but the Anter property was also redeveloped as the Rockport Manor Apartments in the early 1960s. The lady at right is identified as "lovely lifeguard Miss Betty Buckles, 22." (Cleveland Press Archives, Cleveland State University.)

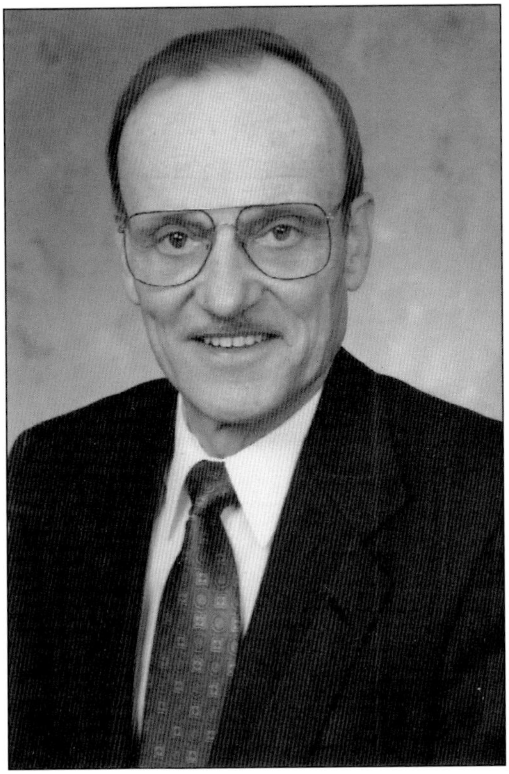

An extensive brochure highlights Karl Kubb's accomplishments as mayor from 1992 to 1999. Earlier mayors' concerns had been paving the roads and keeping up with an ever-growing need for more schools for a surging population. Now the need was for thousands of dollars in grant money for a multitude of projects, including upgrading computers for Y2K compliance, building a senior citizen center, and adding computer terminals to police cars. Kubb also served on the city council and was council president. (Fairview Park Historical Society.)

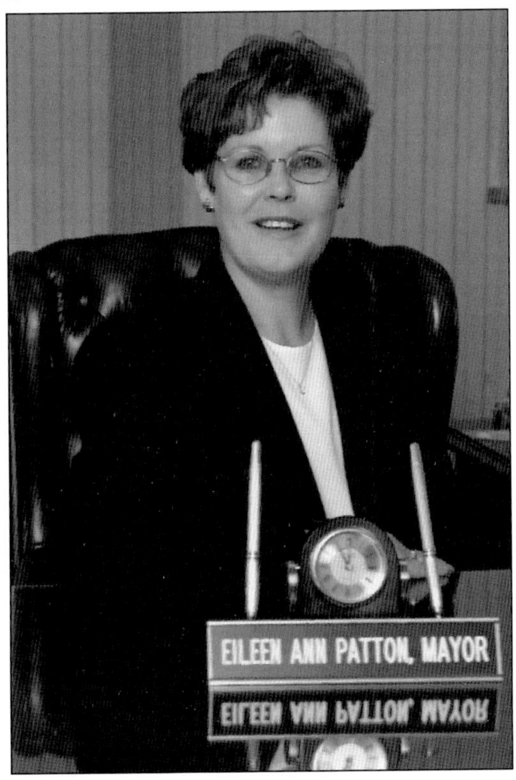

Mayor Eileen Ann Patton ushered Fairview Park into the new century and millennium. One of her early accomplishments was getting rid of the old motels along Lorain Road that were deemed blighted, and they were replaced by office buildings that added to the tax base. She was also part of the very ambitious Gemini Project that built a recreation center and rebuilt schools. She was on the city council for six years before becoming mayor in 2000. (Fairview Park Historical Society.)

Eight

THE PEOPLE

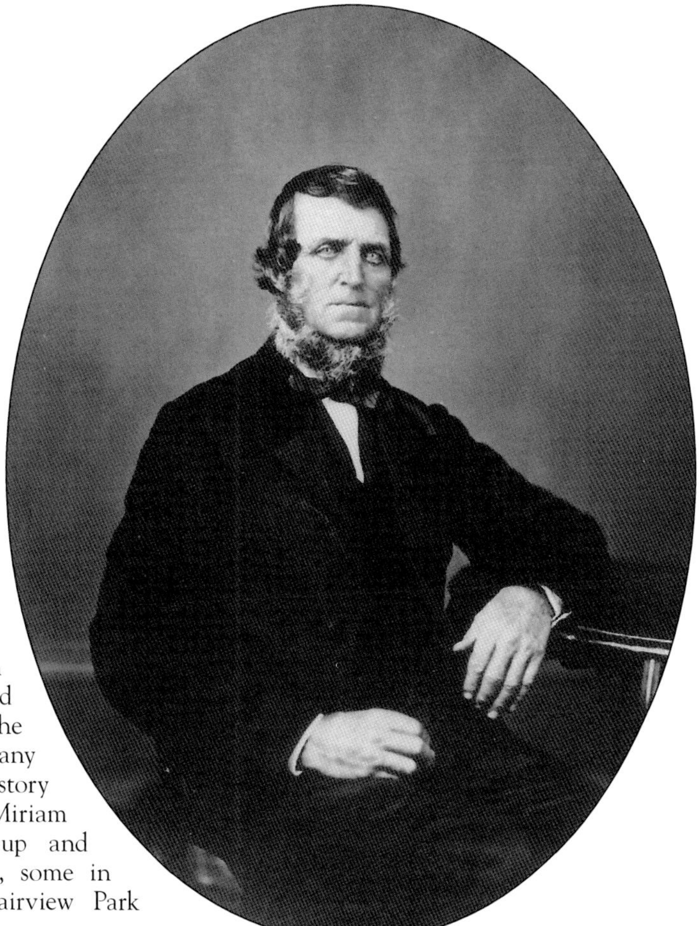

As one of Rockport Township's earliest settlers in 1830, John Place Spencer acquired so much land that his six children each had significant land of their own to develop. The Spencer name comes up many times in early Rockport history as John Place and Electa Miriam Spencer's children grew up and started their own families, some in noted century homes. (Fairview Park Historical Society.)

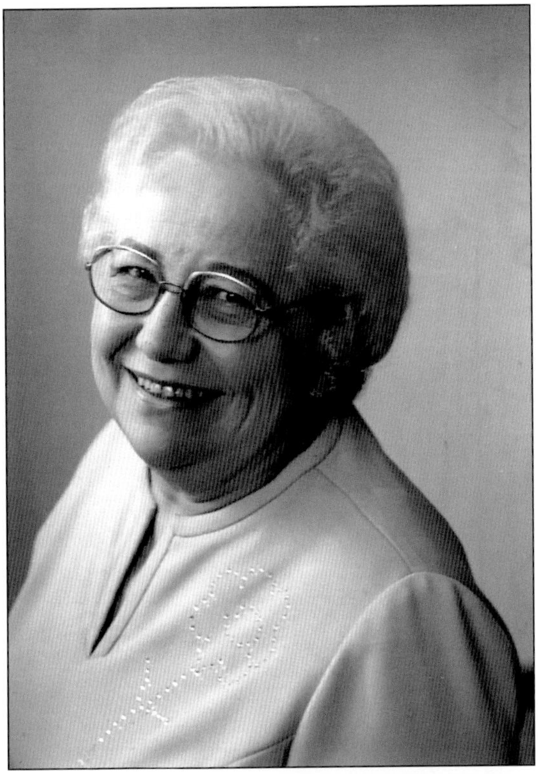

Margaret (Marge) Schaefer was valedictorian for the first graduating class from Fairview High School in 1931. Schaefer had perfect attendance throughout all 12 years. She also wrote the words to the school's alma mater. Schaefer married William Goebelt in 1936, and after retirement in the early 1970s, she wrote the book *Fairview Park in Historical Review.* (Fairview Park Historical Society.)

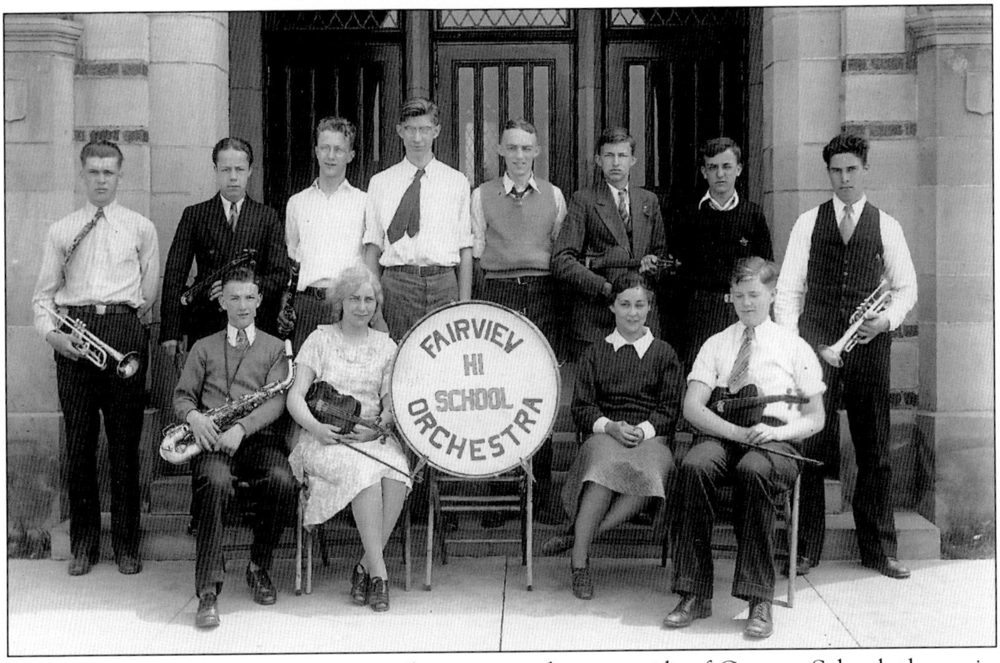

Just like the countless group pictures shot against the same side of Garnett School, the main entrance of the high school became a striking, if overused, background for all the high school photographs. In her senior year, 1931, Schaefer is seated second from the left holding the violin. (Fairview Park Historical Society.)

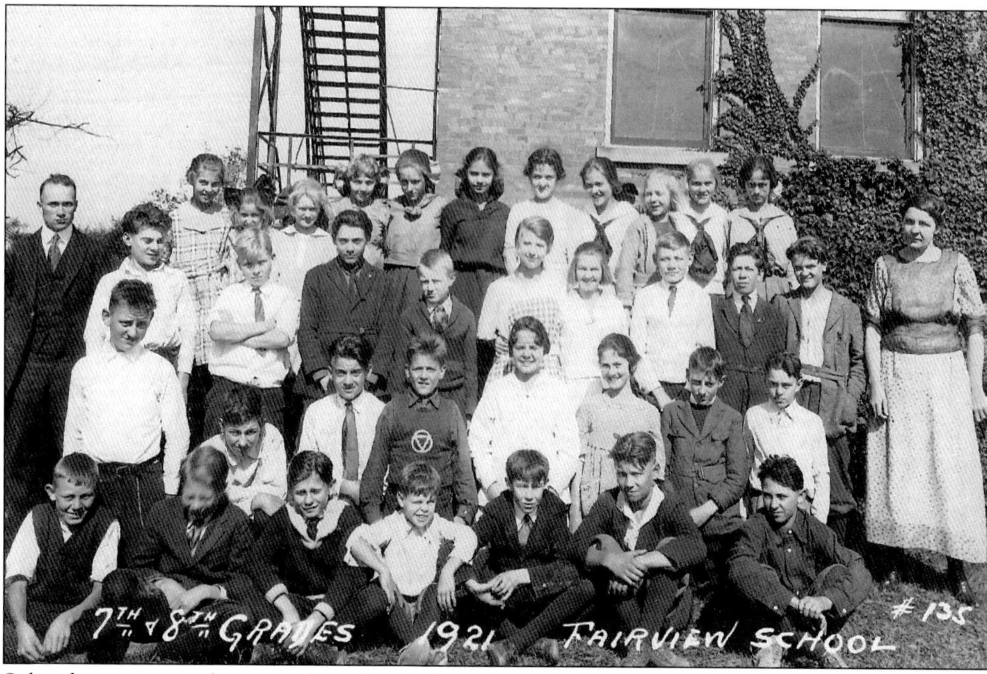

Schaefer is among the seventh and eighth graders of 1921, pictured third from the right in the fourth row. The two teachers are Lewis F. Mayer, who served for 43 years as the Fairview school superintendent, and Anna Baker. (Fairview Park Historical Society.)

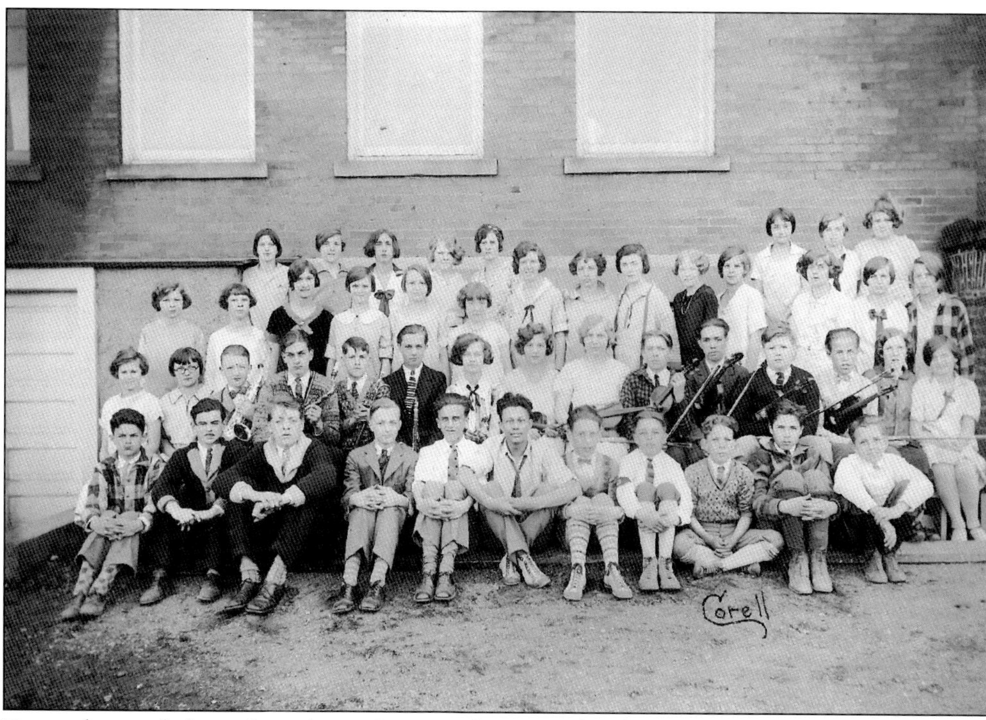

Pictured seventh from the right in the second row is Schaefer in the 1928 Glee Club. (Fairview Park Historical Society.)

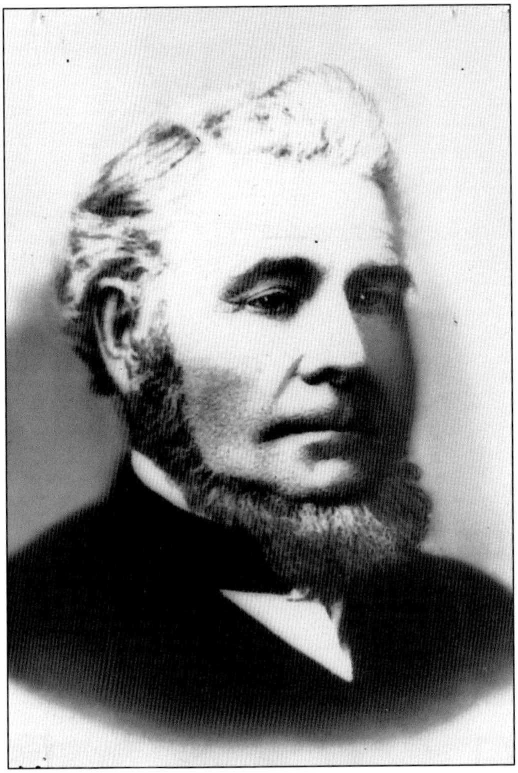

Around 1817, brothers Benjamin and Asahel Mastick came from Massachusetts. No photographs of Asahel seem to be available, but Caroline, shown below, was his wife. The Mastick brothers split 320 acres between them. Benjamin and his first wife, Eliza, settled in the valley just west of the river with Asahel and Caroline on the other side of the river on what is now Puritas Road. They gradually replaced forest with grain fields, which many years later became a golf course. The trees they cleared were fed through the sawmill they built, making lumber for the plank roads. Before there was a bridge, they ferried people across the river. The bridge there now is where Mastick Road changes to Puritas Road. (Fairview Park Historical Society.)

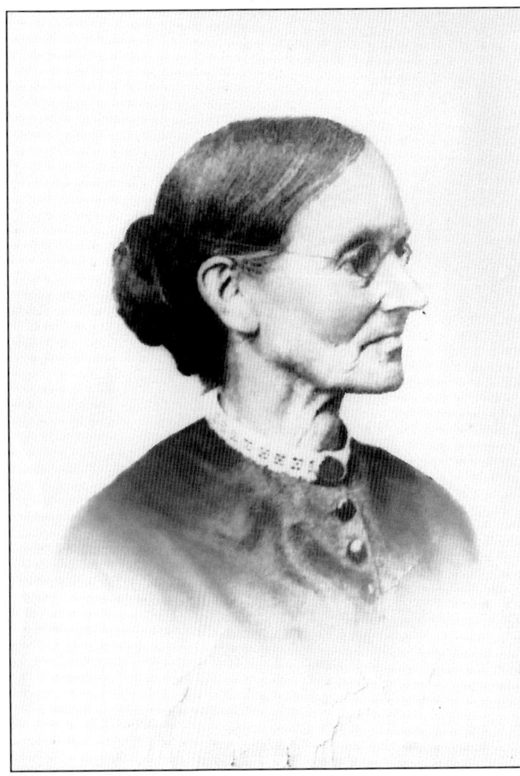

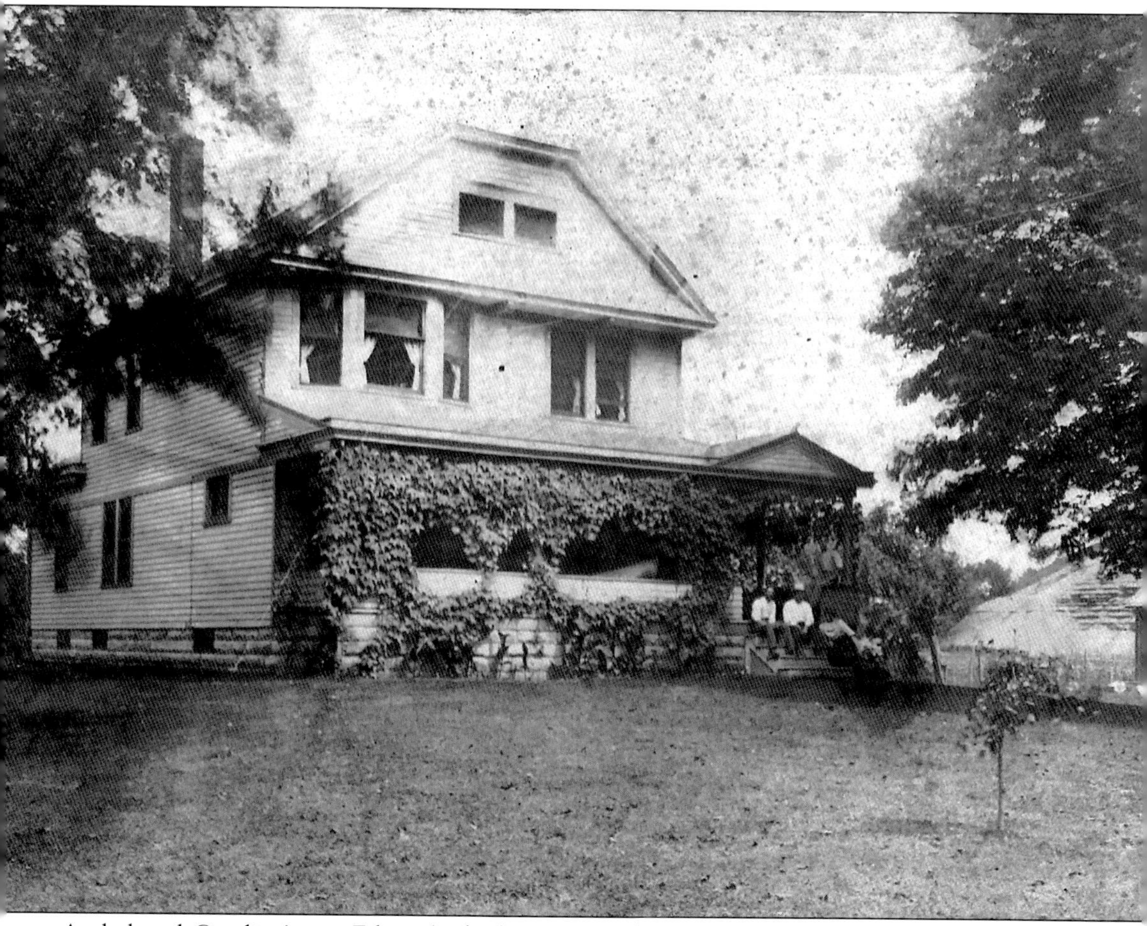

Asahel and Caroline's son Edwin built this 14-room house in 1899 on the land his parents owned, now the Mastick Woods golf course. It had no electric lighting. Heat and lighting were fueled by the natural gas wells on the property. Although Cleveland Metroparks bought all the property when it was established in the early 1920s, Edwin's son (who died in 1960) and daughter (who died in 1954) were allowed to occupy the house as long as they lived. A few times, they were trapped in the house by the overflowing river. (Fairview Park Historical Society.)

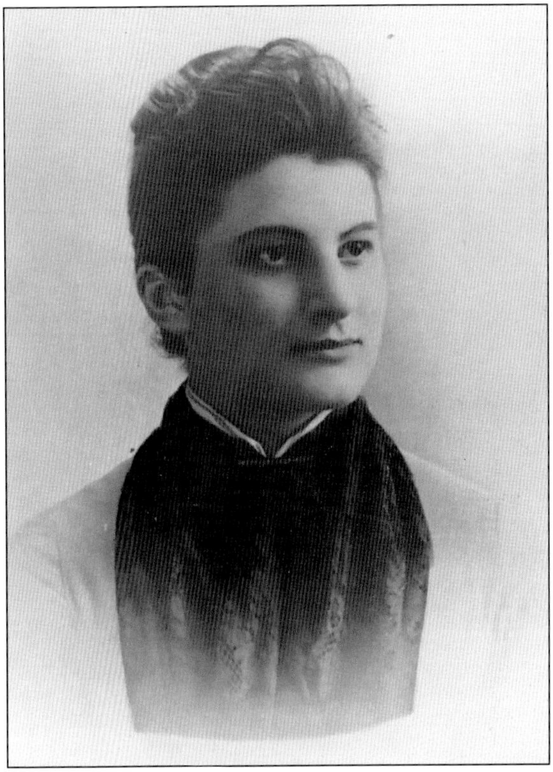

Katherine (Katie) Kaiser came to the Rockport area with her family in 1901. She inspired many people with her volunteer leadership, starting the parent-teacher association as well as the Tonsil Clinic. While the State Street School was being rebuilt, she allowed one of her bedrooms to be used as a classroom for the first four grades. Her death in 1929 brought flags to half-mast and was the biggest funeral Fairview Village had ever seen. (Fairview Park Historical Society.)

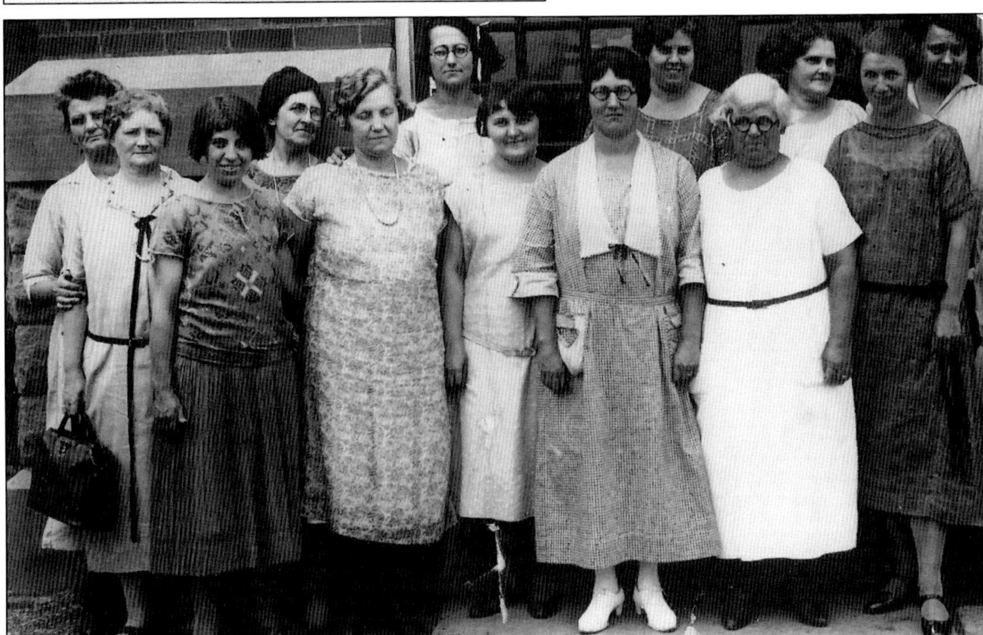

For a few years in the 1920s, a number of local ladies volunteered for the Tonsil or Well-Baby Clinic at Garnett School. The doctors also volunteered their services or worked at reduced rates. Tonsils were examined and children could even be kept there overnight if surgery was necessary. (Fairview Park Historical Society.)

John Kaiser, husband of Katherine, was a successful farmer in the early 1900s and was known for, among other things, making sauerkraut. His land was located at the point where West 210th Street, at the time called Wagar Road, used to dead end at Lorain Road. The eventual extension south of Wagar Road gobbled up a big chunk of his land and ruined his irrigation system, but his wife apparently convinced him to willingly donate the land. (Fairview Park Historical Society.)

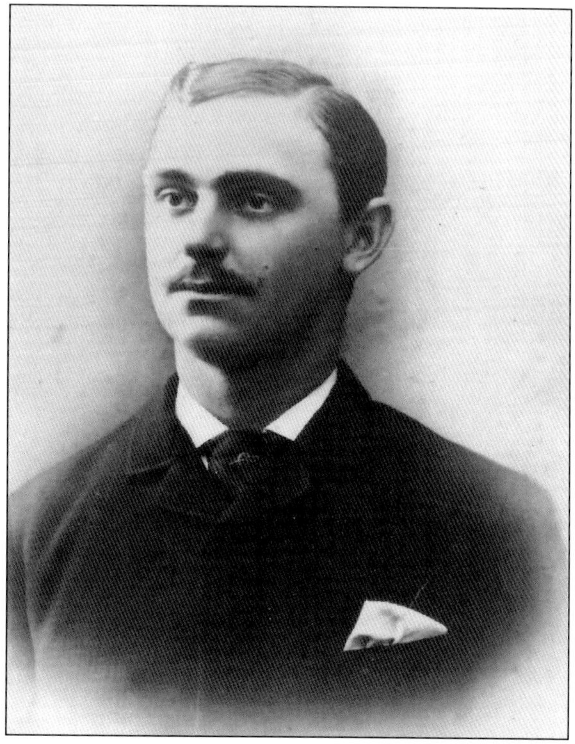

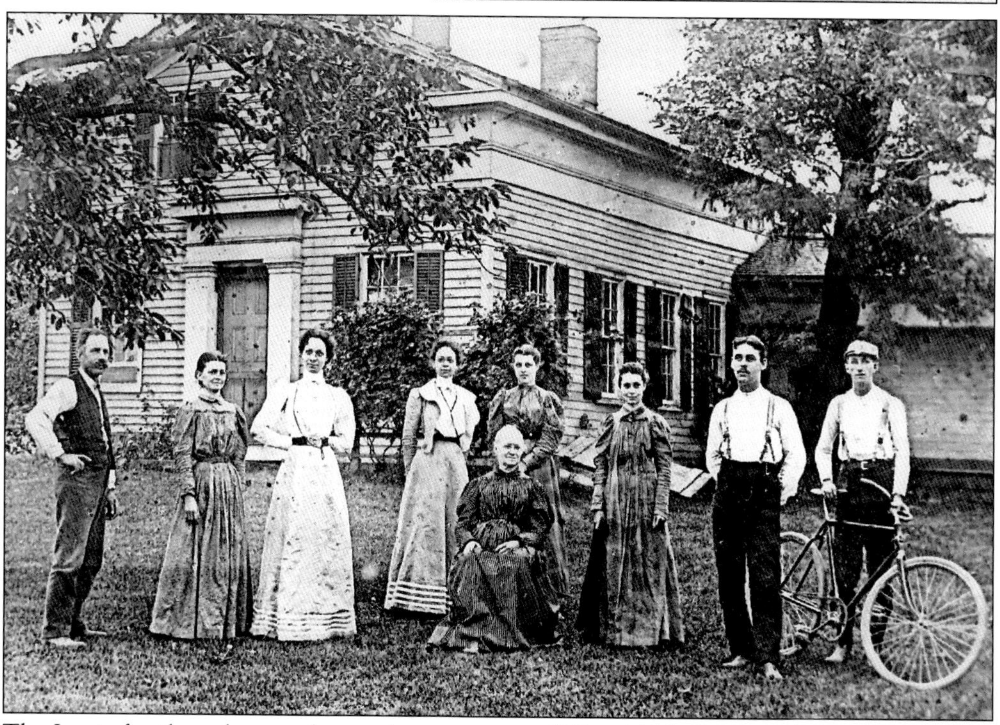

The Lewis family gathers at the northwest corner of West 196th Street and Lorain Road. The house, built in 1847, stood for over 100 years but was replaced by condominiums in the 1960s. (Fairview Park Historical Society.)

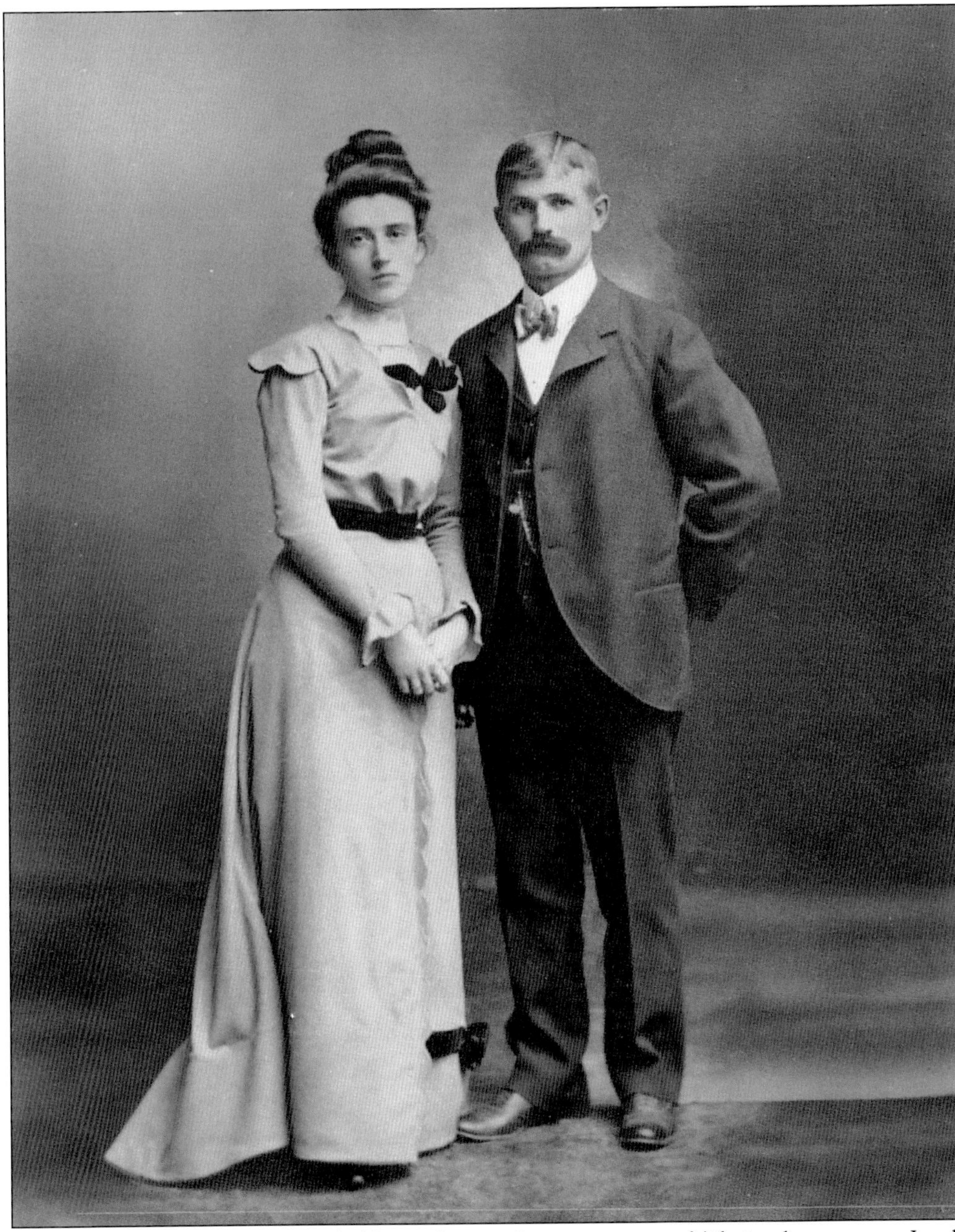

The Biermacher romance sounds like a classic, charming story of life in the country. Jacob Biermacher started working on the Curran farm in 1899 in what was then Parkview Village. It just so happened that Stella Brown was boarding with the Curran family that same year, as local teachers tended to do. One thing lead to another, and Jacob and Stella got married. (Fairview Park Historical Society.)

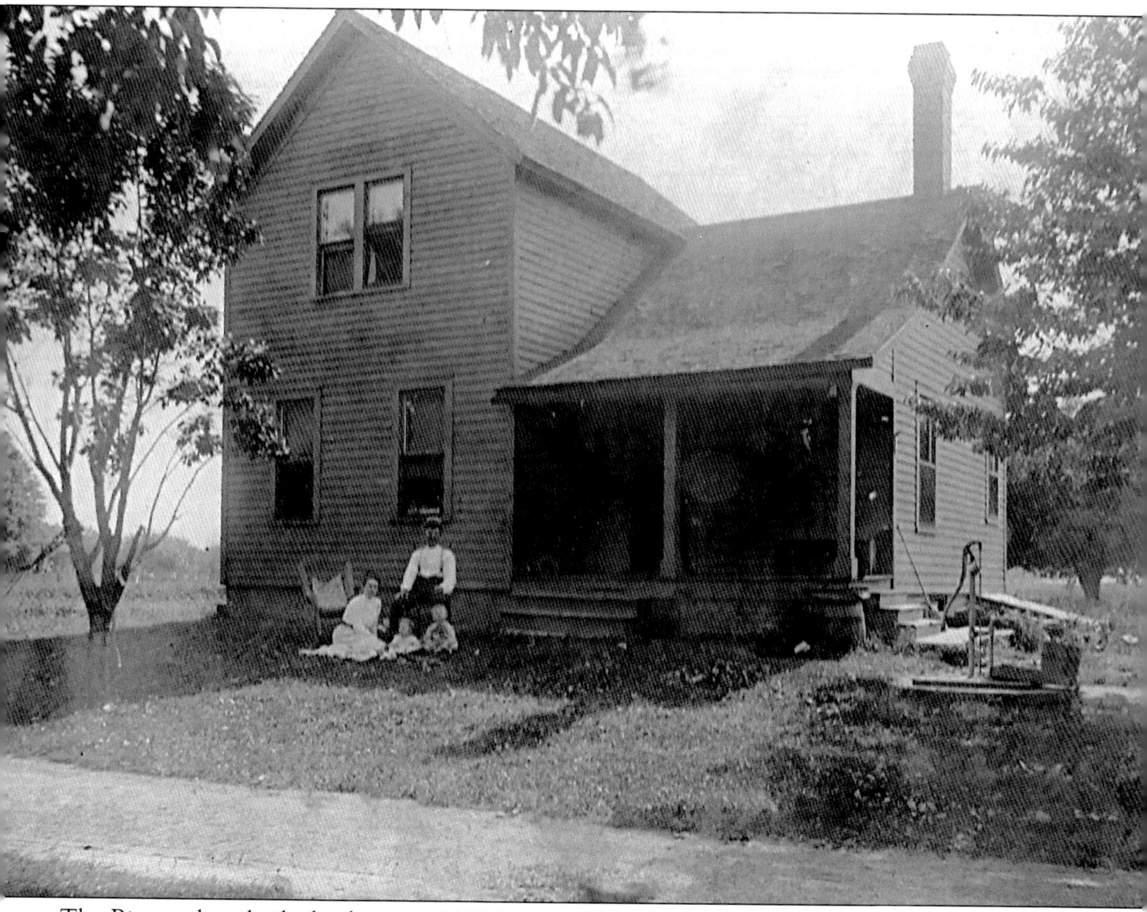

The Biermachers built this home at 21004 Mastick Road, which for a long time was one of the only houses in the area. Their children Gertrude and Ted are also in this photograph. (Fairview Park Historical Society.)

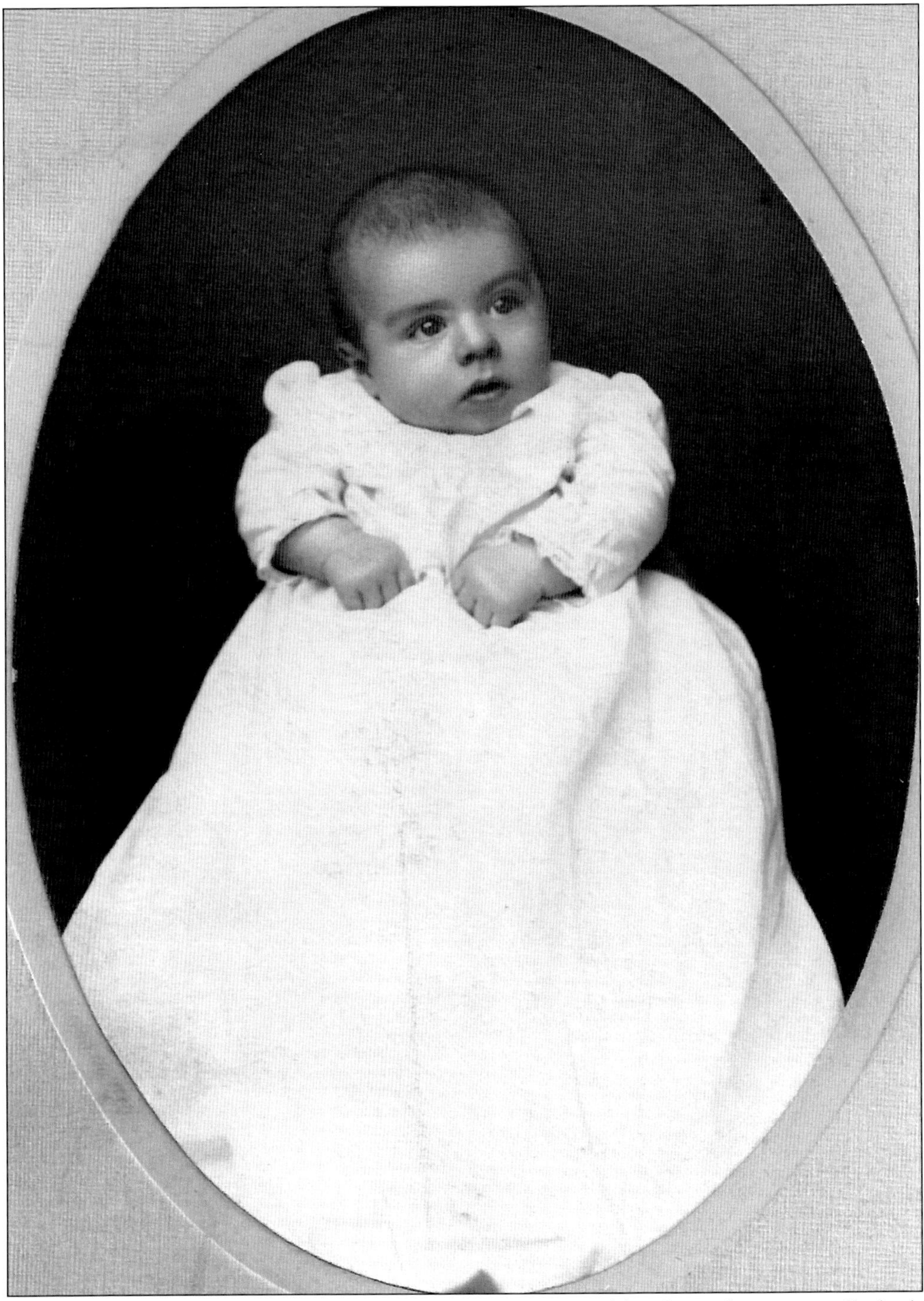

This is Jake and Stella Biermacher's baby Ted. His sister and brother-in-law eventually built another house nearby in 1925. Years later, his daughter, who contributed much to Fairview Park Historical Society, lived in a house around the corner from the original Biermacher homestead, on what is now West 210th Street. For many years, these two houses were the only houses on West 210th Street between Mastick and Lorain Roads. (Fairview Park Historical Society.)

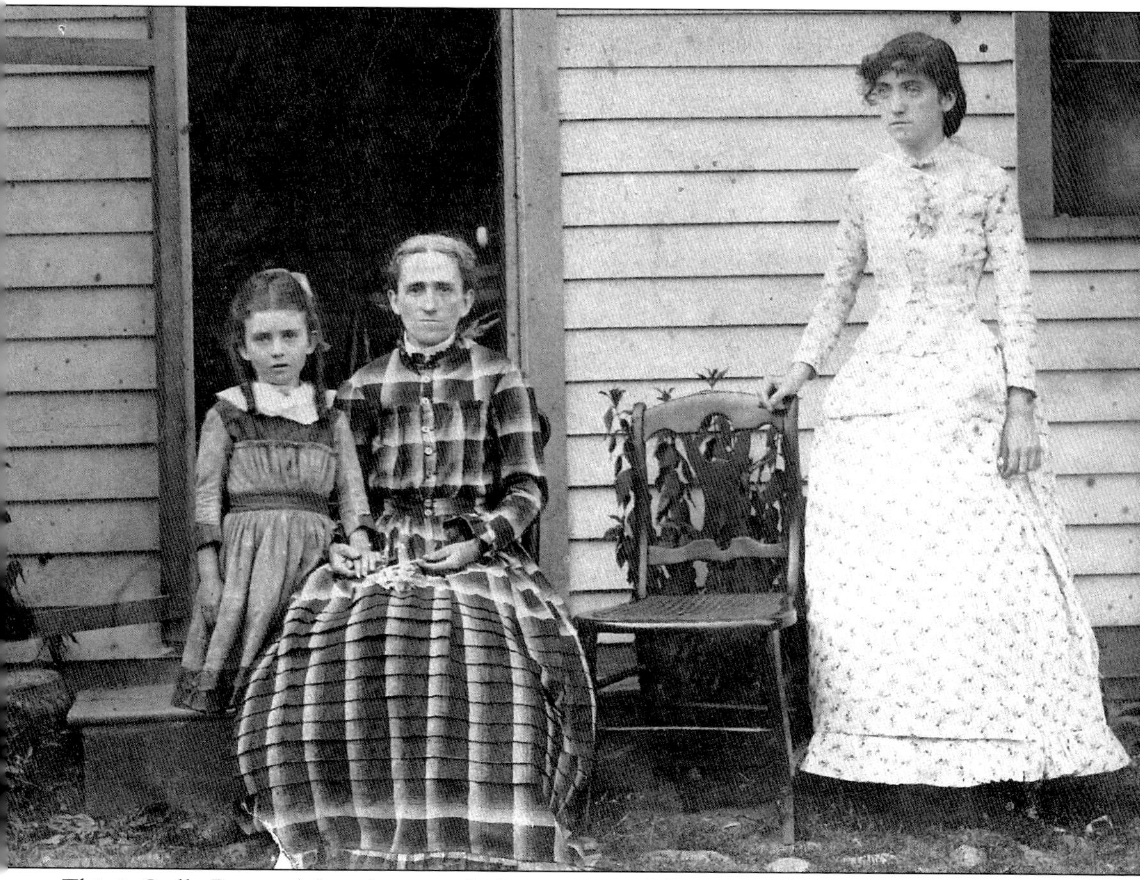

This is Stella Brown, left, a few years before marrying Jake Biermacher, with her mother and older sister Louella. A note on the photograph says the mother made the dresses they wore. (Fairview Park Historical Society.)

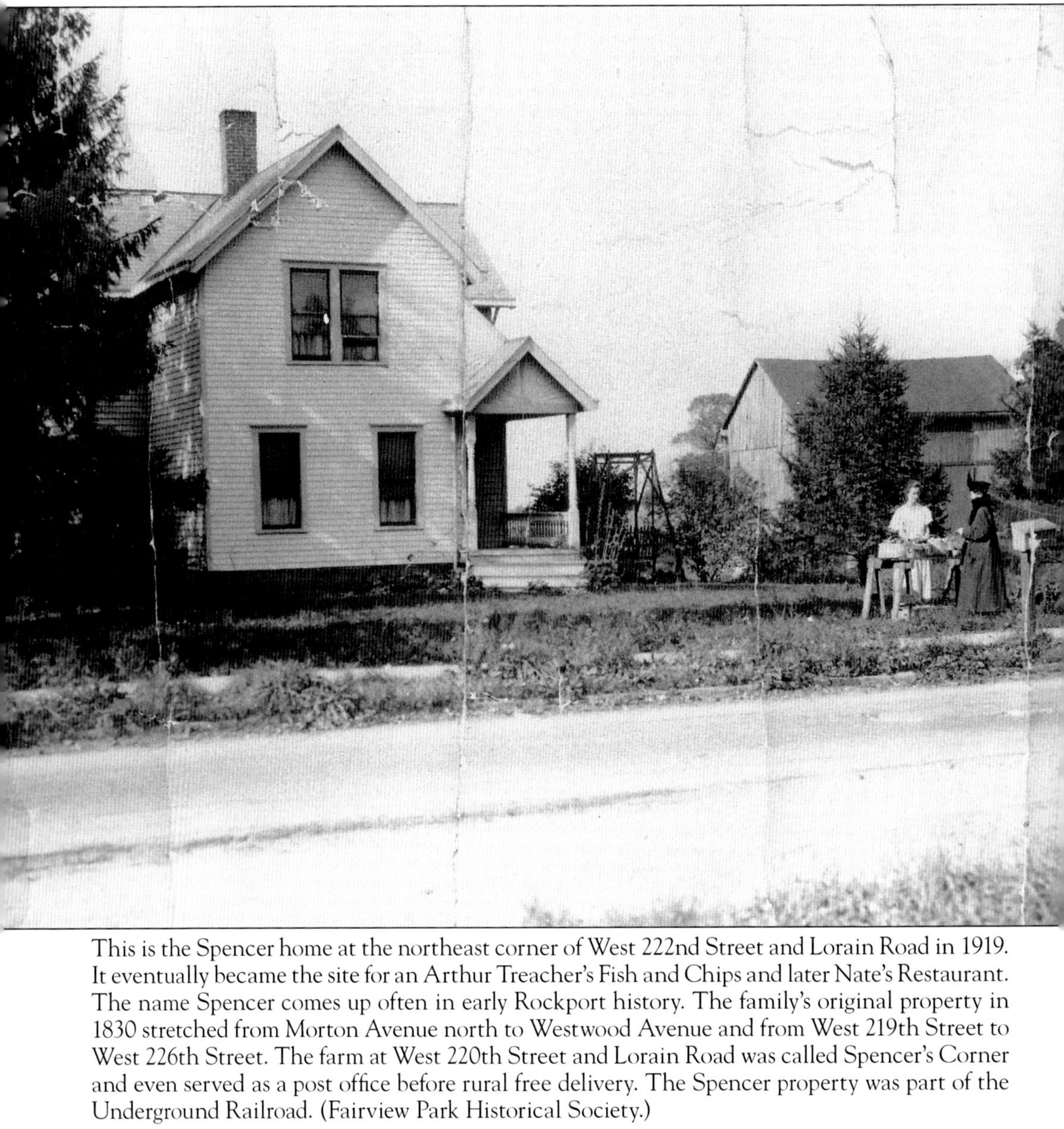

This is the Spencer home at the northeast corner of West 222nd Street and Lorain Road in 1919. It eventually became the site for an Arthur Treacher's Fish and Chips and later Nate's Restaurant. The name Spencer comes up often in early Rockport history. The family's original property in 1830 stretched from Morton Avenue north to Westwood Avenue and from West 219th Street to West 226th Street. The farm at West 220th Street and Lorain Road was called Spencer's Corner and even served as a post office before rural free delivery. The Spencer property was part of the Underground Railroad. (Fairview Park Historical Society.)

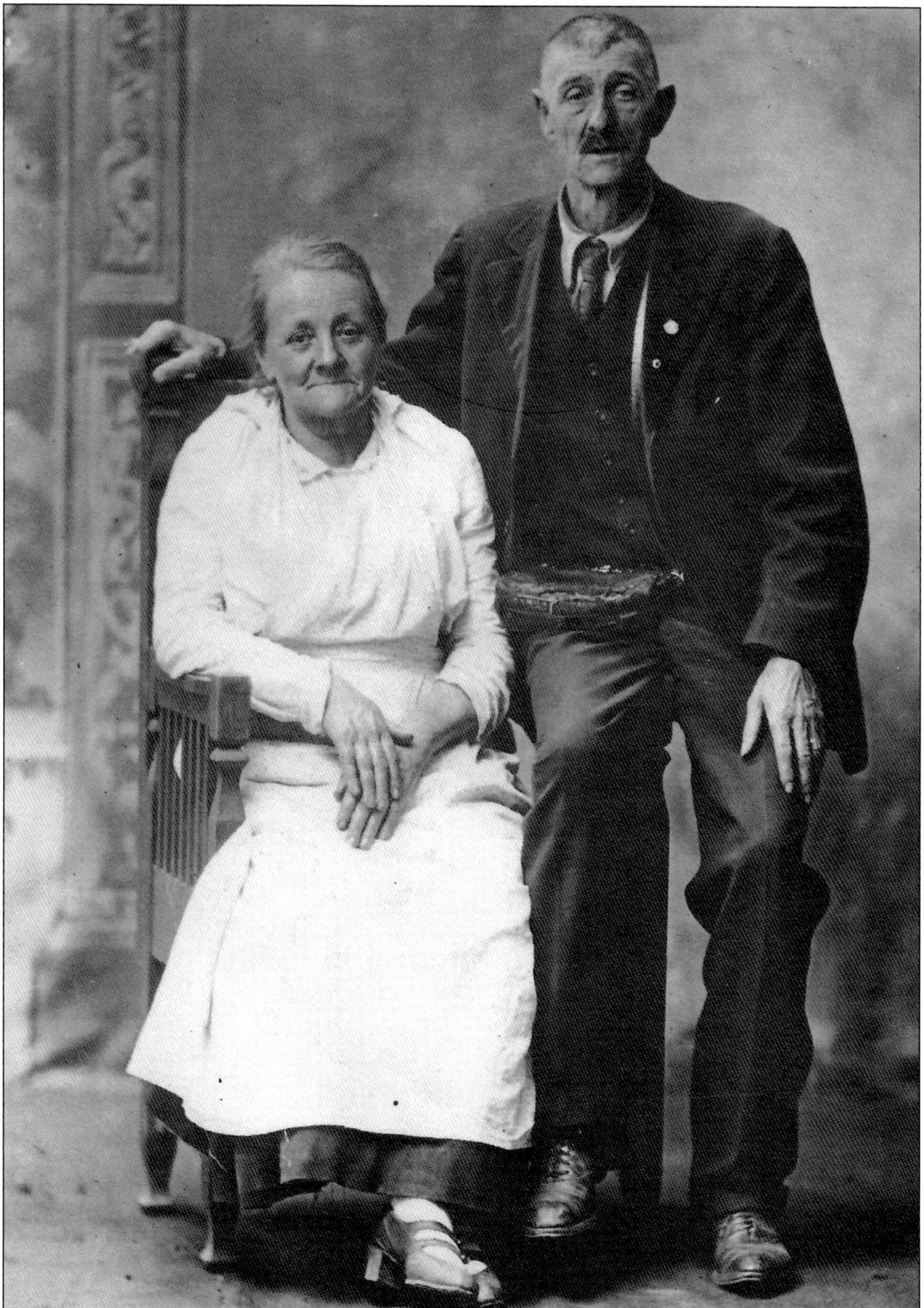

Leonard and Lillian Jordan lived and farmed at 18971 Lorain Road. The note on the back of this picture said they had worked all day at the West Side Market and were very tired, but they stopped at a studio near the market to pose for this portrait to send to their son serving in World War I. (Fairview Park Historical Society.)

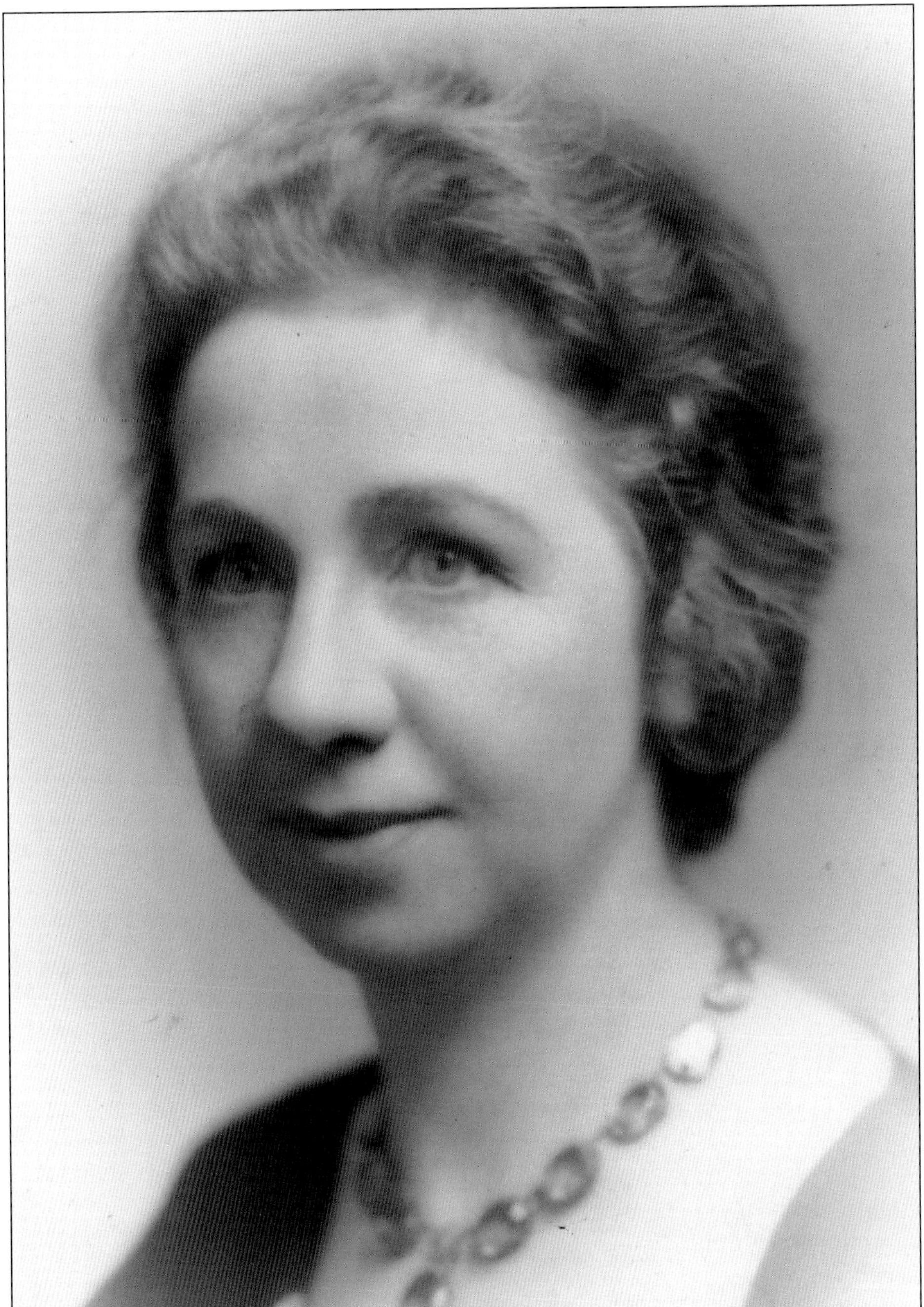

In Josephine Saxer Irwin's 94 years, she certainly had an impact. The fact that she was the first woman on the Fairview Park City Council from 1958 to 1962 certainly shows some real drive. In 1914, about 10 years before this photograph, she rode a horse on the downtown Cleveland Public Square in support of women's suffrage, leading 7,000 women in front of 200,000 spectators. Women could finally vote in 1920. Suffrage was not only a struggle in a male-dominated society, but other women were hesitant. "I despaired until the arrival of my grandchildren's generation," she said in her later years. (Cleveland Press Archives, Cleveland State University.)

In her elder years, Irwin tried to get the Equal Rights Amendment passed, observing, "Now legislation is the only way for equality. Demonstrations have little effect." She was a schoolteacher for a few years before marrying an engineer in 1919 and raising a family, but she clearly was never just another housewife. President of Fairview Park Historical Society from 1971 to 1974, she died in 1984 and is buried in Fairview Park Cemetery. (Cleveland Press Archives, Cleveland State University.)

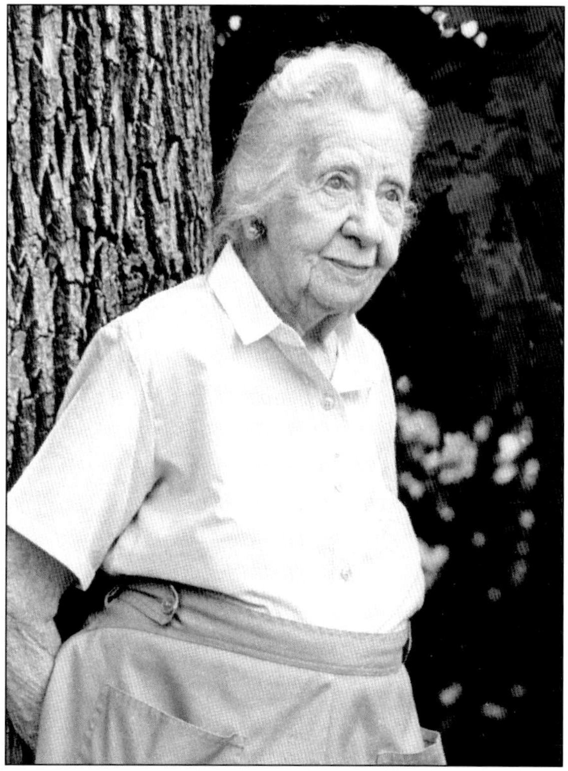

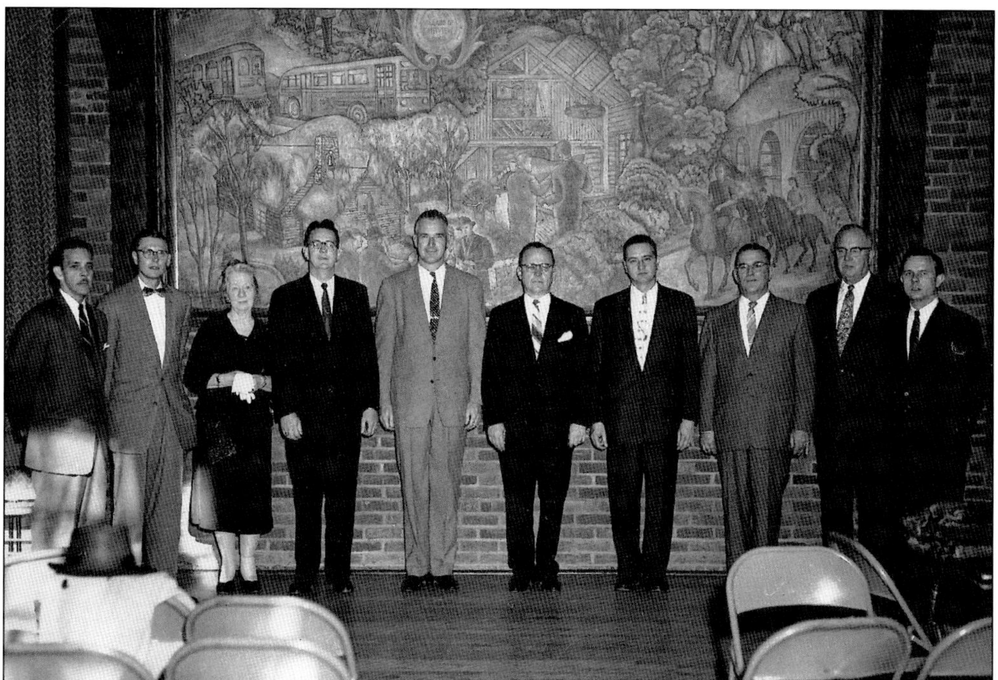

The 1957 city council poses in front of the Bain Cabin mural. Mayor James A. Dunson is in the center and Irwin is the only woman. (Fairview Park Historical Society.)

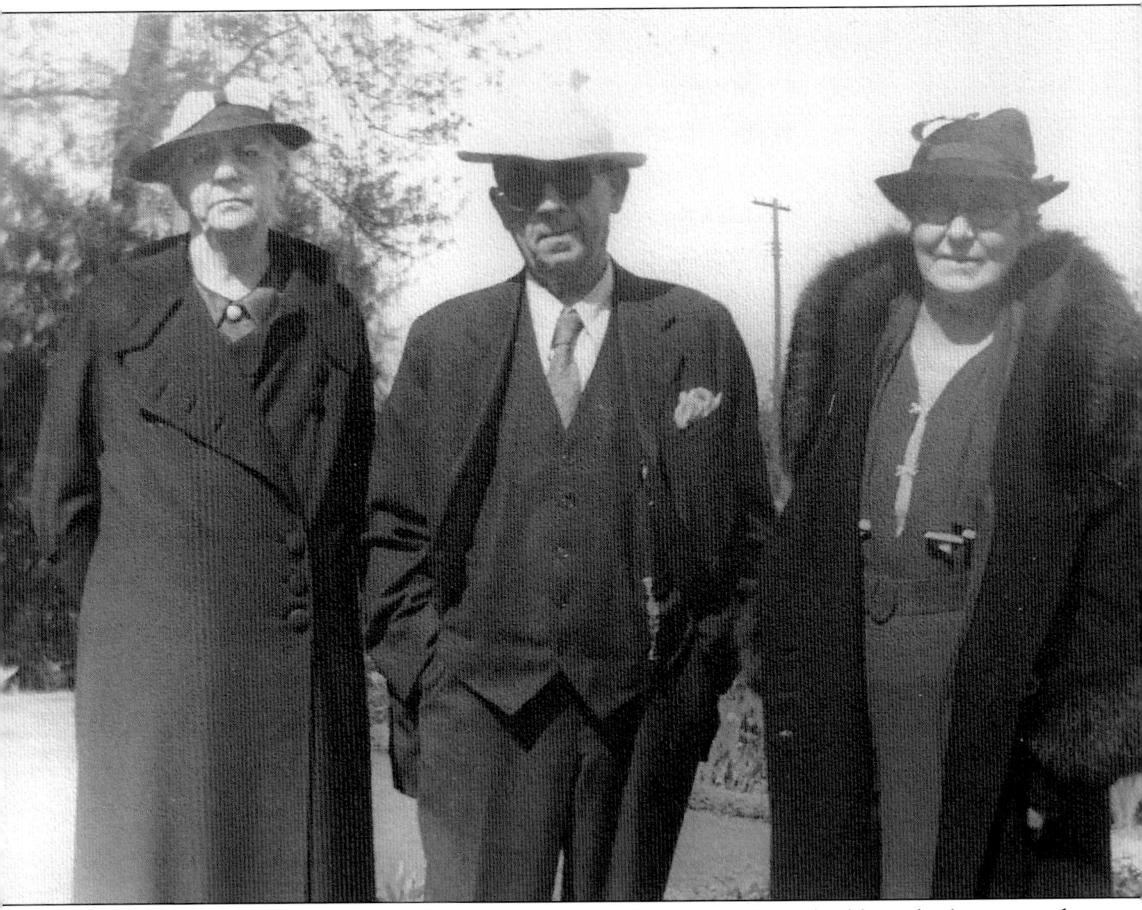

John Baumgardner was one of the early grocers in Fairview Village, building the house on the opposite page with a store in front in 1925. He ran the store with his daughter Verna, on the right, who continued to run it after he died. One of his two sons, J. Orrie, was fire chief from 1944 to 1973 and continued to live in the house after retirement. (Fairview Park Historical Society.)

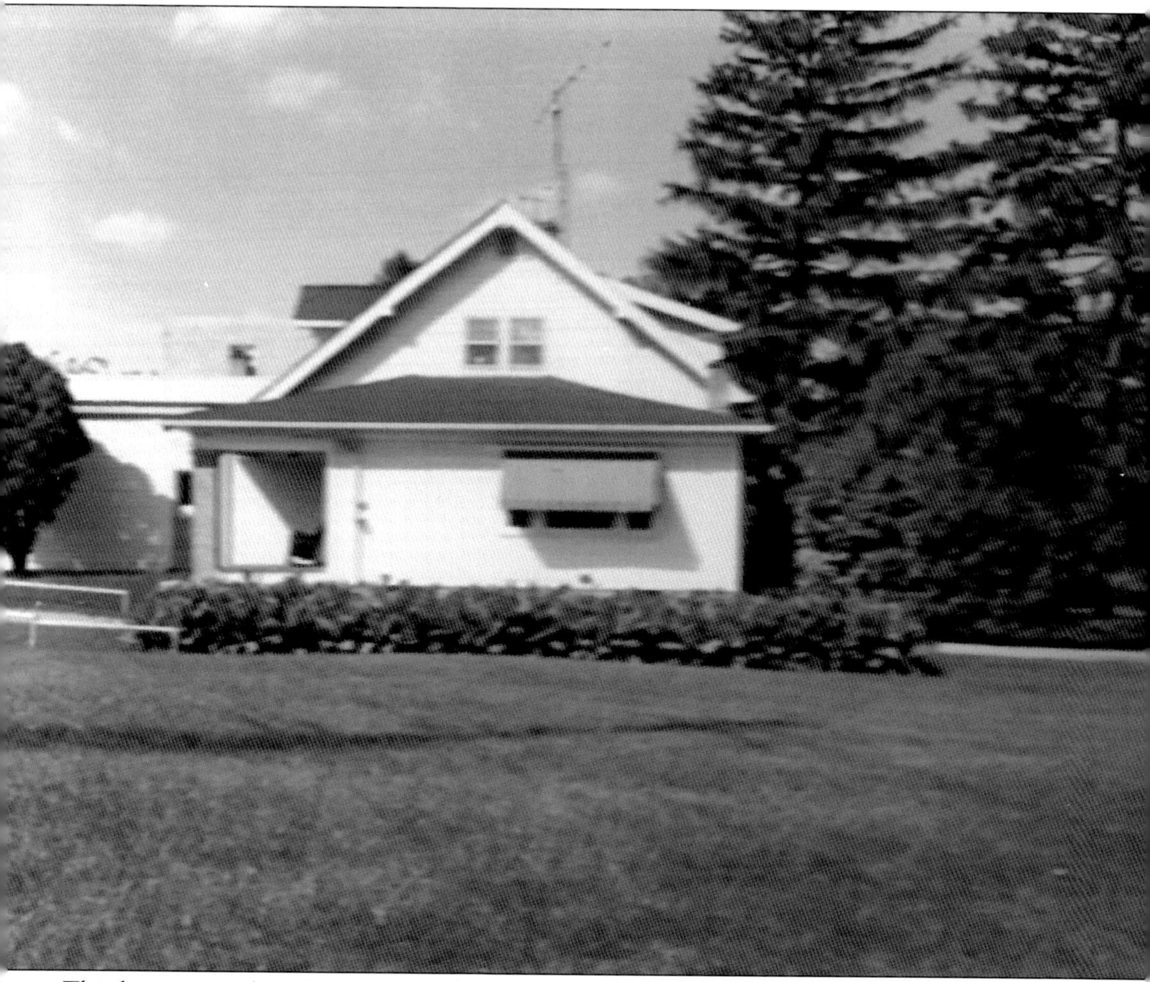

This house is on busy Lorain Road. Long a home to the Baumgardner family, the front used to house their grocery store as well as Cam Tait's meat market. After retired fire chief J. Orrie Baumgardner passed away, it was converted into a resale shop, supporting the American Cancer Society. The lawn was replaced by a small parking lot. (Fairview Park Historical Society.)

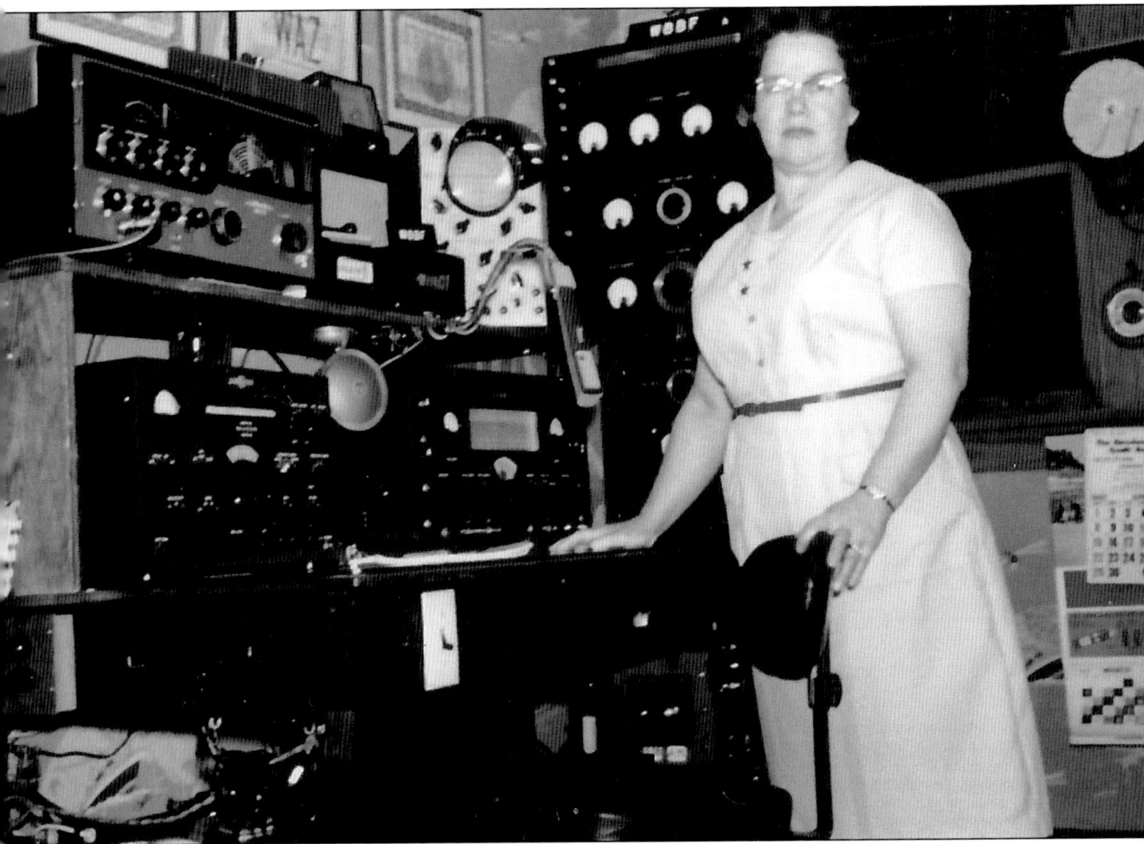

Both fire chief J. Orrie Baumgardner and his wife, Dorothy, were ham radio operators. In addition to enjoying it as a hobby, he helped many people contact family members during World War II and other disasters. (Fairview Park Historical Society.)

Nine

Odds and Ends

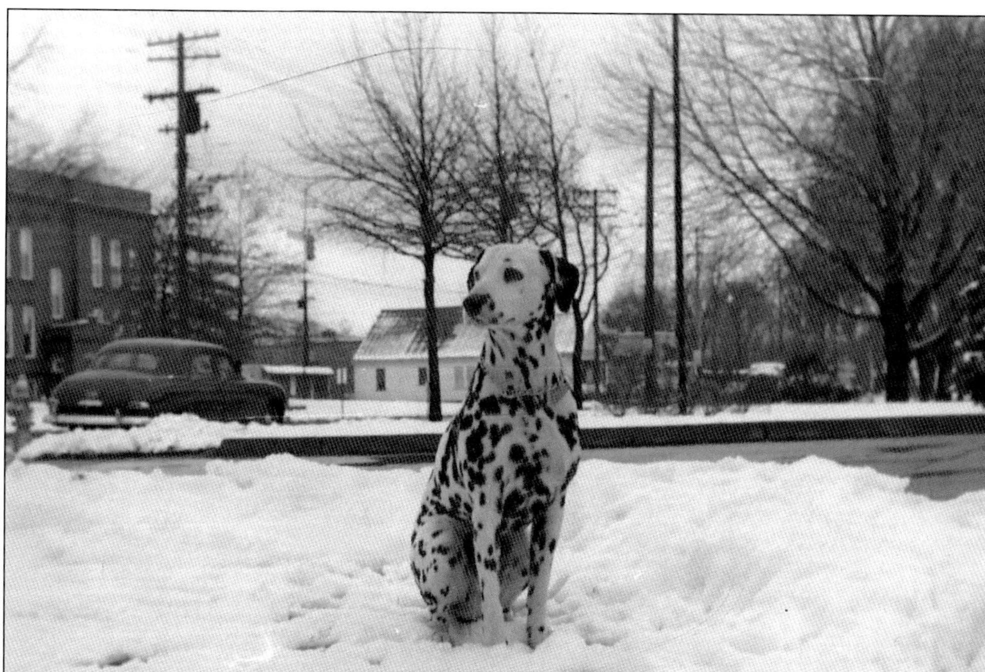

Smokey stands outside the fire station in the 1950s, with old Garnett School still visible across the street. Not only is no firehouse complete without a dalmatian, but also when Orrie Baumgardner, fire chief from 1944 to 1973, retired, so did his dogs. As man and dogs lived out the rest of their lives in the house at West 204th Street and Lorain Road, both were a common sight for a number of years working and playing on the front lawn. (Fairview Park Historical Society.)

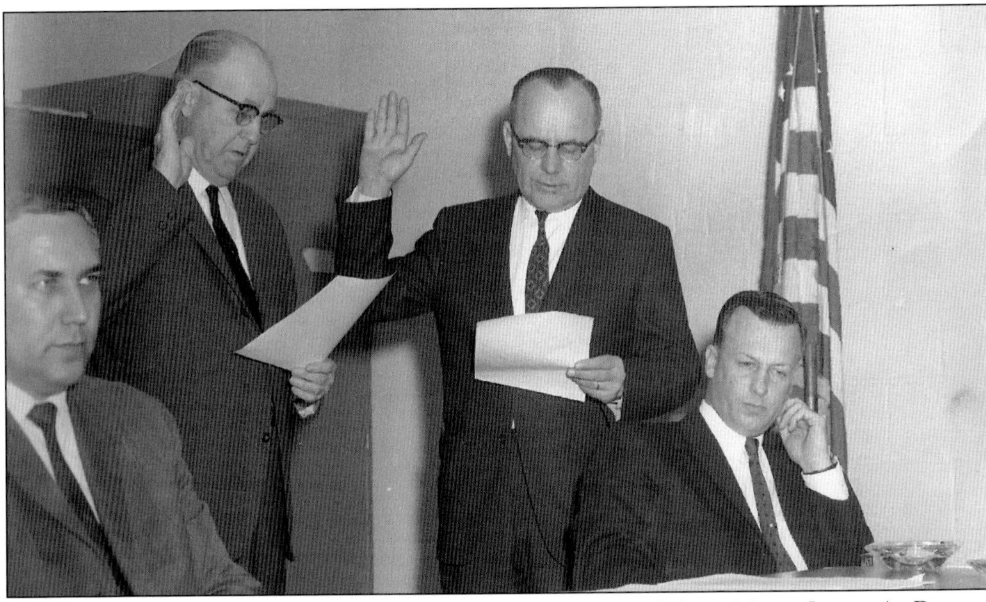

Paul Ungericht (standing, left) takes the oath for city council from Mayor James A. Dunson in 1967. Ungericht was mayor of the one-square-mile Parkview Village until it was annexed to Fairview Park. Parkview became Fairview Park's Ward 5 and Ungericht its councilman, although some people remember Ungericht as a substitute shop teacher at the high school in the late 1960s. The annexation brought lower taxes and better housing and police protection. (Cleveland Press Archives, Cleveland State University.)

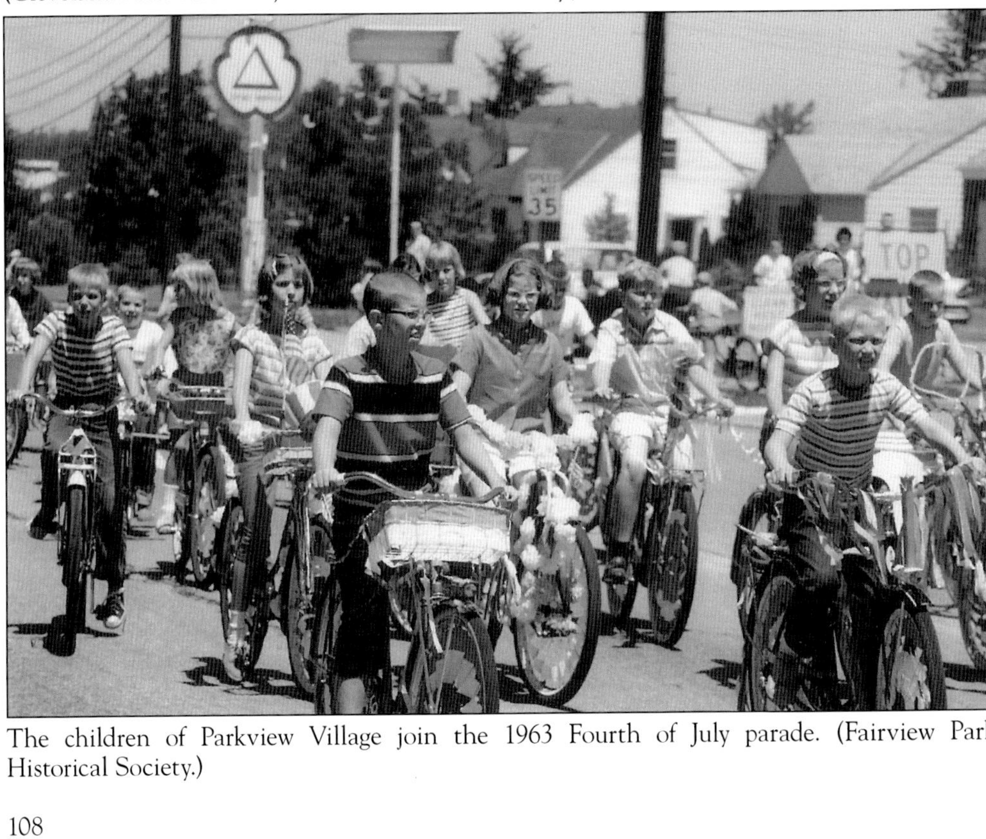

The children of Parkview Village join the 1963 Fourth of July parade. (Fairview Park Historical Society.)

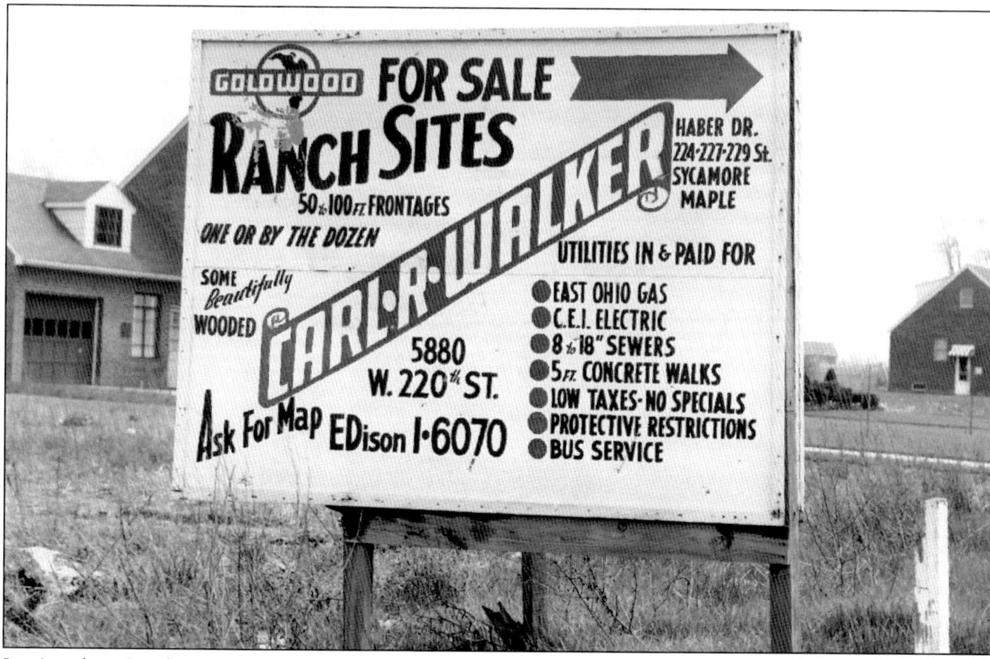

In April 1954, there was still old farmland to develop along West 220th Street. This sign shows the beginnings of the residential street Haber Drive, then a part of Parkview Village. (Cleveland Press Archives, Cleveland State University.)

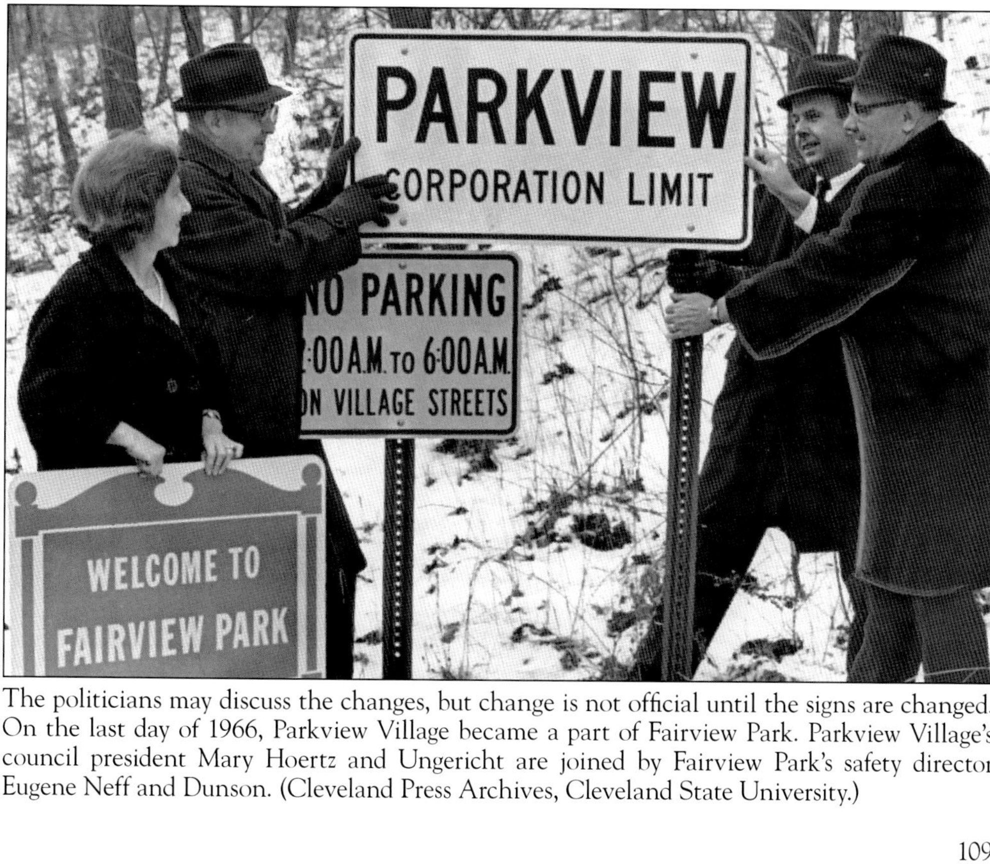

The politicians may discuss the changes, but change is not official until the signs are changed. On the last day of 1966, Parkview Village became a part of Fairview Park. Parkview Village's council president Mary Hoertz and Ungericht are joined by Fairview Park's safety director Eugene Neff and Dunson. (Cleveland Press Archives, Cleveland State University.)

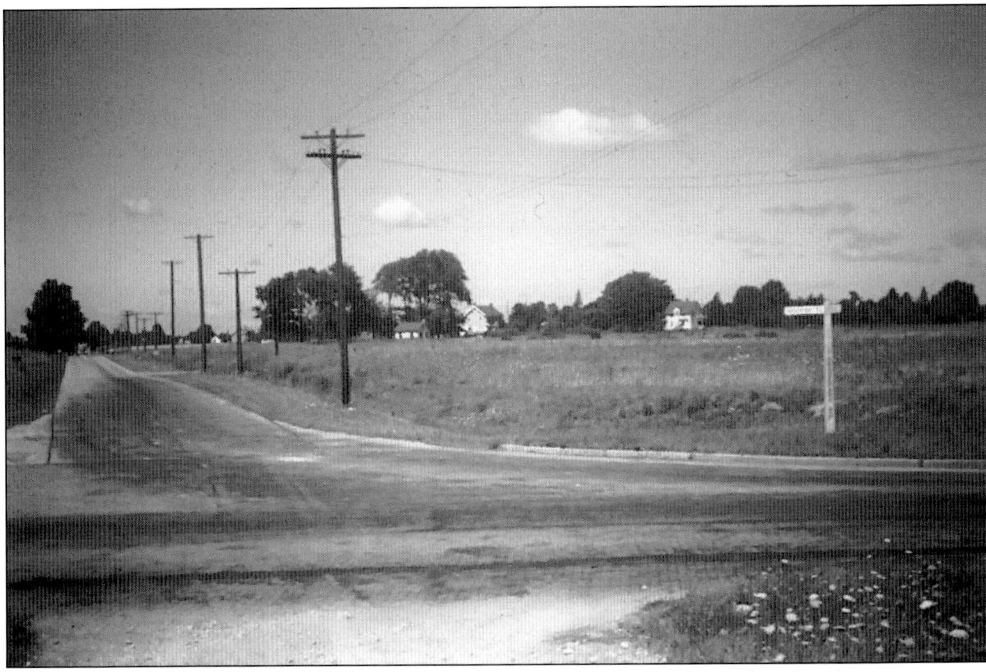

Area development seems to have grown north to south. Rockport Township development started on the lakefront, while the southern area that became Fairview Park and Parkview Village was isolated farmland. Lorain Road became a major street, but Brookpark Road, the southern border of Fairview Park, has remained the least developed. Hopkins Airport and the river valley certainly kept Brookpark from being more than the southern edge of town. The photograph above looks north from the American Legion's Clifton Post in 1948. The bottom photograph was shot to the west at the same time from the same point. In the opposite direction, the concrete Brookpark Bridge was built in 1934, the same year that the new steel Lorain Road bridge was built, a compromise between the concrete and steel industries. (Courtesy of William Robishaw.)

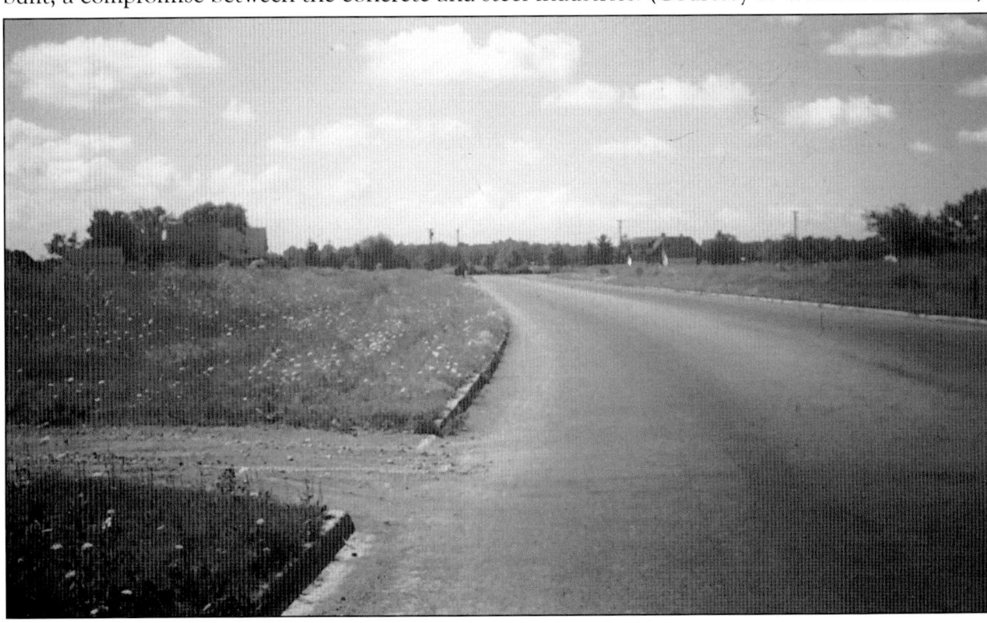

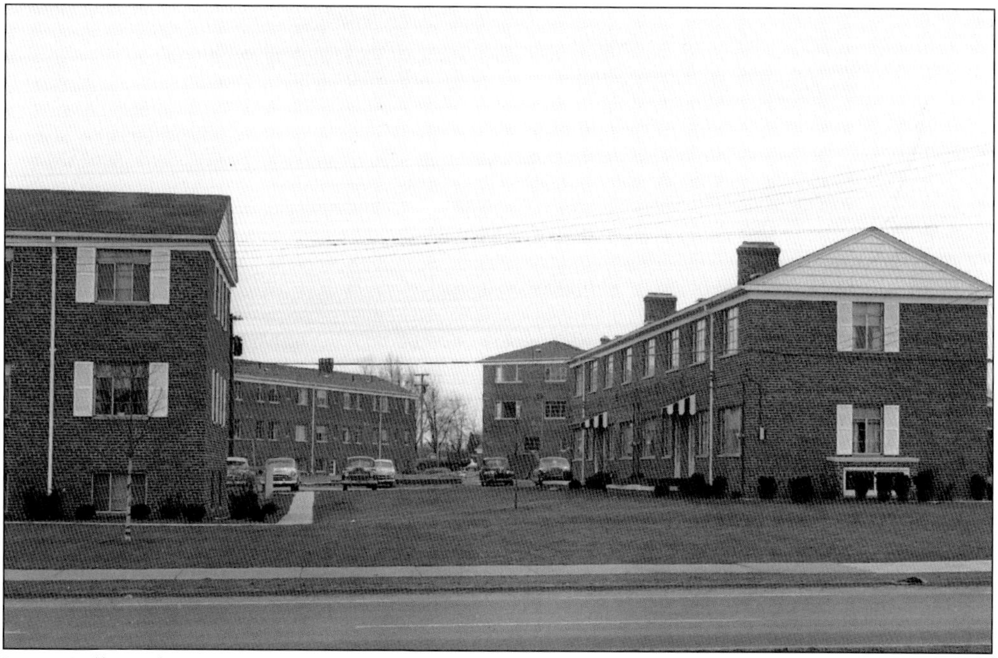

Lawn Village, later renamed Aberdeen Commons, is 12 acres of apartments and townhouses built on Lorain Road in the early 1950s between West 223rd and West 224th Streets, stretching back to Morton Avenue. (Cleveland Public Library.)

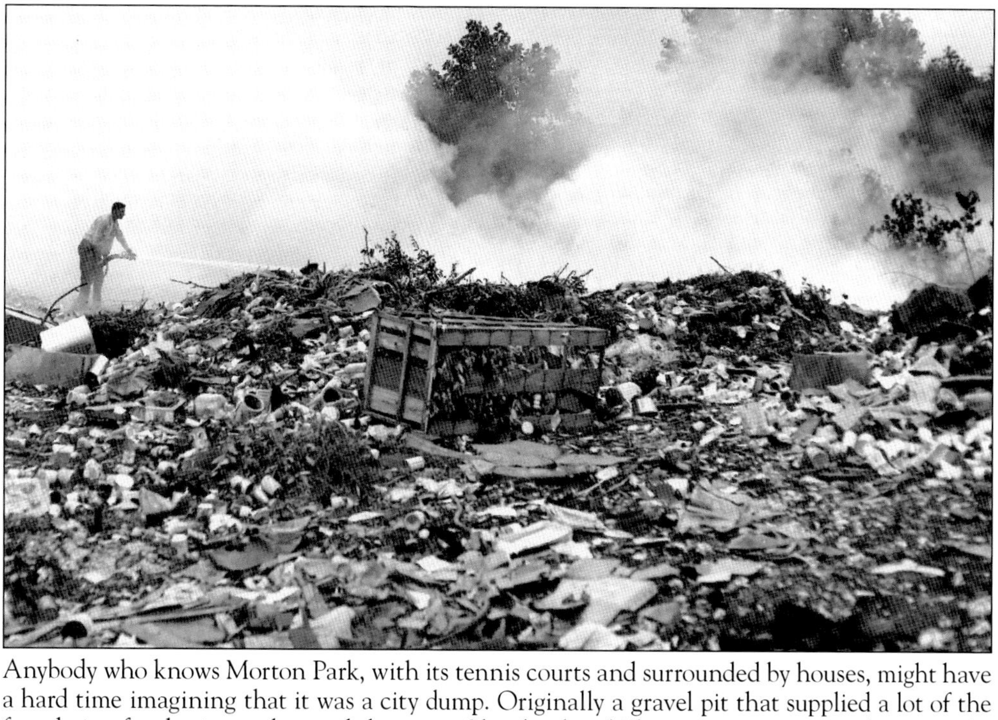

Anybody who knows Morton Park, with its tennis courts and surrounded by houses, might have a hard time imagining that it was a city dump. Originally a gravel pit that supplied a lot of the foundation for the interurban rails between Cleveland and Elyria, it was considered as a site for Gilles-Sweet School before it was built a few blocks away in 1925. (Cleveland Press Archives, Cleveland State University.)

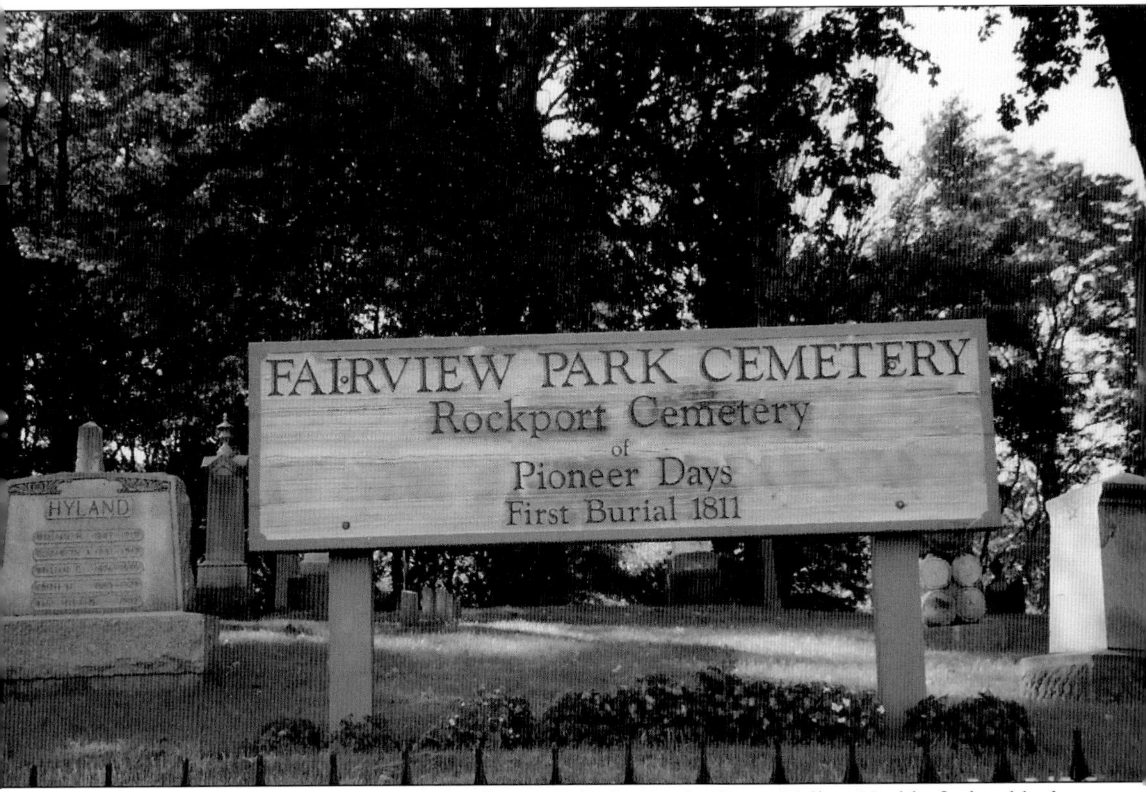

Along this stretch, Lorain Road closely parallels the Rocky River Valley. Usable flatland before the hill drops down varies from areas large enough for parking lots to just a few feet, but Fairview Park Cemetery has long held down a small, serene patch of land. Familiar names appear in the cemetery, like Spencer, Mastick, Eaton, Potter, as well as Fred Gilles and John H. Sweet, whom the school was named after. Going back at least to 1830, some of the earliest graves are of Revolutionary War soldiers from the area. (Fairview Park Historical Society.)

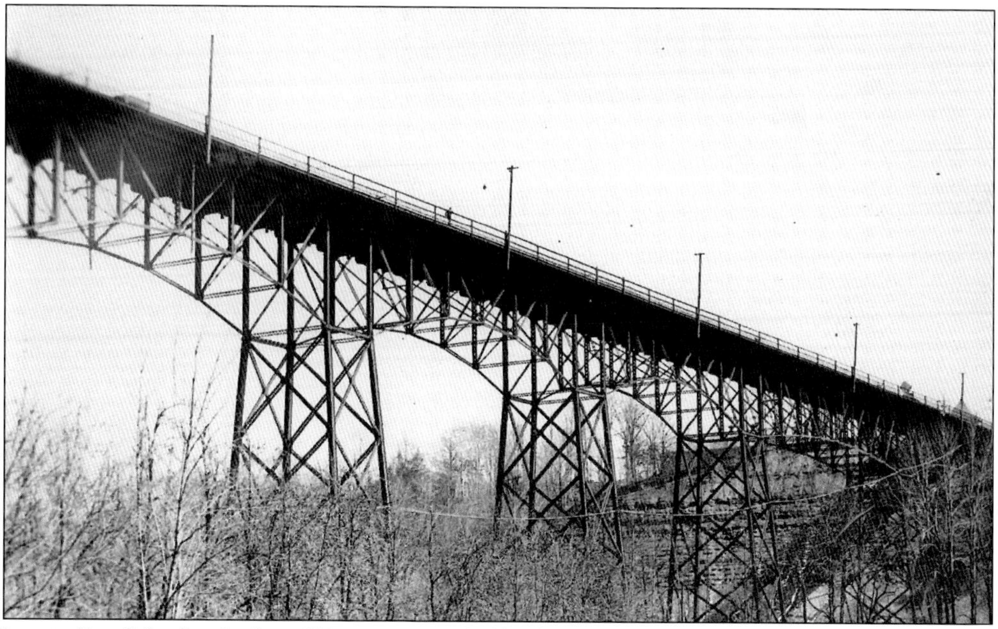

Lorain Road's bridge, built in 1934, was preceded by this iron bridge built in 1895 so the interurban could cross the valley. This bridge's opening prompted the street name change from Coe Ridge to State Street long before it was changed again to Lorain. Lorain Road was designated Ohio Route 10 in the 1930s to attract state funding to help pay for the new bridge. (Fairview Park Historical Society.)

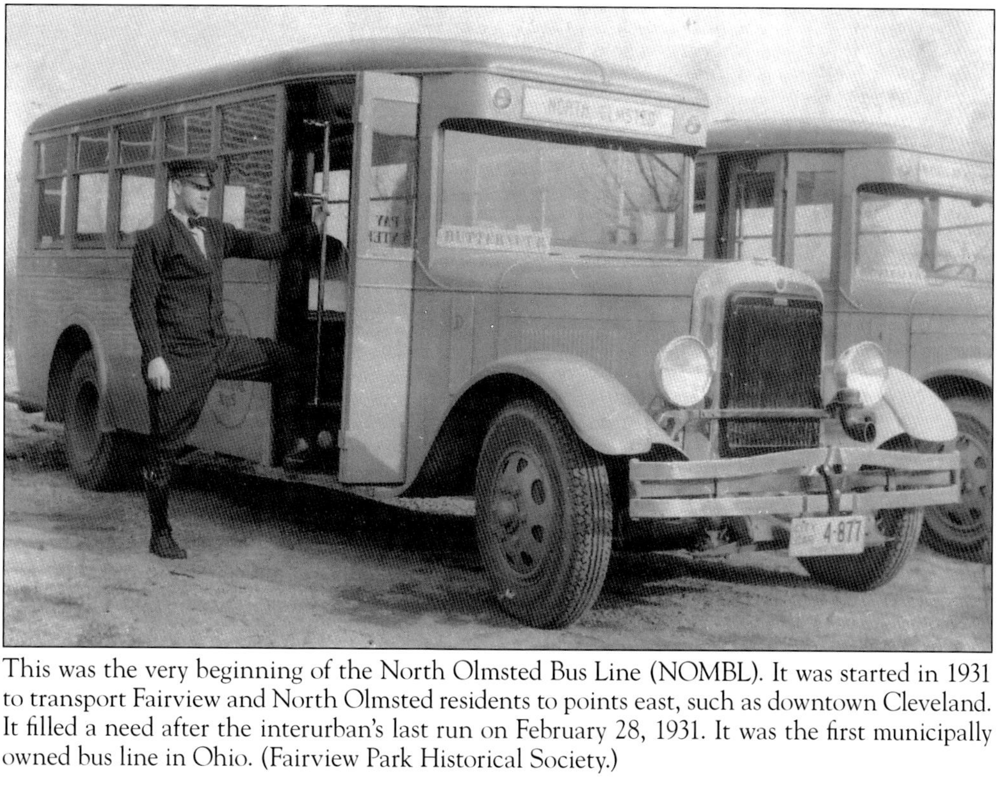

This was the very beginning of the North Olmsted Bus Line (NOMBL). It was started in 1931 to transport Fairview and North Olmsted residents to points east, such as downtown Cleveland. It filled a need after the interurban's last run on February 28, 1931. It was the first municipally owned bus line in Ohio. (Fairview Park Historical Society.)

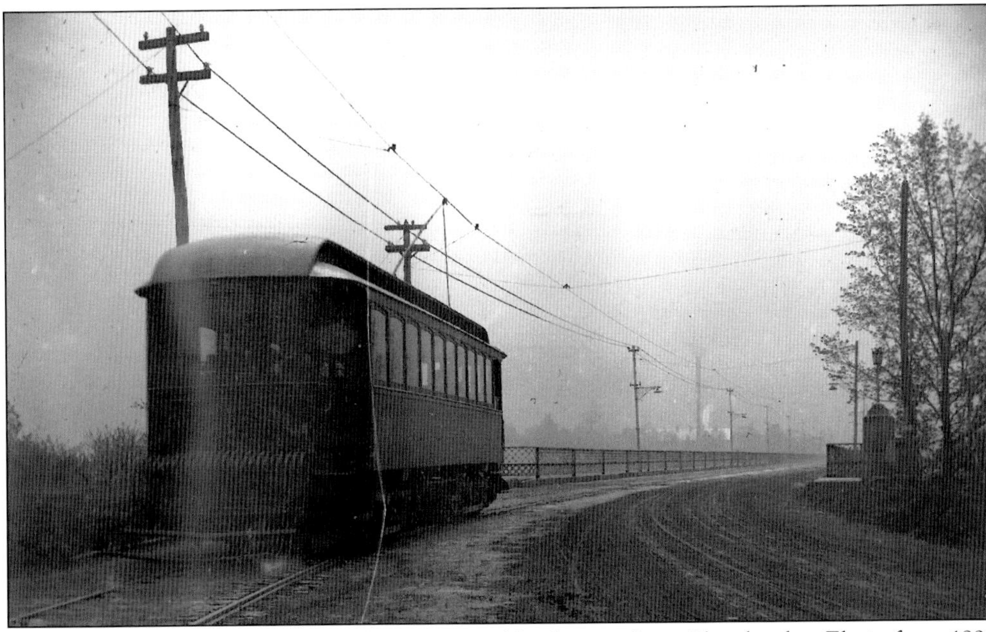

This interurban coming off the old Lorain Road bridge ran from Cleveland to Elyria from 1895 to 1931. Essentially extensions of city streetcar lines, electric interurbans were an improvement over steam. There was no pollution, and they were cheaper to operate. When paved roads arrived, the tracks were harder to maintain, and so the interurban outlived its usefulness. (Fairview Park Historical Society.)

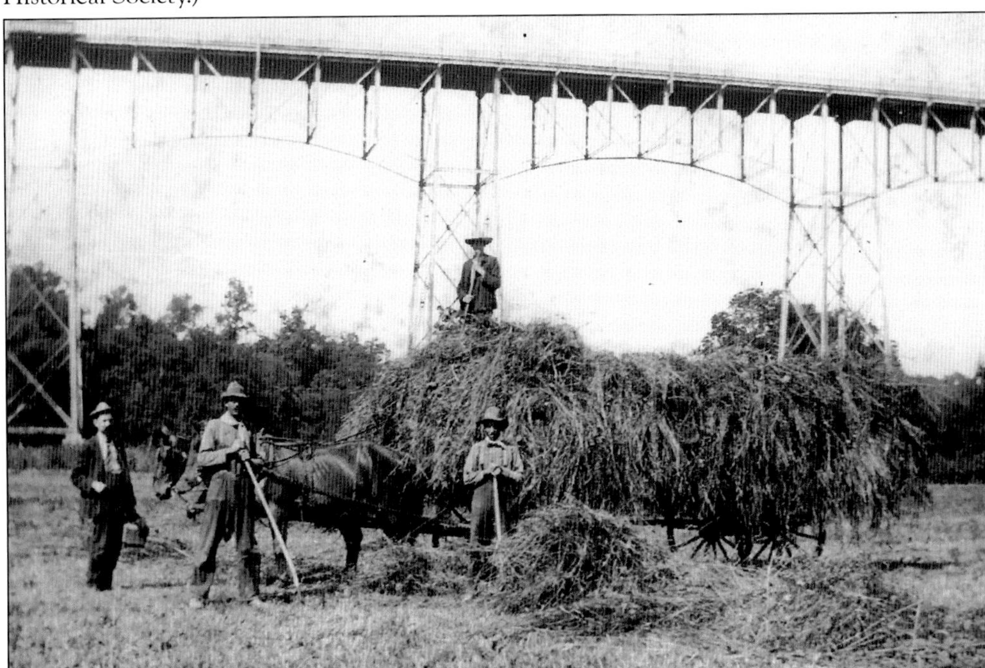

Pictured here is the older bridge, which existed from 1895 to 1934, but one could easily imagine today that farmers once gathered hay in the valley beneath Lorain Road. (Fairview Park Historical Society.)

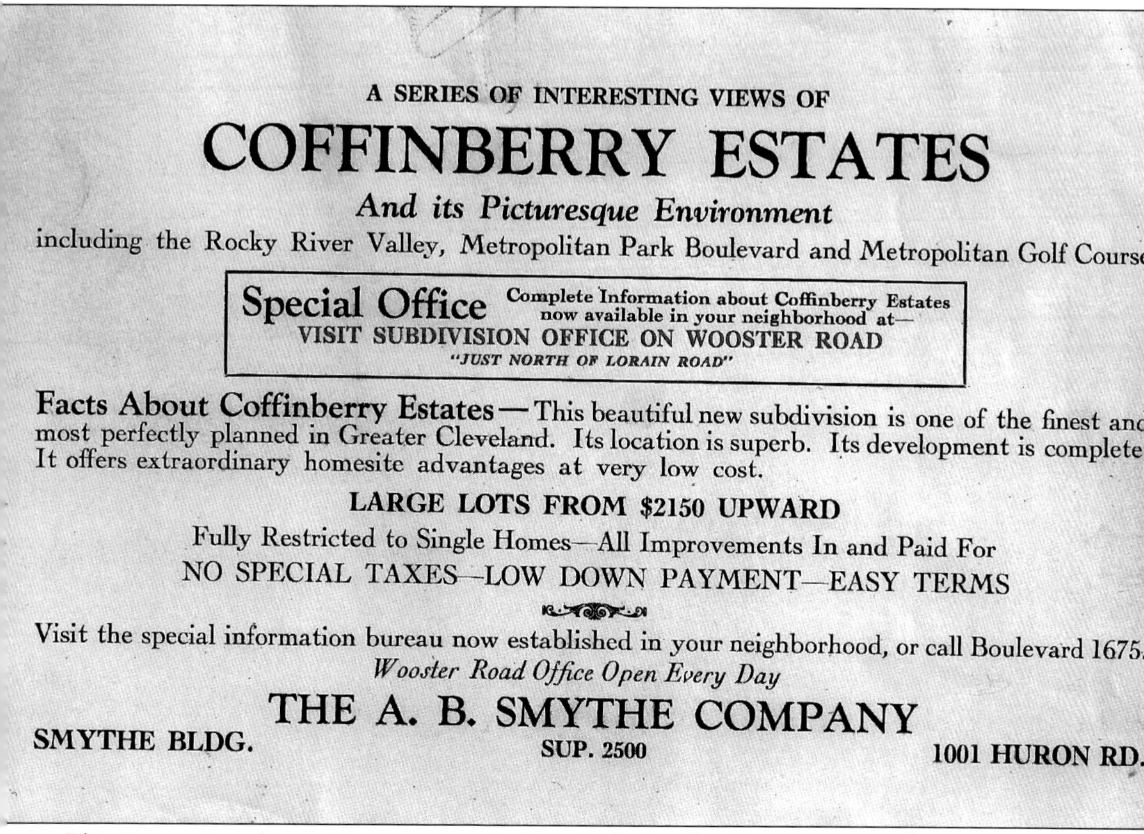

A SERIES OF INTERESTING VIEWS OF

COFFINBERRY ESTATES

And its Picturesque Environment

including the Rocky River Valley, Metropolitan Park Boulevard and Metropolitan Golf Course

Special Office Complete Information about Coffinberry Estates now available in your neighborhood at—
VISIT SUBDIVISION OFFICE ON WOOSTER ROAD
"JUST NORTH OF LORAIN ROAD"

Facts About Coffinberry Estates—This beautiful new subdivision is one of the finest and most perfectly planned in Greater Cleveland. Its location is superb. Its development is complete. It offers extraordinary homesite advantages at very low cost.

LARGE LOTS FROM $2150 UPWARD

Fully Restricted to Single Homes—All Improvements In and Paid For

NO SPECIAL TAXES—LOW DOWN PAYMENT—EASY TERMS

Visit the special information bureau now established in your neighborhood, or call Boulevard 1675.

Wooster Road Office Open Every Day

THE A. B. SMYTHE COMPANY

SMYTHE BLDG. **SUP. 2500** **1001 HURON RD.**

This is now just the northeast corner of the suburb. It is hard to imagine today, seeing the Coffinberry area as a fully developed neighborhood, that it was originally marketed as an area with room to build one's dream home. It was extolled that the relatively new Lorain Road, Detroit Road, and Hilliard Road bridges allowed easy access to Lakewood and Cleveland. (Fairview Park Historical Society.)

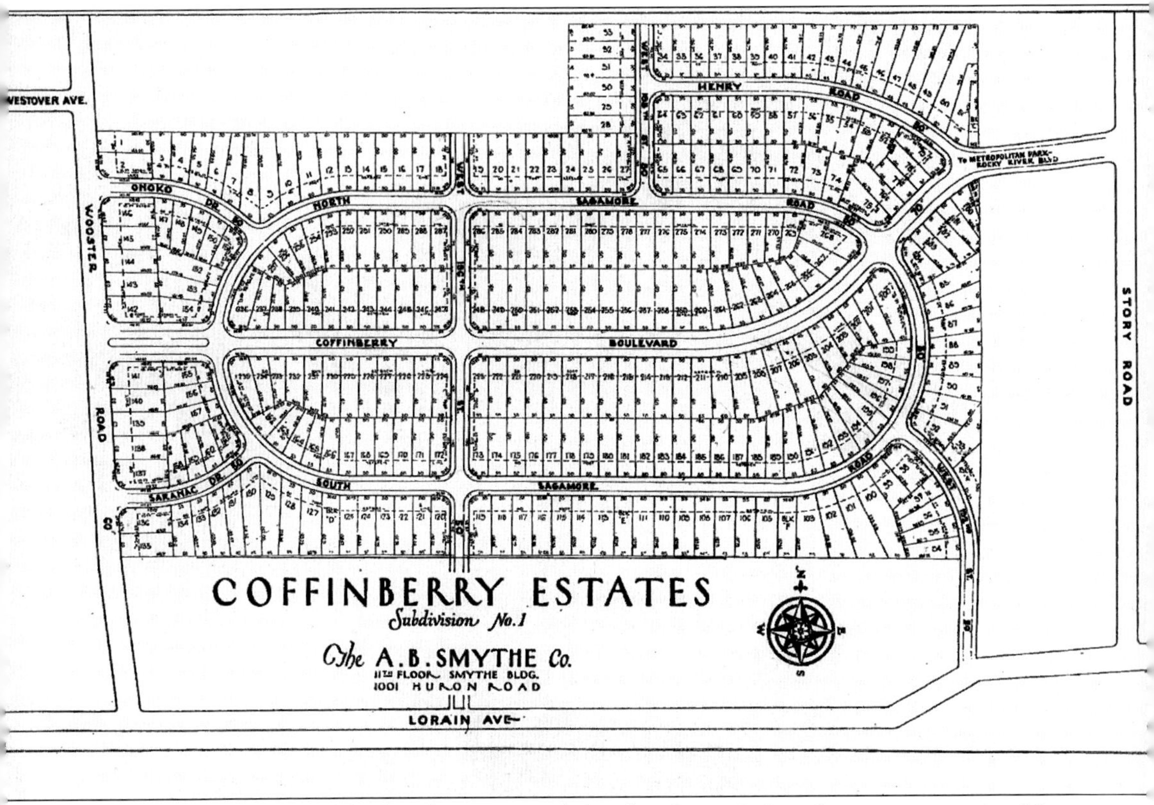

The Coffinberry neighborhood was named for the Great Lakes shipping executive Henry Coffinberry, with both his first and last names becoming names of streets in the neighborhood. His company proved metal could be made to float, building the first iron-hulled steam freighter on the Great Lakes, the *Onoko*, a prototype of the modern Great Lakes freighter, as well as the steel *Saranac*. Both ship names are also Coffinberry-area street names. (Fairview Park Historical Society.)

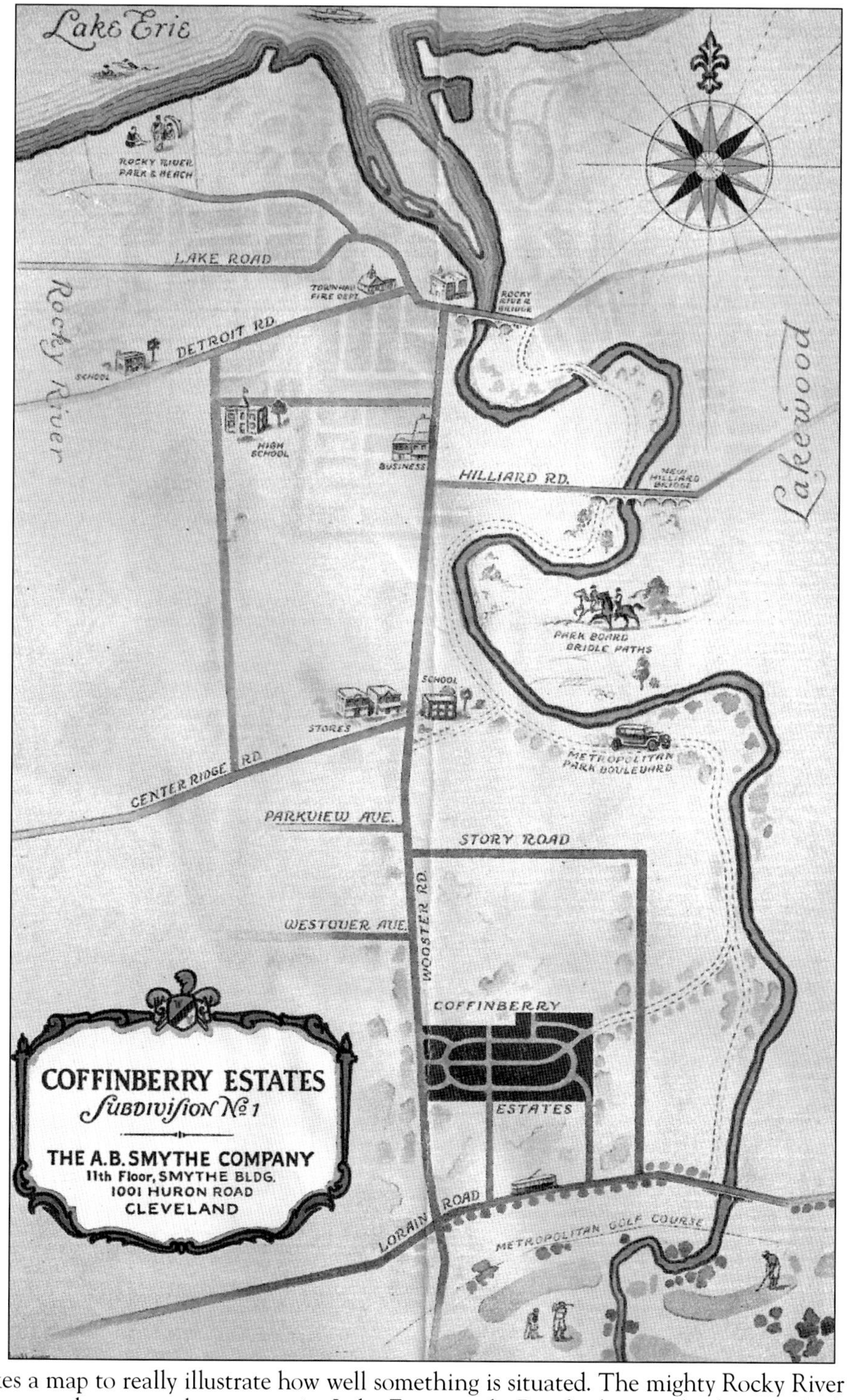

It takes a map to really illustrate how well something is situated. The mighty Rocky River long had its popular namesake town at its Lake Erie mouth. But further south, the river had been a hindrance to traveling east. The map shows how conveniently located Coffinberry was to everything, including bridges. (Fairview Park Historical Society.)

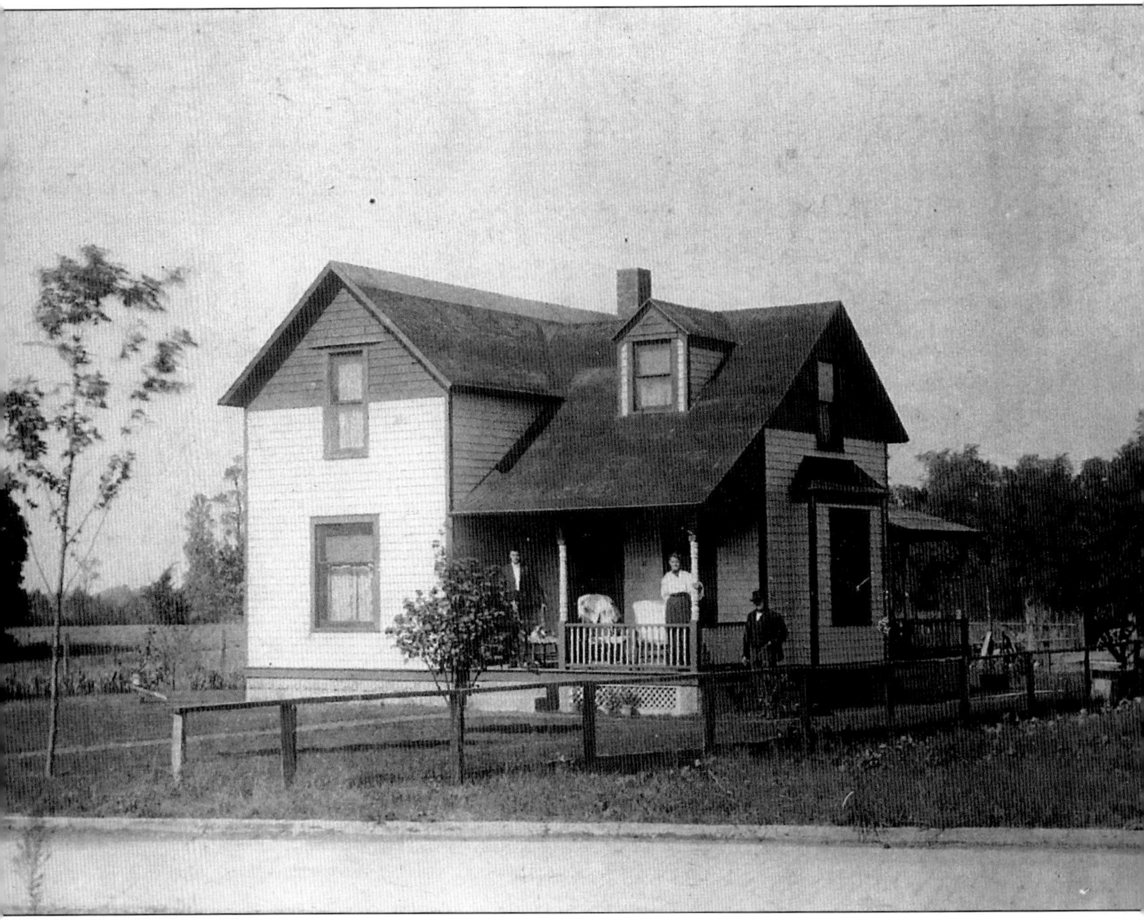

This house continued to stand at the corner of West 204th Street and Lorain Road into the 1990s. But here in the 1920s, West 204th Street did not exist yet. (Courtesy of Sue Lachendro.)

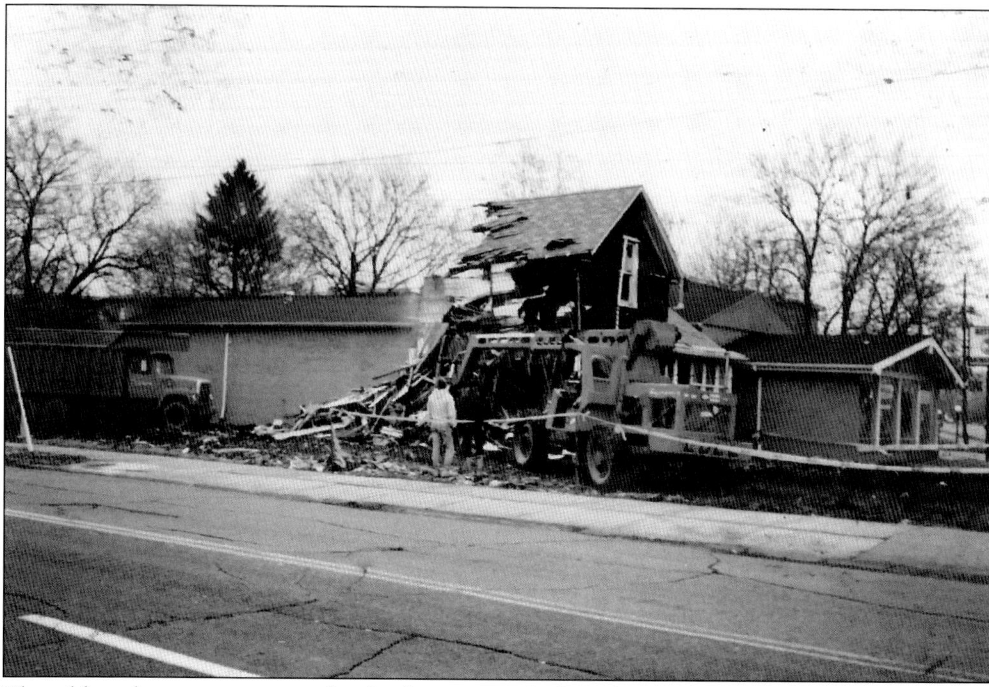

The old and new coexist in the final moments before the last few blows to the remaining fragments at West 204th Street and Lorain Road. (Courtesy of Sue Lachendro.)

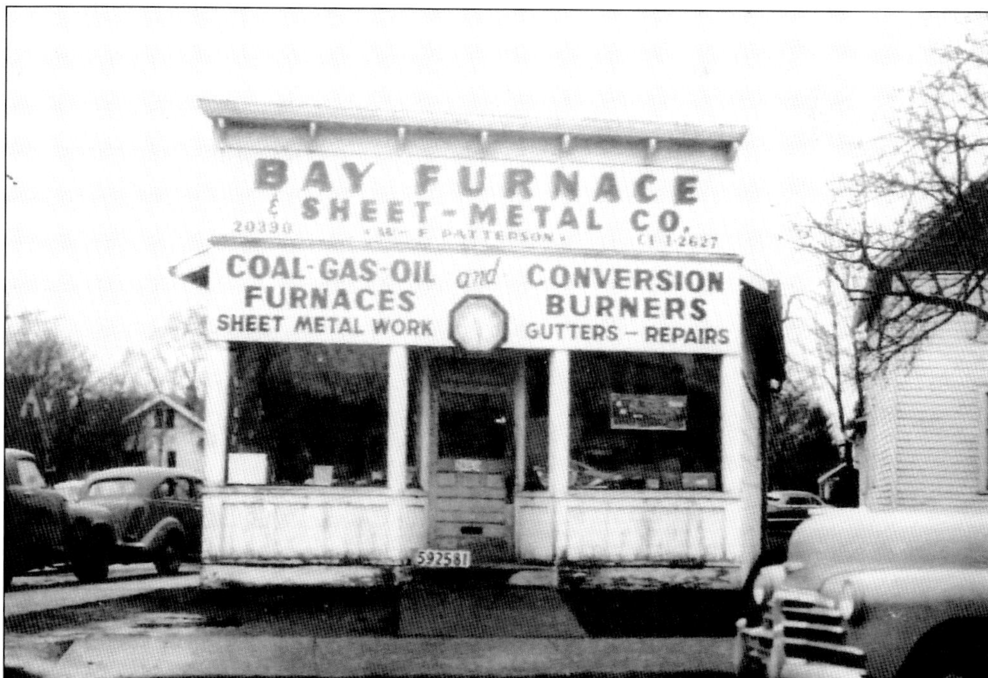

Bay Furnace and Sheet Metal Company started in Bay Village in 1944 and eventually returned there. But in between, it spent a few years in Fairview Park, developing the corner next to the house on the opposite page. (Courtesy of Sue Lachendro.)

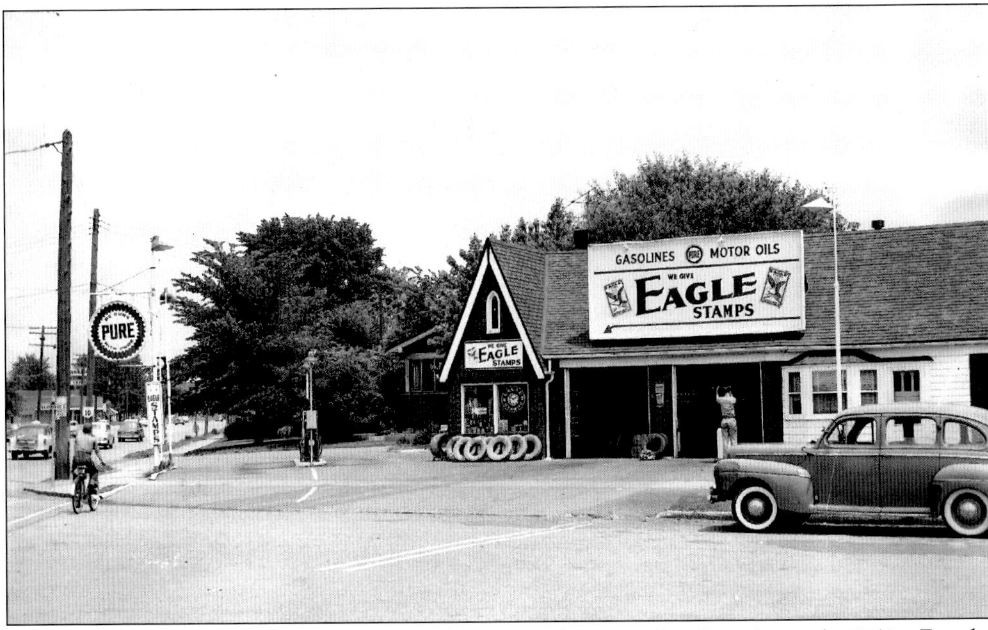

This was Suesse gas station at West 213th Street and Lorain Road in the early 1950s. For the record, when the city name change was put before the voters in the late 1940s, the name Fairview Park got 1,040 votes, Fairview City got 661, Fairhaven got 224, Fairpark got 240, Rockport got 144, Fairdale got 55, Westbridge got 56, Fairville got 117, Riverview got 110, New Fairview got 112, and City of Fairview Village got 123. (Fairview Park Historical Society.)

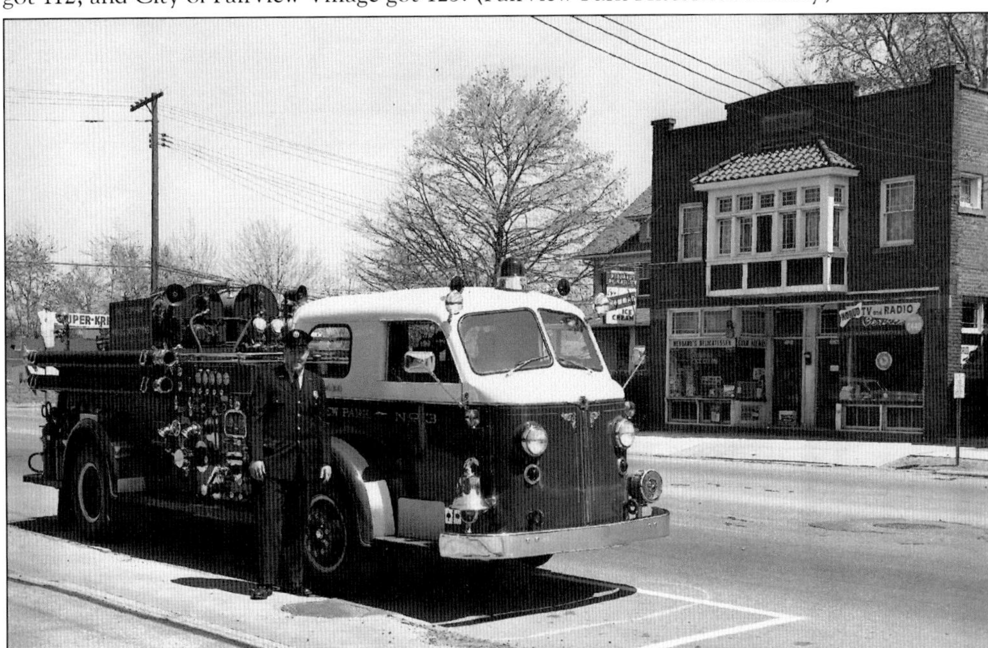

A routine inspection by the fire department in May 1956 allows for another random street scene. Here are two of the businesses that have called this building at West 228th Street and Lorain Road home over the years: Hebbard's Delicatessen and Korud TV and Radio Service. (Fairview Park Historical Society.)

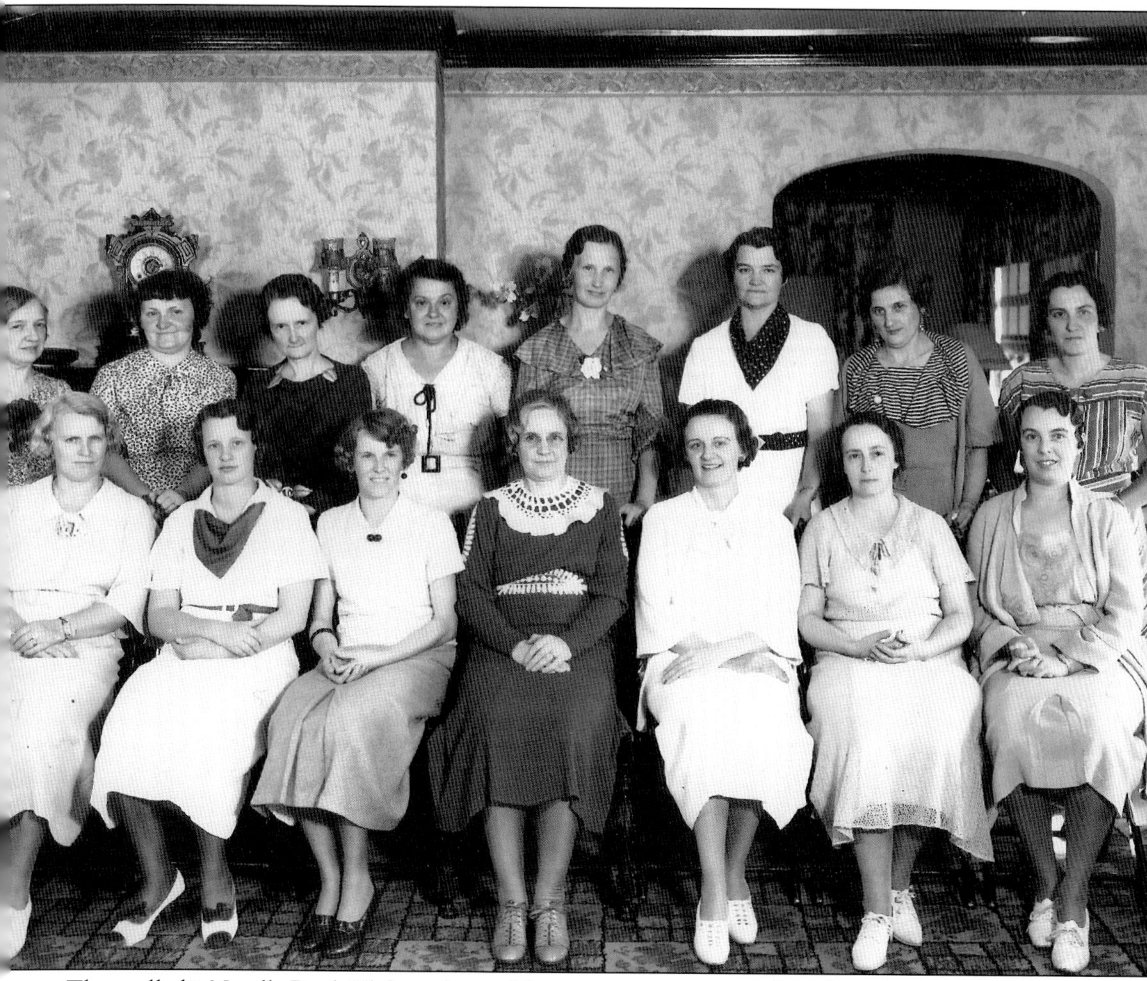

They called it Needle Book Club, and monthly meetings were at members' homes. This particular month, the hostess was the lady at the right of the first row, a Mrs. Faus or Fause, whose husband was a dentist. Apparently it was not merely a book discussion group, because the guest speaker, in the front row center, was the wife of the principal of a Cleveland school for boys with behavior problems. (Fairview Park Historical Society.)

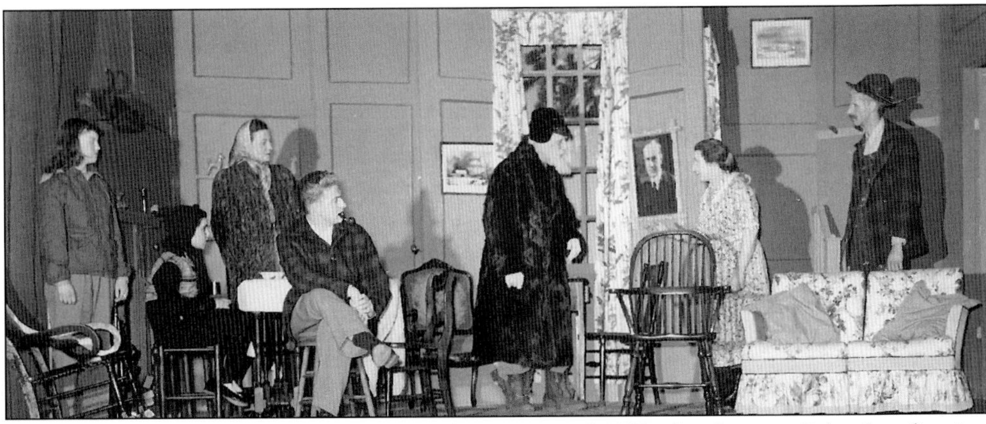

Since the high school did not have an auditorium until 1952, the Garnett School auditorium was the village's stage. Local people got to perform as the Fairview Players. In every photograph of their productions, the stage lighting casts very prominent shadows, so they were not exactly professional lighting designers. This production in April 1948 was a comedy called *January Thaw*. (Fairview Park Historical Society.)

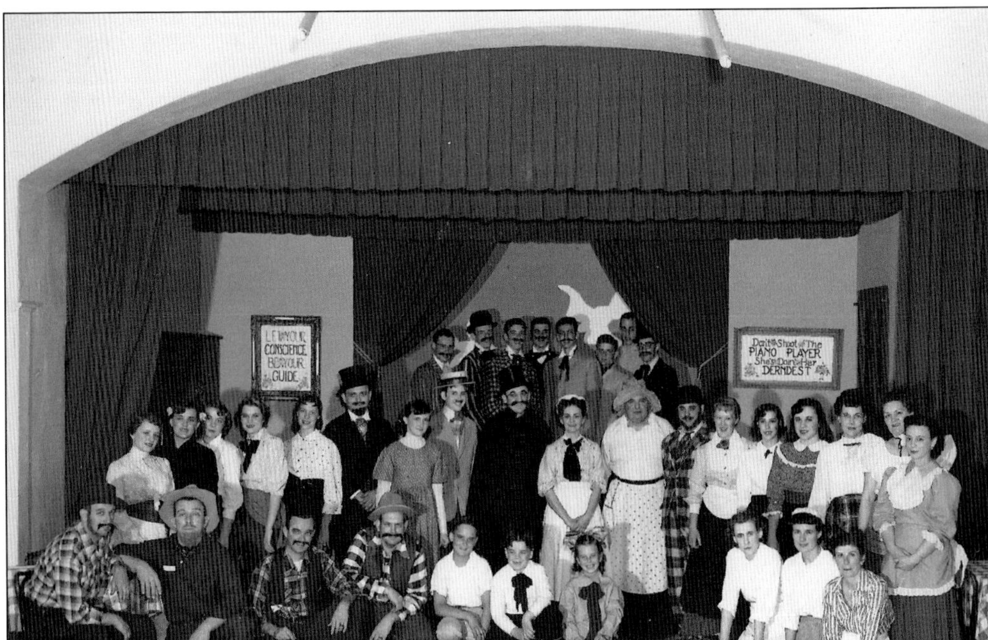

In 1952, Fairview Players presented an original musical comedy about the gold rush called *Thar's Gold in Them Thar Hills*. (Fairview Park Historical Society.)

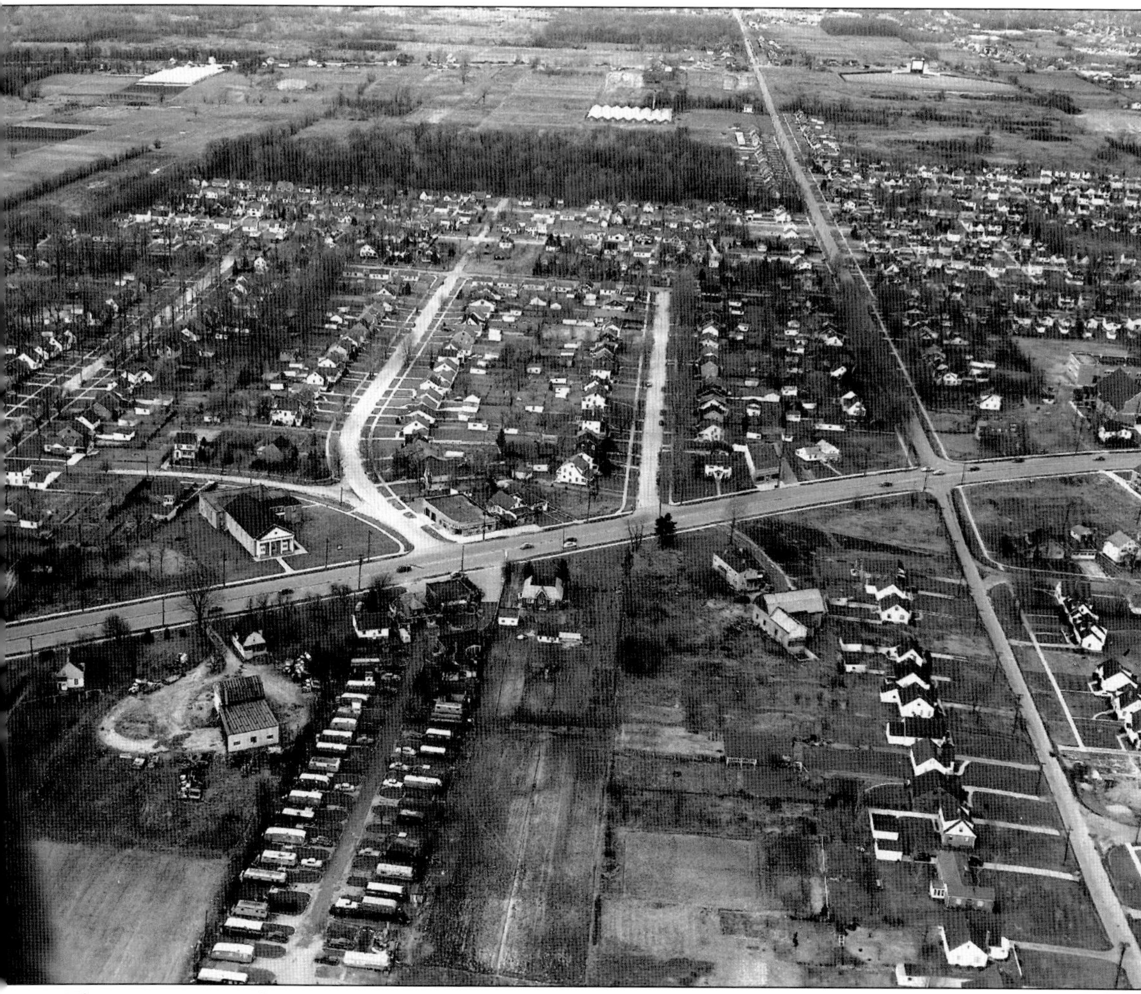

This perspective of West 210th Street and Lorain Road, shot on March 25, 1954, dramatically shows how much of southern Rocky River along the top of the picture was still farmland. That left Fairview to differentiate itself as a separate suburb, even without the advantage of Rocky River's lakefront. (Fairview Park Historical Society.)

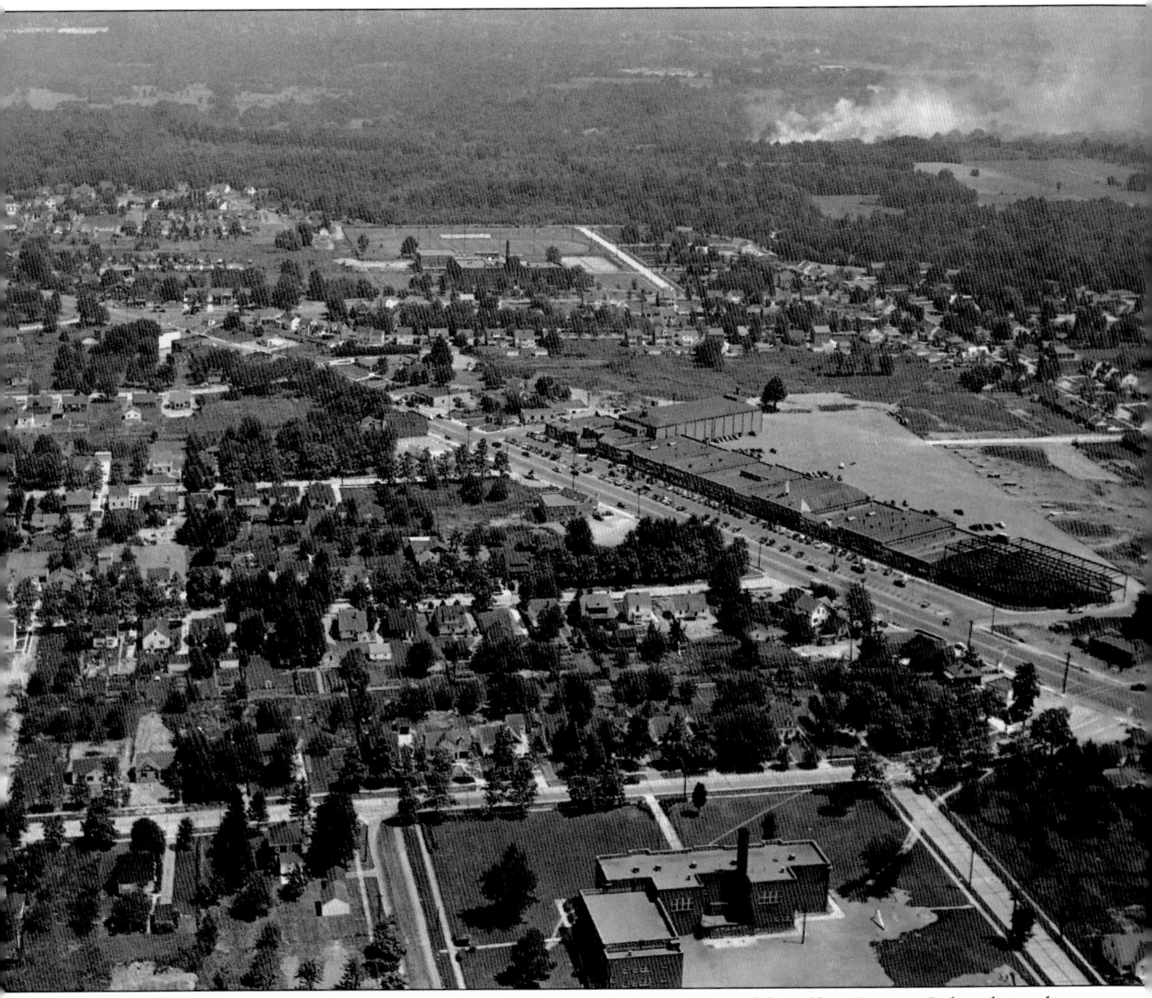

Various changes can be seen in this 1951 aerial shot. The old Gilles-Sweet School is along the bottom. The north wing (left) was added the year before, and the south wing was added the following year. The three-year-old shopping center dominates the center right of the photograph, with a new store being built on the west end. The smoke in the upper-right corner is a trash-burning operation in the valley. (Courtesy of Adam Pangrace.)

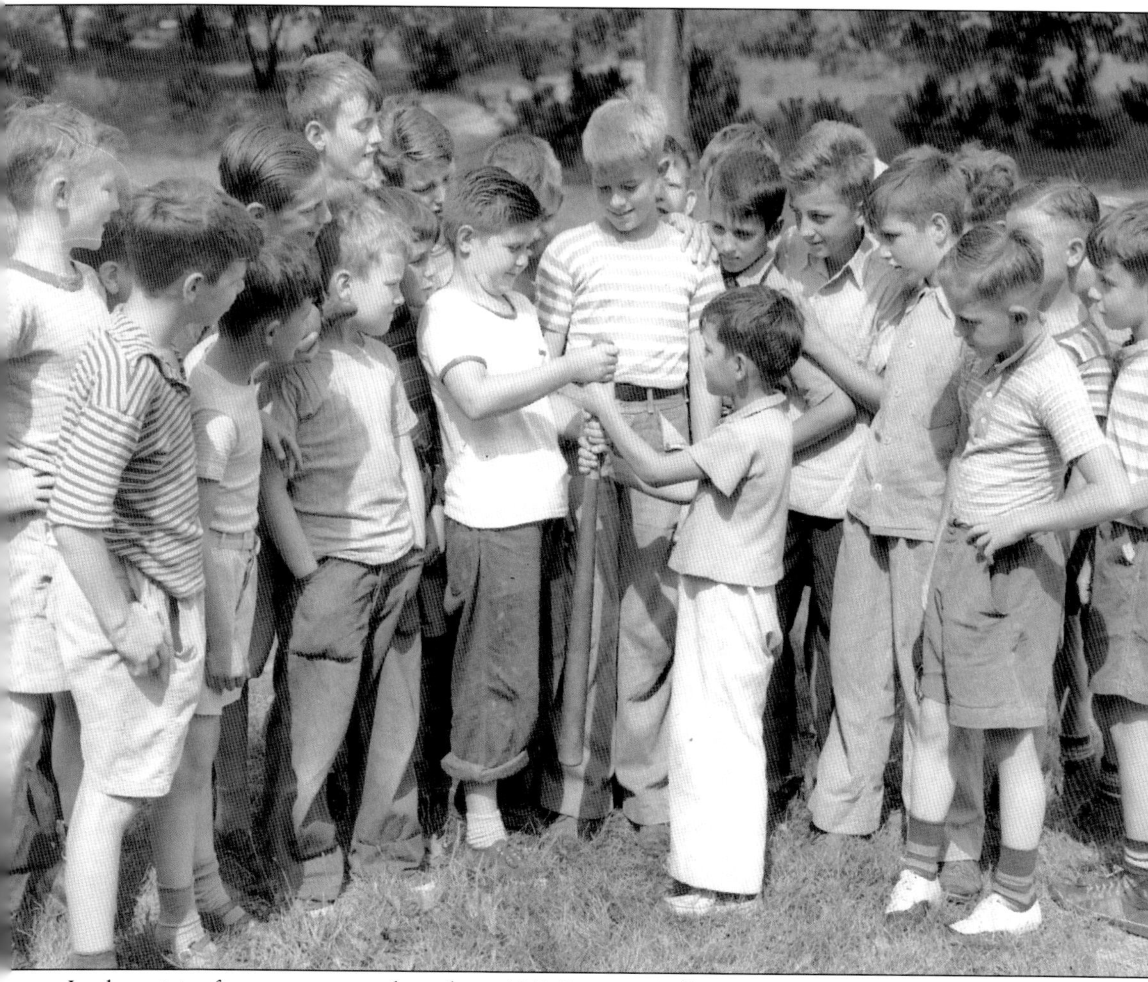

In the spirit of true sportsmanship, these 1942 Fairview Village summer recreation participants choose sides in a peaceful way, since they are neither rival suburbs nor rival countries. To the left of the bat is Joseph Dorogi, and to the right is Donald Kenzig. (Cleveland Press Archives, Cleveland State University.)

BIBLIOGRAPHY

Goebelt, Margaret Schaefer. *Fairview Park in Historical Review.* Cleveland, OH: John S. Swift Company, 1978.

Iezzi, Anthony J. *History of Saint Angela Merici Parish.* Fairview Park, OH: St. Angela Merici Parish, 1999.

Jones, Florence Hays. *Fifty Years of Action.* Fairview Park, OH: Fairview Baptist Church, 1974.

Pfingsten, Ralph A. *From Rockport to West Park.* Rocky River, OH: John Marshall High School Alumni Association, 2004.

Van Tassel, David D., and John J. Grabowski. *The Encyclopedia of Cleveland History.* Bloomington, IN: Indiana University Press, 1987.

Index